DYNAMIC STUDIES IN REVELATION

BRINGING GOD'S WORD TO LIFE

FRED A. SCHEEREN

WESTBOW
PRESS
A DIVISION OF THOMAS NELSON
& ZONDERVAN

Chart used with permission of Mike McCormick
Permission of Dr. David Hurtado

Scripture taken from the Holy Bible, NEW INTERNATIONAL VERSION®. Copyright © 1973, 1978, 1984 by Biblica, Inc. All rights reserved worldwide. Used by permission. NEW INTERNATIONAL VERSION® and NIV® are registered trademarks of Biblica, Inc. Use of either trademark for the offering of goods or services requires the prior written consent of Biblica US, Inc.

Scripture quotations taken from the Holy Bible, New Living Translation, Copyright © 1996, 2004. Used by permission of Tyndale House Publishers, Inc., Wheaton, Illinois 60189. All rights reserved.

Scripture taken from the New King James Version. Copyright © 1979, 1980, 1982 by Thomas Nelson, Inc. Used by permission. All rights reserved.

Scripture taken from the King James Version of the Bible.

Scripture quotations taken from the New American Standard Bible®, Copyright © 1960, 1962, 1963, 1968, 1971, 1972, 1973, 1975, 1977, 1995 by The Lockman Foundation. Used by permission. (www.Lockman.org)

WestBow Press books may be ordered through booksellers or by contacting:

WestBow Press
A Division of Thomas Nelson & Zondervan
1663 Liberty Drive
Bloomington, IN 47403
www.westbowpress.com
1 (866) 928-1240

Because of the dynamic nature of the Internet, any web addresses or links contained in this book may have changed since publication and may no longer be valid. The views expressed in this work are solely those of the author and do not necessarily reflect the views of the publisher, and the publisher hereby disclaims any responsibility for them.

Any people depicted in stock imagery provided by Thinkstock are models, and such images are being used for illustrative purposes only. Certain stock imagery © Thinkstock.

ISBN: 978-1-4908-6439-6 (sc)
ISBN: 978-1-4908-6438-9 (e)

Library of Congress Control Number: 2015900370

Printed in the United States of America.

WestBow Press rev. date: 01/27/2015

DEDICATION

I DEDICATE THIS book to my lovely wife, Sally, who is a Jewish believer. She has stood by me over the years and raised our sons in our God-loving home. The comfort of sharing our friendship and our love for Christ has encouraged me greatly in creating this series of dynamic studies of various books of the Bible. Sally's participation in our small group studies has added a much deeper dimension of richness to the discussions. Thank you for sharing your heritage, training, and knowledge.

CONTENTS

ACKNOWLEDGMENTS

MY FRIEND, BOB Mason, who at the time I began the Dynamic Bible Studies series was in his second career as the pastor of small groups at the Bible Chapel in the South Hills of Pittsburgh, suggested the overall structure of each study. Realizing our group was doing more in-depth work than most, he asked that I include several important segments in each lesson—most specifically, the warm-up and life application phases.

Bob suggested a great resource called the *New Testament Lesson Planner* from InterVarsity Press. I have augmented this with commentaries by Dr. Charles Missler from Koinonia House, the *Wiersbe Bible Commentary*, *Because the Time is Near* and *the MacArthur Bible Commentary* by Dr. John MacArthur, *Escape the Coming Night* by Dr. David Jeremiah, the *Bible Commentaries* of J. Vernon McGee, *Authentic Christianity* by Gordon Haresign, and the whole of Scripture itself. To make the utilization of the whole of Scripture more efficient, I have also leaned heavily on the Libronix Digital Library, perhaps the most advanced Bible software available, and other resources to help us understand how the New Testament and the Tanakh (Old Testament) fit together as one cohesive document.

I have also enjoyed the input and encouragement of my friend, Ron Jones, as I have continued to prepare these studies. Ron is a former high school principal and administrator. He is also a committed believer and daily student of God's Word. His background in education coupled with his love of God and His Word has made him a powerful force for good. It has been my privilege to work with him in presenting a series on the book of Revelation to our ABF (Adult Bible Fellowship) group at the Bible Chapel. He and I prepared separate studies on this book and then alternated in presenting them to the class. I believe that both we and the ABF members benefited from this collaboration. While our studies were prepared separately, they were remarkably similar primarily due to the high regard in which we each hold the Word of God.

In addition, it has been my privilege to discuss many of the Jewish customs and practices of the time when this book was written with my friend, Rabbi Jeff Kipp. Rabbi Kipp is outstanding among Jewish Rabbis in that he has realized that Jesus of Nazareth is indeed Yeshua Ha-Maschiach, the Jewish Messiah. Being able to discuss and review certain points of the text, customs and practices involved has been an invaluable resource.

I would also like to express my appreciation to my two proof-readers. This included Cynthia NiCastro, an intelligent, ardent and devoted student of the Scriptures and a meticulous grammarian as well as my wife Sally, a Jewish believer and Ivy League educated lawyer who was law review in law school, worked for the Superior Court of the State of Pennsylvania and is now in private practice.

May God bless you, inspire you, teach you, and change your life for the better as you work through these lessons.

PREFACE

WELCOME TO WHAT I hope you will find to be a most enjoyable study of the book of Revelation, part of the Judeo-Christian documents which we have come to know as the Bible.

As we consider how this book fits into the whole of the New Testament and the Tanakh (the name used by Jews for the Old Testament, used here to emphasize the Jewishness of the Scriptures), we need to realize a number of things. We should stand in awe of this collection of 66 books, written over thousands of years by at least 40 different authors. Every detail of the text is there by design. It explains history before it happens, and comes to us from outside the dimension of time. It is, in short, the most amazing, most authenticated, and most accurate book available in the world.

If this claim is not strong enough, add to it the indisputable fact that the words contained therein have changed more lives than any others now in existence.

I intended this particular study to be used in a small group setting, however, it can also be adapted to a larger group or individual study.

While the Judeo-Christian Scriptures are demonstrably perfect, my prepared studies are not. There is no way I or anyone else could possibly incorporate the depth of the text into individual sessions. I simply desire to provide a vehicle for others to use in their investigation of the Scriptures as they incorporate these timeless truths into their lives.

Speaking of small groups, Dr. Chuck Missler, a former Fortune 500 CEO, said "I experienced more growth in my personal life as a believer by participating in small group bible studies than anything else." I believe you may find this to be true in your experience and encourage you to be an active participant in such a mutually supportive, biblically-based group.

GROUND RULES

I DESIGNED THE first portion of each study to encourage readers to think about their personal situation. I designed the second portion to help people understand what the text says and how it relates to the whole of Scripture. And finally, each lesson ends with a discussion designed to help people apply that lesson.

You will notice that, in most instances, I have included the citation, but not the actual text of the Scripture we are considering. I did this on purpose. I believe we all learn more effectively if we have to dig out the text itself. As a byproduct of that exercise, we become more familiar with this marvelous book.

Scripture references are preceded or followed by a question or series of questions. Again, this is on purpose. I have also found that people seem to learn most effectively when employing the Socratic Method. That is, instead of telling someone what the text says and how it relates to other texts and life, they will remember it better if they answer questions about it and ferret out the information for themselves.

In a few instances, I have inserted additional commentary or partial answers to some of the questions to help the group get the most out of the study.

In addition, I added various scriptural references, intending that they be read out loud as part of the session. Shorter passages might be read by one participant, while anything over two or three verses might serve everyone better if one member reads one verse and another reads the next until the passage is completed. This keeps everyone involved. After reading these passages, I intend that how they relate to the primary Scripture at hand in Revelation be seriously considered. At times, this relationship seems to be available and obvious on the surface. In many other instances, the interconnectedness of the whole of Scripture and its principles are most effectively understood through deeper thought, discussion, and prayer.

In commenting on and discussing the various passages, questions, concepts, and principles in this material, it is not required that any particular person give his or her input. The reader of any passage may, but is not pressured to, give his or her thoughts to the group. This is a group participation exercise for the mutual benefit of all involved and many people in the group giving their insight into a certain verse or question will often enhance the learning experience.

I also have two practical suggestions if you work through this book in a small group setting. Every time you meet, I suggest you review the calendar and agree upon the next scheduled meeting as well as who will bring refreshments. This will help the group to run a lot more smoothly while enhancing everyone's enjoyment and expectations.

INTRODUCTION TO THE BOOK OF REVELATION

THIS BOOK OF the Bible was written by John, one of the disciples of Jesus. It was produced about 95 AD during the reign of the Roman Emperor Titus Flavius Domitian. The emperor had demanded that he be worshipped as "Lord and God," and the refusal of the believing Jews and Gentiles to do so led to severe persecution often involving torture and death. It was Domitian who sent John to a Roman penal colony off the coast of Asia Minor for refusing to worship him. Life on this island inhabited only by condemned criminals banished to work in the stone and marble quarries was hard.

As Gordon Haresign says in his excellent book *Authentic Christianity* "Banishment to the mines meant hard labor, scourging, scanty clothing, and insufficient food. By night the prisoners slept on the bare ground in dark, dungy prisons, and by day they worked under the lash of military overseers. While banishment was a terrible fate, it was to be the apostle's lot for about eighteen months until the death of Domitian in A.D. 96."

One has to imagine that Domitian would have been surprised to learn that his maltreatment of John, who by this time was an old man and ultimately the last of the apostles to die, resulted in God using the situation to communicate vital messages to His followers.

The book of Revelation seems to be a book of mystery for most of humanity. Even believers often approach it with awe, wonder, questioning, and even a little confusion.

However, this need not be so.

First, and foremost, the book is an "unveiling" of a person. That person is Jesus Christ, the Alpha and the Omega.

The key to understanding the book of Revelation is in the whole of Scripture itself. The book itself consists of 404 verses. Discerning the meaning of these verses requires an in-depth study of the Old Testament. Since most people today do not have sufficient grounding in the Tanakh, they are at wits end in trying to decipher just what God is trying to get across in this final book of the Bible.

Realizing this difficulty experienced by most people in the world today, even those with a background of faith, we will take a step-by- step look at this mysterious book.

Engaging in this process will require diving into the Old Testament verses that are alluded to in Revelation. Indeed, over 800 allusions are made to the Scriptures that were in existence prior to the time of the birth of Jesus. In addition to applying these verses we will come to understand some exciting attributes of the design and structure of the book that should give us a further sense of awe and wonder as we see the hand of the Greatest Power of the Universe at work.

It should be of no uncertain interest to us that this book, and only this book of the Bible promises a special blessing to those who read it and take heed to what we are told.

Revelation 1:3 says "God blesses the one who reads the words of this prophecy to the church, and he blesses all who listen to its message and obey what it says, for the time is near." NLT

Revelation 22:7 says "Blessed is he that readeth, and they that hear the words of this prophecy, and keep those things which are written therein: for the time is at hand." KJV

As we engage in this study we are making a number of overt presuppositions:

1. God means what He says and says what He means.

2. The Bible is an integrated whole. Every detail is there by design. (Matthew 5:17-18)

3. Nothing in Scripture is trivial. All things therein are presented for our learning. (Romans 15:4)

4. God is His own interpreter through the means of His Word.

While each chapter of this book has lessons for our daily life, it also deals with prophecy. It is this very prophetic element that has led to so much controversy surrounding some of the conclusions learned people have drawn from their study of the text over the years.

Prophecy itself is an interesting and alluring field of study for the believer and non-believer alike. It is one of the tools utilized by God to essentially prove himself on a statistical basis. (See Composite probability theory in appendix A.) For example, there are hundreds of prophecies about the first coming of Jesus Christ in the Old Testament, which the Jews call the Tanakh, that were fulfilled in Him. The statistical probability surrounding this makes it impossible for Scripture to be untrue or for Jesus to not be just who He claimed. No honest and thinking mathematician can deny the claims of Christ based upon these facts alone.

Biblical prophecies go beyond the person and work of the Jewish Messiah, Yeshua Ha-Maschiach, who we call Jesus Christ. They extend to world events. In fact, with the aid of mathematics, we find that the reestablishment of Israel as a nation was accurately prophesized to the day thousands of years before the event took place. According to J. Barton Payne writing in the Encyclopedia of

Biblical Prophecy, the whole of the Judeo Christian documents which we call the Bible:

- Contain 8,362 predictive verses;

- In which 1,817 predictions are made;

- About 737 separate matters.

The prophecies about Jesus and His first coming have already been fulfilled. As mentioned, there are hundreds of them. In a sense, this is easy for us to see now that we have the benefit of hindsight and history.

What is more difficult, however, is the interpretation of prophecies about things yet to come. While the first coming of Christ is confirmed by hundreds now fulfilled prophecies, His second coming receives even greater attention in the New and Old Testament documents.

There are over 1,845 references to Christ's second coming and future rule on earth in the Old Testament. In the Old Testament itself, 17 of the books give great prominence to the event. The New Testament simply adds to this. Here we find that the second coming of Jesus is mentioned in 23 of the 27 books and that there are 318 references to it in the 216 chapters making up the whole.

In our study we hold to a high view of Scripture. We believe what it says in II Timothy 3:16-17 where we read "All Scripture is inspired by God and is useful for teaching the truth, rebuking error, correcting faults, and giving instruction for right living so that the person who serves God may be fully qualified and equipped for every good work." GNT For more helpful information on how to avoid error and understand what God is communicating to us in the mysterious book of Revelation please take the time to review "How to Avoid Error" in appendix B of this guide.

We would be remiss to not note that there are also three other positions that some "theologians" take in regard to the book of Revelation. These positions can only be held if one adopts a somewhat lower view of God's Word and couples that view with a knowledge of history that is wanting.

The four major views of the book of Revelation are often characterized as:

1. Preterist, which says that the book applied only to the time period in which it was written.

2. Historical, which says that the book is only one of history.

3. Idealist, which says that the book is one of allegory.

4. Futurist, which says that while the book had application to the time when it was written as well as to our lives today, it is also prophetic.

We should note that the book of revelation itself claims the latter view to which we adhere. See:

Revelation 1:3

Revelation 22:7

Revelation 22:10

Revelation 22:18-19

Revelation 10:11

Even though serious students of the Biblical text hold a high view of God's Word, it is still possible for them to arrive at slightly different conclusions after a diligent study of prophecy. When engaging in the study of Eschatology, which is of the last things, one must not only be diligent, but open to learning and tolerant of divergent opinions that are not counter to the whole of Scripture.

There are many essentials of faith and life for the believer. One must personally trust in Jesus Christ for life now and the hereafter. A believer is also called to live a life that is consistent with the Word of God. These are givens. However, all believers will not agree on the timing of the second coming of Christ or when and where certain battles might take place and the timing of other events or the identity of certain personages surrounding these events.

While all believers may not agree on these things, it does behoove one to study them to the extent they:

1. Are comfortable that their understanding and position is true to the Word of God.

2. Are humble enough to continue to engage in positive relationships with committed believers with slightly divergent views of eschatology.

3. Gratefully and humbly participate in the times to come even if things don't occur when they think they will.

Chuck Missler, internationally known and respected Bible scholar, feels that the return of Jesus will occur prior to the events described as "The Tribulation" in the book of Revelation. Other competent and sincere Bible scholars feel that the return will take place at a slightly different time. Chuck's response to them in speaking of this event and specifically about what is known as "The Rapture" is "That's ok; we'll explain it to you on the way up." Chuck is doing his best to be right about his scholarship, as should we. He is also humble enough to know that the important thing is to trust the Messiah and to have a personal effective relationship with Him. Any details about the future will become clear at the right point in time.

This study will help us all gain a better understanding of the past, present and future of all believers, whether Jewish or Gentile. And, most importantly, it will help us learn more about the ultimate destiny of everyone who trusts in Yeshua Ha-Maschiach, the Jewish Messiah who we call Jesus Christ.

Since the book of Revelation holds so many "secrets" and concepts that relate specifically to our ultimate destiny I suggest that we each approach it not only with awe, but with scholarship aided by the power of the Holy Spirit. Don't rely on what is presented in this study alone. Proceed as suggested in Acts 17:11. Search the Scriptures yourself on a daily basis to be sure that you know the Author of your faith on an intimate personal basis and that you fully experience the abundant life available through Him.

As part of this investigative effort the student of Revelation will encounter concepts and symbols whose meaning may not be immediately apparent. I suggest that such serious students make extensive use of a good concordance. Doing so will take the diligent student to most every book of the Bible. By following these words and concepts through the whole of the New and Old Testaments one gains a greater understanding of the grandeur of the plan of God not only for the world at large but for each follower of Jesus Christ on an individualized basis. In the end, what this supernatural book means to you and your life will be the greatest secret unraveled by everyone who studies it.

Supplement to Revelation Introduction

Revelation:

1. 404 Verses in Revelation

2. 800+ Allusions to Old Testament Scriptures

Whole of Scripture:

1. 8362 Predictive Verses

2. 1817 Predictions are Made

3. 737 Separate Matters

Jesus Christ:

1. Over 300 References to First Coming in OT.

2. Over 1845 References to Second Coming and Rule on Earth (OT and NT Combined)

- Prominent in 17 Books of Tanakh.

- Mentioned in 23 of 27 New Testament Books

Four Major Views

1. Preterist

2. Historical

3. Idealist

4. Futurist (The one claimed in the text itself.)

A UNIQUE PROMISE
REVELATION 1:1-3

Opening Prayer

Group Warm-Up Question

What outlandish predictions about the future have you heard at one time or another?

Human beings seem simply enthralled and enchanted by the possibility that they might know the future. Many charlatans have used this predilection to their own financial advantage. Indeed, Edgar C. Whisetianat published a short book that was very popular in the 1980's. That is, it was very popular until 1989. The title was "88 Reasons Why the Rapture Will Be In 1988." While the author and his group were obviously discredited, they did mislead many people in the process of raking in a lot of money. (See Mark 13:32 and Acts 1:6-7)

Jesus Christ himself warned people about scams like this. And, of course, He did better than that. Through His Word he provided us with a roadmap for daily life now and in the time to come. The book of Revelation is part of that road map.

Read Matthew 24:1-51 to see part of what Jesus had to say about His return.

Please list the things we learn from this passage.

1.

2.

3.

4.

5.

6.

7.

8.

9.

10.

11.

12.

13.

14.

15.

16.

17.

18.

19.

20.

21.

22.

23.

24.

25.

26.

27.

28.

29.

30.

31.

32.

33.

34.

How do you feel and what are your thoughts having read this passage and having made such a long list?

Reread: Matthew 24:35

What key truth do we learn from this verse?

Why is it so important that we remember this truth?

Read: Revelation 1:1-3

Reread: Revelation 1:1

What did John call his writing in this book?

What is this book about?

For whose benefit did God provide the book of Revelation?

The Holy Spirit inspired John to use the term *doulos* in the original Greek, or bond slave in referring to God's servants in this verse. (See Exodus 21:5-6 and Deuteronomy 15:17)

Why is it important that God refers to His followers as "His servants?" What does this mean to you?

Why is it important to realize that God also referred to John, obviously an important man, as "His servant?"

How did God deliver this revelation to John?

What did God want us to learn from the book of Revelation?

The term Revelation is *apokalypsis* in the original Greek (apocalyspsis in Latin) and is the source of our modern English word *apocalypse*. While this has become a synonym for chaos and catastrophe in our day, the actual meaning of the original word simply means "unveiling." When used as a verb it means "to uncover, to reveal or to make manifest."

Let's also read Revelation 1:1 in the NKJV.

Revelation 1:1

"The Revelation of Jesus Christ, which God gave Him to show His servants— things which must shortly take place. And He sent and signified *it* by His angel to His servant John,"

Here we should note:

1. This Unveiling is not just that of certain events. It is also that of a person, Jesus Christ.

2. The unveiling has been signified. That is it is delivered in signs such it can be deciphered by one who diligently studies and applies the whole of Scripture. (As we noted in our introduction)

Before we go further, we should also ask one more important question. That is, when did John say that the things in this book would happen?

The answer to this question is more involved than one can determine by simply reading the translation in English. The NLT says these things will happen "soon." The KJV says they will "shortly come to pass." To get to the root of what this means one must go back to the original Greek. Here we find that what has been translated "shortly" was *"en taxei."* This is the root of the word tachometer and means that these things will come to pass rapidly after they begin. It does not mean that they will happen shortly after the book was written.

How does this knowledge of the depth of the Greek involved impact your thoughts about the book of Revelation?

Does this understanding make you take the book even more seriously since once the prophetic events spoken of in the book start happening things will begin rolling along at a rapid pace?

Reread: Revelation 1:2

How much of the information John received from the angel did he report on in this book?

What were the ultimate sources of the information John was passing on in this book?

Reread: Revelation 1:3

What is promised to those who take the time to study the book of Revelation?

What three things must one do to receive the promise made in Revelation 1:3? The promise in this case is conditional.

1.

2.

3.

How did John show a sense of urgency in what he wrote?

How does it make you feel to know that God wants us to know what the future holds?

The book of Revelation also contains important statements as to ways in which a believer can be blessed. Seven specific ways can be found in this book of the Bible alone. Please read each of the references listed below and write down who is blessed, why they are blessed, and how they are blessed.

Read: Revelation 1:3

Who is blessed?

Why are they blessed?

How are they blessed?

Read: Revelation 14:13

Who is blessed?

Why are they blessed?

How are they blessed?

Read: Revelation 16:15

Who is blessed?

Why are they blessed?

How are they blessed?

Read: Revelation 19:9

Who is blessed?

Why are they blessed?

How are they blessed?

Read: Revelation 20:6

Who is blessed?

Why are they blessed?

How are they blessed?

Read: Revelation 22:7

Who is blessed?

Why are they blessed?

How are they blessed?

Read: Revelation 22:14

Who is blessed?

Why are they blessed?

How are they blessed?

Application Questions

What commitment can you make today that will help you get the most out of your study of the book of Revelation?

How can you alter your life-style this week so that you can more honestly say that God calling you "His servant or His follower" is an accurate reflection of you and your life?

Close in Prayer

WEEK 2

GETTING THE LAY OF THE LAND
REVELATION 1:4-8

Opening Prayer

Group Warm-up Question

How did you feel the first time you realized that someone loved you?

Read: Revelation 1:4-8

Reread: Revelation 1:4

To whom did John write this letter?

Note: The reference to Asia refers to the Roman province of Asia, or to what we might call Asia Minor in the modern day country of Eastern Turkey.

What unusual two-fold blessing did John bestow upon his readers in the second sentence of verse 4?

Grace or *charis* was a common Greek greeting. In this instance it refers to more because of its source in God. Here it refers to the unmerited favor of God. (Ephesians 2:8-9)

Peace or *shalom* refers to the peace of God in this instance. This inner peace is deeper and better than any other type of peace or contentment. (John 14:27)

What is being communicated to the readers of this letter when they realize the emotional depth of receiving a blessing of God's grace and peace?

How do you feel when realizing the depth of love behind this letter?

How is God described in this verse?

How is the Holy Spirit referred to?

This appears to be an allusion to Isaiah 11:2. The Holy Spirit is spoken of as the Seven Fold Spirit; part of the trinity. How do you identify the seven characteristics of the Holy Spirit when you put Isaiah 11:2 together with Revelation 1:4?

1.

2.

3.

4.

5.

6.

7.

Reread: Revelation 1:5

In what three ways is Jesus described in this verse?

1.

2.

3.

Read the following verses to see the honored position of Jesus as the Firstborn. Please note what you learn from each.

Colossians 1:15

Colossians 1:18

Romans 8:29

What three things does Revelation 1:5 say Jesus did and/or does for us?

1.

2.

3.

How do you feel knowing that Jesus, in all of His majesty, has done these things for you when you did not deserve it? Please discuss each separately and the impact it has on you personally.

How should we act in the light of these three things God has done for us?

Reread: Revelation 1:6

What honor has Jesus bestowed upon all believers?

As kings and priests what do believers owe to God?

How long will the rule and glory of God last?

It is quite significant that believers are honored to serve God as Kings and priests. In the whole of scripture this honor is bestowed on only two other personages. (See Isaiah 11:1, Hebrews 6:20, and Hebrews 7:1-3)

What, in your opinion, is the import of believers being given the honor of serving God in this fashion?

Note: We will learn much more about the great importance of believers serving God in this fashion in Revelation chapters four and five.

Reread: Revelation 1:7

This statement refers to the second coming of the Lord Jesus Christ to earth.

This event is not the same as what is referred to in Greek as the *Harpazo* or the Rapture in English.

The order, according to Scripture is:

1. The Rapture.

2. The Second Coming.

We see the rapture spoken of in the following verses:

I Thessalonians 4:13-18

I Corinthians 15:50-55

Revelation 3:3

Revelation 16:15

Matthew 24:37-44

I John 3:1-3

Isaiah 26:19

Daniel 12:13

This will be an event with worldwide impact, but experienced only by those who have found new life by trusting Jesus.

The event spoken of in Revelation 1:7 is what is referred to as the Second Coming.

It is spoken of hundreds of times in the Old and New Testament. This will be a very public event witnessed by the whole world and particularly by a repentant nation of Israel.

Read the following verses to see this.

Daniel 7:13-14

Zechariah 12:8-12

Revelation 19:11-15

Matthew 24:30-31

The second coming of Jesus Christ will climax the period known as the tribulation, which we will examine in greater detail as we study Revelation 6-19.

We should note that all godly Bible students do not agree on the timing of the events leading up to the second coming and the establishment of God's eternal kingdom as seen in Revelation 21-22.

Much of this discussion takes place around the timing of the rapture. There are some godly people who believe that believers will go through the tribulation. For more information on this view you might want to take a look at the book *Christians Will Go Through the Tribulation* by Jim McKeever or *A Case for Historic Premillennialism: An Alternative to "Left Behind" Eschatology* by Craig L. Blomberg and Sung Wook Chung. While some students will find this material of interest, it is decidedly not light bedtime reading.

Other committed believers believe that the rapture will occur about half way through the tribulation period.

The majority report, however, at least in North America, is that the rapture is expected to occur prior to the tribulation. Those holding this view point to the following verses, among others, to support their position:

Revelation 3:10-11

I Thessalonians 1:10

I Thessalonians 5:9-10

It is also interesting to note that at a certain point the group of believers referred to as "the church" disappears from mention in the book of Revelation. They are not seen between Revelation 3:22 and Revelation 22:16.

Regardless of the timing of these events it is encouraging to know that believers will be part of the victorious fray against the enemies of God. We see this in Revelation 17:14 where it says "They will fight against the Lamb; but the Lamb, together with His called, chosen, and faithful followers, will defeat them, because He is Lord of lords and King of kings." GNT

We must be wise enough to say that we do not know the specific timing of these events. We do know that according to a high and literal view of scripture:

1. There will be a time when believers are taken up from the earth.

2. There will be a time of great trial and tribulation on the earth unlike any that has ever been seen before. Daniel indicates that this period of time will last seven years. (Daniel 9:25-27)

Understanding the application of this passage from Daniel in its intricacies will require more explanation as we see it in the light of the rest of scripture and history. We will do this in greater depth later in our study.

In the book of Revelation we also see measurements of time that coincide with this seven year time period. Those below refer to half of the period. As with the prophecy about the duration of the Great Tribulation in Daniel, understanding the intricacies of these verses will require more explanation as we see them in the light of the rest of scripture and history.

Revelation 11:2-3

Revelation 12:6

Revelation 12:14

Revelation 13:5

3. Jesus Christ will come again and rule for one thousand years on earth.

4. Jesus Christ will ultimately establish His eternal kingdom along with a new heaven and a new earth.

5. Believers must be prepared to remain faithful to Jesus regardless of the timing of these events.

6. God will empower believers through the Holy Spirit to endure.

7. The rewards awaiting the faithful followers of Jesus Christ are immeasurable.

Reread: Revelation 1:8

How does God describe Himself in this passage?

As with so much else in Revelation, there is more going on here than meets the eye.

Take a look at the following verses to see this playing out.

Revelation 1:4

Revelation 1:8

Revelation 4:8

Revelation 11:17

Revelation 15:3

Revelation 16:7

Revelation 16:14

Revelation 19:6

Revelation 19:15

Revelation 21:22

Revelation 2:8 (Jesus speaking)

Revelation 21:6 (Jesus speaking)

Revelation 1:17-18 (Jesus speaking)

Revelation 22:13 (Jesus speaking)

This concept does not exist only in the book of Revelation. It exists throughout the whole of scripture. Read the following verses to see a few examples:

Isaiah 41:4

Isaiah 44:6 (Note the allusion to the coming work and dual roles of the coming Messiah)

Isaiah 48:12-13

John 1:1-5

By describing Himself in this way God is:

1. Demonstrating His eternal nature.

2. Demonstrating that he has the power to work out His purposes in human history.

3. Showing that He is unlimited by time.

4. Demonstrating that He can do anything. He is all powerful.

5. Demonstrating the deity of Jesus Christ by applying the same description and title to Him as to the Father. (See also John 10:38, John 14:9-11)

Application Questions

What is one way you can show your gratitude for all Jesus has done for you today?

What can you do right now to prepare for the imminent return of Jesus Christ?

Close in Prayer

WEEK 3

NEWS FLASH
REVELATION 1:9-20

Opening Prayer

Group Warm-up Question

What do you think Jesus might have looked like as a man? Why?

Read: Revelation 1:9-20

News Flash: Before we delve into the meat of this session we should consider an important hypothesis. The idea for our consideration is that the second and third chapters of Revelation are the most important chapters in the whole book in terms of our daily lives. These chapters contain seven letters to seven specific churches in existence at the time the book of Revelation was penned. Jesus himself lays out the preparation for chapters two and three in the passage we will consider today. To get an idea of why Jesus might have given the messages to these churches such prominence, consider the following list.

Seven Reasons the Seven Letters are Important

1. Each letter is written to an actual church with certain characteristics.

2. Each letter was also to be read to all of the other churches.

3. Each letter applied to each church to some extent.

4. Every community of believers today also deals with the topics mentioned in the seven letters to some extent.

5. Each letter therefore contains information that is relevant to every community of believers and applies to us today.

6. Each letter applies to us individually today, although perhaps to varying degrees.

7. Some researchers feel that the letters are also prophetic and that in the specific order presented lay out the history of the church.

When we get to the letters themselves, we will realize that they all share common design elements.

Seven Common Design Elements in Each of the Seven Letters

1. Each letter specifically identifies a particular church.

2. In each letter Jesus Christ specifically refers to Himself by a certain title for an express purpose that is relevant to the church in question.

3. Each letter contains a commendation. (Some by inference.)

4. Each letter expresses a concern. (Again, some by inference.)

5. Each letter contains an exhortation.

6. Each letter contains a promise to the Overcomer.

7. Each letter proclaims that it is for all believers and says "He that hath an ear, hear what the Spirit says to the churches."

It is also of some interest that each church seems to have been somewhat surprised at what Jesus had to say about it. In fact, those that thought they were doing great found out something was lacking. Those that thought they were not doing well enough were doing better than they thought. Why do you think this was the case?

How can we as believers or members of a fellowship of believers avoid being surprised at how we are viewed by Jesus Christ?

Reread: Revelation 1:9

In what way was John a companion of his readers?

What did John mean when he spoke of this shared suffering and patient endurance?

(Remember, John was exiled to the island of Patmos by the Roman emperor Domitian from A.D. 86 to A.D. 96.)

Have you experienced such suffering and/or endurance? Please explain.

Why was John where he was when he received this revelation?

How do you think you would respond and fare if exiled on an island for ten years?

John refers to himself by name five times in the book of Revelation.

You can see this in:

Revelation 1:1

Revelation 1:4

Revelation 1:9

Revelation 21:2 (KJV)

Revelation 22:8

As we know from our study of the Scriptures, nothing is there by accident. It is all by design.

Why do you think John is referred to as he is in the above verses?

What impact might this have had on the readers in the first century?

What impact might this have on people now who are students of history?

Might this have had something to do with John's status as part of the "inner circle" of disciples in personal contact with Jesus when he walked the earth and the respect with which he was therefore accorded? How so?

Reread: Revelation 1:10

What kind of voice did John hear in his vision?

What kind of an impact do you think this voice that sounded like Niagara Falls or other great cataracts had upon John?

John refers to being in the spirit four times in the book of Revelation. We can see this in:

Revelation 1:10

Revelation 4:2

Revelation 17:3

Revelation 21:10

Dr. Charles Missler says that every believer lives in two locations and that an imbalance can lead either to mysticism or materialism. What do you think of his statement? Please explain.

It has been said of some people that they are so spiritual that they are of no earthly good. What do you think of this statement? Please explain.

How can believers maintain a healthy and effective balance in their spiritual and temporal lives?

Reread: Revelation 1:11

What was John commanded to do?

There are certainly many other churches mentioned in the scriptures and many more existed that were not mentioned. (Over 100 existed at the time.) Why do you think Jesus directed his letters to the particular churches mentioned in Revelation 1:11?

Many students of the Judeo Christian Scriptures tell us that the problems, successes, and situations experienced by these seven churches mirror what every fellowship of believers or church has or will experience. Every letter is therefore applicable to every church and every believer to at least some degree.

Reread: Revelation 1:12

When John turned around, what objects did he see?

Reread: Revelation 1:13

Who did John see standing behind him?

How was the Son of Man dressed?

It is interesting to note that the title "The Son of Man" is used 85 times in the Gospels to refer to Jesus Christ. 83 of these references were made my Jesus Christ Himself.

It is also interesting to note that the great historian, Josephus, tells us that the priests were in fact girded about the breast (and not the loins) as we see the Son of Man here.

Reread: Revelation 1:13-16

What was the overall appearance of the Son of Man?

Read:

Daniel 7:9

Daniel 7:13-14

Matthew 17:1-9

Revelation 19:12

How do these passages coincide with the description of Jesus in Revelation 1:13-16?

Reread: Revelation 1:14

Read:

Hebrews 4:13

Isaiah 66:18

Proverbs 5:21

Putting these verses together, what seems to be the significance of the way in which the eyes of Jesus are described in Revelation?

Reread: Revelation 1:15

Brass, in scripture is symbolic of sin.

Read: Numbers 21:6-9

This passage might have been hard to understand until Jesus explained it to Nicodemus.

Read: John 3:14-15 to see this.

Having made the connection between the Son of Man being lifted up on a pole like the serpent to save people from sin and so they might have eternal life, the stage is set for John 3:16, perhaps the most famous verse in the Bible.

- John 3:16

16 For God so loved the world that He gave His only begotten Son, that whoever believes in Him should not perish but have everlasting life. NKJV

Reread: Revelation 1:16

Also read:

Hebrews 4:12

Ephesians 6:17

What does the sword in John's vision in Revelation symbolize?

Why is this so important?

Reread: Revelation 1:17

How did John react to seeing the Messiah in all of His radiance and glory?

How do you think you would respond if you turned to the side and saw the Son of Man standing beside you?

In this passage we see an interesting progression of four actions taken by John. They are:

Revelation 1:10 "I heard."

Revelation 1:12 "I turned."

Revelation 1:12 "I saw."

Revelation 1:17 "I fell at His feet."

Does this progression and pattern have any application to us today? How so?

Reread: Revelation 1:17-18

How and why did Jesus reassure and comfort John?

What does it mean to you that Jesus Christ, in all of his power, splendor and majesty, took the time to comfort John, admittedly an old man by this time, when he was frightened?

What did Jesus say about himself?

Of the titles used by Jesus so far in Revelation, which one means the most to you? Why?

Reread: Revelation 1:18

Also read:

Isaiah 41:4

Isaiah 44:6

Isaiah 48:12

Revelation 1:8

Revelation 1:17-18

Revelation 2:8

Revelation 22:13

What do we learn about Jesus Christ when we put these verses together?

What kind of a personal sense do you get when you consider these verses and concepts?

Reread: Revelation 1:19

What did Jesus tell John to do?

In Revelation 1:19 we also see what amounts to an outline of the book of Revelation as a whole.

"Write down what you have seen" (The Vision of Christ)

"The things which are" (The Seven Churches in Chapters 2 and 3)

"The things that will happen" (Revelation 4-22)

Reread: Revelation 1:20

What did Jesus explain to John about the meaning of the seven stars and seven golden lampstands?

Jesus seemed to be saying that He walked among the seven churches and at the same time held them in the palm of His hand. What does this mean to you?

As we noted earlier in this series, the keys to unraveling the mysteries of Revelation are presented in the text of the Judeo Christian scriptures themselves. This is one very obvious example.

What overall impression does the passage under consideration today give you of Jesus Christ?

Application Question

In what ways can you remind yourself of the awesome nature and power of Christ on a daily basis this week?

Prior to Engaging in the upcoming studies on each of the seven churches one might do well to read the following passages:

1. In preparation for studying the letter to the church in Ephesus read Acts 18-20 and Ephesians Chapters 3 and 5.

2. In preparation for the study of the letter to the church in Smyrna read Acts 15.

3. In preparation for the study of the church in Pergamos read Numbers 22-24, Numbers 33, Acts 15, and 1 Corinthians 6.

4. In preparation for the study on the letter to the church in Thyatira read 1 Kings 16, 1 Kings 21, 2 Kings 9:36.

5. In preparation for the study of the letter to the church in Sardis read Galatians and Romans.

6. In preparation for the study of the letter to the church in Philadelphia read First and Second Thessalonians.

7. In preparation for the study of the letter to the church in Laodicea read the book of Colossians.

Close in Prayer

LETTER TO THE FELLOWSHIP OF BELIEVERS IN EPHESUS
REVELATION 2:1-7

Opening Prayer

Background

The reader of today must often wonder why Jesus would bother to write a letter to the church in Ephesus. After all, in modern times the town of Ephesus seems to be little more than a desolate place of admittedly impressive ruins.

However, it was not always so.

Tacticus, a famous Greek military writer, recorded that Ephesus was founded about 1400 B.C., when a temple was built to the ancient Hittite fertility deity who later became identified with Diana. (This Greek military writer was so highly thought of that the word "Tactics," stemming from his name, today is used to denote one's strategy in all areas of life.) The city was colonized by settlers from Athens around 1100 B.C.

In the middle of the 6th century B.C. the city was captured by the Lydians. The Lydian King, Croesus, is still famous today for his personal wealth and the wealth he brought to the city. In Greek and Persian cultures the name of Croesus became a synonym for a wealthy man. Croesus' wealth remained proverbial beyond classical antiquity: in English, expressions such as "rich as Croesus" or "richer than Croesus" are used to indicate great wealth to this day. Croesus is credited as being the first person to issue gold and silver coins as a means of exchange and to foster commerce.

The Lydians were routed by the Persians in 541 B.C. and subsequently joined with other cities in forming the Ionian confederation. They were involved in the Peloponnesian and Persian wars. During those conflicts the city of Ephesus served as a key naval base. In 334 B.C. Ephesus fell to Alexander the Great and became part of his far-reaching empire.

The government in Ephesus was very developed. They sported their own municipal administrative structure and senate, even when they came under the influence of Rome. So prominent were they that the Romans made the city the Roman capital in the province of Asia. This city of great influence, wealth, size, military importance, and center of power was where the church of Ephesus was located. It was, in fact, the largest city of its day in the New Testament period.

As we think of Ephesus in the first century A. D. we should picture a harbor metropolis similar to the most developed such city one can imagine today.

Because of its position and development Ephesus was called "The Queen of Asia." The city proper was extremely beautiful and the chief harbor of proconsular Asia, located, near the mouth of the river Cayster (now the Lower Meander). It was the principal line of communication between Rome and the eastern provinces. Trade with Greece and Italy ran through the port regularly.

Interestingly, even at this point in its history, the end of its prominence was being fomented by the unintentional actions of the Romans. Their legions had cut down all the trees in the area. When the root systems of these trees were gone they no longer held the soil in place during periods of rain and snow. Consequently, the runoff and silt began to fill in the proud harbor. Eventually, years later, the shoreline would be six miles of swampy land beyond where it lay at the height of the city's development. Sea traffic eventually had to be rerouted to Smryna, the second city to receive a letter directly from Jesus Christ in the book of Revelation.

The architecture of Ephesus was superb. The theatre was 495 feet in diameter and held 25,000 people. The Marble Way, lined with statues and fountains, ran from the temple of Artemis through the city to the Megnesia Gate. The Arcadian Way, another main road running from the theatre to the harbor, was 1735 feet long and 70 feet wide. It was lined with columns and shops and was illuminated at night.

The Ephesian goddess Artemis, sometimes called Diana, is not quite the same figure as was worshiped in Greece. The Greek Artemis was the goddess of the hunt. The Ephesian Artemis was a goddess of fertility and was often pictured as draped with eggs or multiple breasts, symbols of fertility, from her waist to her shoulders.

The Temple of Diana (Artemis) was the most outstanding architectural feature of the city. It was one of the "seven wonders" of the ancient world and was four times larger than the Parthenon at Athens. It was erected on a platform 425 feet by 220 feet. The temple building itself was 340 feet by 165 feet and had 120 Ionic columns, each of which was 60 feet high.

The temple of Diana was the center of much activity. It functioned as what some say was the first bank in the world under the direction of the chief temple priests. Harlotry associated with the worship of Diana also took place here. (See *Authentic Christianity* by Gordon Haresign) Local artisans engaged in the very lucrative business of making and selling silver models of the temple and of the goddess herself.

The aforementioned temple harlotry was big business. The preaching of the apostle Paul over a period of two years resulted in many residents of the town choosing a new life in Jesus Christ. These new believers then no longer patronized the temple harlots nor did they buy models of the temple or the goddess. Instead of visiting the temple of harlotry they spent time with their families and in home Bible study groups. Instead of buying idols they gave money to feed the hungry and help the poor.

This led to a great decline in the revenue received by the pagan artisans, the harlots, and the priests. To them, this was an intolerable situation. This economic issue was the impetus for the uproar against Paul in 58 A.D. and for his turbulent departure from the city.

Speaking of Paul, we should note that this bold man always attacked the great centers of power. He carried the message of a new life in Christ to the crossroads of culture, commerce, religion, and government. His boldness in proclaiming the good news and in influencing his world serves as an example for us all.

Paul did return to the area for a final farewell to the Elders in the church at Ephesus. However, he sent for them to meet him in the rival city of Miletus. (Acts 20:16-38) This may have been to avoid causing another uproar in Ephesus or because of the many dredgings the harbor at Ephesus was already going through as a result of the Roman deforestation and erosion.

The apostle John reportedly returned to Ephesus to live after the death of Domitian. He is reported to be buried there as were Timothy and Mary (the mother of Jesus).

Group Warm-up Questions

Why does love, even the most fervent and committed love, sometimes grow cold over time? How can we prevent this from happening?

Read: Revelation 2:1-7

Reread: Revelation 2:1

How does Jesus refer to himself in this verse?

Why do you think He refers to Himself in this fashion?

For help with this we need only to access the whole of Scripture. As we noted in earlier sessions, Scripture itself holds the key to understanding the symbols and metaphors we may encounter elsewhere in God's Word.

Read: Revelation 1:20

How does this verse help us understand what Jesus is saying in Revelation 2:1?

As we noted in the previous session, Jesus seems to be saying that He is not only walking among the believers, He is holding them and their fellowships in the palm of His hand. Does thinking about things in this fashion give you any more insight? How so?

Before we proceed, we might do well to consider the significance of the churches being held in the "right" hand of Jesus. Throughout the scriptures we continually see references to the right hand. This obviously had significance to the people reading the text then. It also obviously had significance to the Holy Spirit, who made sure it was in the text, and it must therefore be important enough for us to understand. A few of the many verses in the book of Revelation where we see this type of symbolism are:

Revelation 2:1

Revelation 1:16

Revelation 1:20

It is clear from our study of the Old and New Testament Scriptures that the "right [hand]" was often a symbol for strength. We can see this in the following verses. (Be sure to include the KJV.)

Revelation 1:17

Exodus 15:6

Psalm 44:1-3

Isaiah 62:8

Psalm 118:15

Psalm 118:16

Psalm 98:1

Psalm 73:23

Isaiah 41:13

Psalm 17:7

Isaiah 45:1

In addition, a person of high rank who put someone on his right hand gave him equal honor with himself and recognized him as possessing equal dignity and authority. This can be seen in:

Matthew 22:44

Mark 14:62

Romans 8:34

Hebrews 8:1

1 Peter 3:22

Ephesians 1:19-21

What do we learn about Jesus Christ from these verses?

What do we learn about God's interaction with believers from these verses?

Reread: Revelation 2:2-3

What does Jesus first remind the Ephesians about?

Why do you think He begins His letter to them first with comfort and then with this statement?

What impact might it have had on the Ephesians to see most pointedly that Jesus knows ALL the things that they do?

Jesus goes on to list the things the Ephesians are doing with which he is pleased. Please list them below. (There are seven.)

1.

2.

3.

4.

5.

6.

7.

By the way, it behooves us to know that the Greek word used for "labor" or "hard work" in verse two means to "toil to the point of exhaustion." The word translated "patience" literally means "endurance under trial." The Ephesian believers were working very hard during some extremely tough times.

In verse two, we also see that the Ephesians were doing a good job of ferreting out the false teachers that they had previously been warned about in the following portions of scripture:

2 John 1:7-9

Acts 20:28-31

1 John 4:1-6 (This verse, in particular, relates to the heresy called Gnosticism, which says that Jesus had a spiritual body and not a physical one. In short, this deceptive doctrine ultimately denies the incarnation, and subsequently His sacrificial death and resurrection. In the end, it fully opposes the plan of God, the opportunity for believers to have a personal relationship with Jesus Christ, and the second birth of believers culminating in our resurrection.)

2 Corinthians 11:1-4

2 Corinthians 11:12-15

Reread: Revelation 2:4

The Greek word describing the love of the Ephesians toward Jesus is *protos*. *Protos* means first in rank and honor; the chief or principal; the superlative; the greatest in quality or degree, surpassing all others.

What great complaint did Jesus have against the believers in Ephesus?

There are actually two specific things for which Jesus is taking the Ephesians to task. What are they?

Why is each of these actions, on its own, so important?

Why did these two actions occur concurrently? What made them happen together? What was the psychological, spiritual, and emotional mechanism?

How could this be possible when they were doing the seven things He first commended them for?

Some would say that the believers in Ephesus were too busy with the business of the King to have time for the King Himself.

Can this happen to people and churches today? How so?

Read:

Psalm 51:12

Jeremiah 2:2

2 Corinthians 11:2

1 John 4:19

Luke 10:38-42

What insight do these verses provide in terms of the love God wants to see from us?

Reread: Revelation 2:5

What does Jesus first tell the Ephesians about what has happened to them in this verse?

Why was it important for Him to tell them how far they had fallen?

What was the solution that Jesus presented to the Ephesians?

What exactly do you think Jesus meant by telling them to "turn back to me and do the works you did at first?"

Curiously, this was the only solution He presented to them. Why was this the only way they could please Him?

Jesus tells the Ephesians that they must "repent." This word has gotten short shrift in today's world. It is often avoided. However, it simply refers to a changing of the way; a change in direction. Why do people in the world today so often want to avoid the use of the word "repent?"

What does Jesus tell the Ephesians He will do if they do not change their ways, love Him and each other as they did at first, and do the works they did at first?

Why must love and action come together as Jesus commands?

Read: James 2:14-20

How does this relate to Revelation 2:5?

If love, commitment, and action do not occur together, what does this indicate?

What does Jesus say He will do if the Ephesians do not get their act together?

What does it mean that He will "remove your lampstand from its place among the seven churches?"

Does this seem harsh? After all, the Ephesians were doing seven good things.

Question: Does this mean that the seven good things the Ephesians were doing were pointless unless done in combination with the things they were lacking?

Read: 1 Samuel 15:22

How does this verse tie in with Revelation 2:5?

How does this apply to our lives as individuals?

What do we learn about the unchanging character of God when we see this same concept in 1 Samuel, written about 1200 years before Revelation was written, and yet still applying to us today, about 3200 years after Samuel was penned?

Can this sort of difficulty with works and real obedience occur with individuals or churches today? How so?

Is the solution for this dilemma, when experienced today, the same as when Jesus sent his letter to the believers in Ephesus? Please explain.

Read: Revelation 2:6

What one great attribute did the Ephesians have in their favor, in addition to the seven mentioned in the first part of Jesus letter to them?

Why did Jesus hate, actually hate, the deeds of the Nicolaitans so much?

Did Jesus hate the Nicolaitans or the *deeds* of the Nicolaitans?

If Jesus disliked what the Nicolaitans were doing, we had better understand their practices so that we can avoid them. The word "Nicolaitan" has its root in two Greek words:

Nicao which means to Conquer, overcome, or rule.

Laos which refers to the Laity (believers not part of the leadership), or people.

The name actually means to conquer the people. This group claimed apostolic authority and is believed to have been a sect that "lorded it over" the believers thus attempting to rob them of their freedom in Christ. History also records that this group was spiritually corrupt and actually engaged in idolatry and sexual sin. It was this group that brought into being the groups that we know today as clergy and laity. We see no such division in Scripture.

We can see this difficulty clearly highlighted in III John 9-11

- 3 John 9-11

9 I sent a brief letter to the church about this, but Diotrephes, who loves to be the leader, does not acknowledge our authority.

10 When I come, I will report some of the things he is doing and the wicked things he is saying about us. He not only refuses to welcome the traveling teachers, he also tells others not to help them. And when they do help, he puts them out of the church.

11 Dear friend, don't let this bad example influence you. Follow only what is good. Remember that those who do good prove that they are God's children, and those who do evil prove that they do not know God.

All believers are to serve as kings and priests as we see in the verses below.

- 1 Peter 2:9

9 But you are not like that, for you are a chosen people. You are a kingdom of priests, God's holy nation, his very own possession. This is so you can show others the goodness of God, for he called you out of the darkness into his wonderful light.

- Revelation 1:6

6 He has made us his kingdom and his priests who serve before God his Father. Give to him everlasting glory! He rules forever and ever! Amen!

All believers have equal access to God through Jesus Christ and they do not need some professional priest, minister, or pastor to mediate on their behalf as we see in Hebrews 10:19

- Hebrews 10:19

19 And so, dear brothers and sisters, we can boldly enter heaven's Most Holy Place because of the blood of Jesus.

What problems have arisen over the centuries from this practice of elevating certain people to positions of negative power or priesthood (virtual or literal) over other believers? Please list as many as you can think of.

1.

2.

3.

4.

5.

6.

Do you think Jesus feels the same way today about the deeds of certain individuals or groups as he felt about the Nicolaitans? How so?

Why does this bother our Lord so much?

What are the negative consequences of this type of problem?

We do, of course, see people with certain gifts placed in roles of leadership. However, these people even with their admittedly important and crucial roles, are no better than those with other gifts. Dealing correctly with this concept has a direct impact upon the health of any small or large group of believers. Read the following verses to see what God has to say about gifts within the fellowship of believers:

Romans 12:4-12

1 Corinthians 12:4-31

1 Peter 4:10

Reread: Revelation 2:7

Who else did Jesus want to benefit from this letter?

What great promise does Jesus give to those who are victorious in and for Him?

What do you think it means to be victorious in the sense Jesus is talking about?

Read:

Mark 13:13

Hebrews 11:32-40

Might someone die in the cause of Christ and yet still be "victorious?"

Read: John 16:33

What insight, comfort, inner peace, and confidence does Jesus' statement provide?

Read: 1 John 5:4-5

Just who are the victorious overcomers?

Application Questions

What is one step you can take this week to be sure that your relationship with Jesus Christ has the proper place of prominence in your life?

If you are in a position of leadership in the body of believers, how can you be sure that your view of yourself is enshrouded in true biblical humility as you perform your vital functions in the service of both Jesus and others who follow Him?

How can you, in a positive and legitimately humble fashion, help other believers who are in a position of leadership to remain humble and to keep Jesus Christ in the proper place of prominence in their lives?

Close in Prayer

LETTER TO THE CHURCH AT SMYRNA
REVELATION 2:8-11

Opening Prayer

Group Warm-up Question

How does talk of death and dying affect you?

Background to Smyrna

The name of the city comes from the Greek word *Smurna* which comes from the Hebrew root that is translated "myrrh." Myrrh was a bitter gum and costly perfume which exudes from a tree or shrub in Arabia and Ethiopia. It was used in embalming (John 19:39) and is associated with suffering and death. The fragrance of Myrrh can only be extracted by crushing the bark or branches of the tree itself. The approbation of death was quite appropriate to the trials and persecutions experienced by the earlier believers in the city.

Smyrna was founded about 3000 B.C. It is the only great city of ancient Roman Asia to survive until the present day. Today, it is called Izmir and is the third largest city in Turkey with a population of 300,000. It exports tobacco, grapes, figs, cotton, olives, and olive oil. Its' excellent harbor aids in the export of the produce from the surrounding farms and was a major factor in the city's prominence two thousand years ago.

About 900 B. C. the city fell into the hands of the Ionians and began the most glorious phase of its history. During that period the poet Homer was born, lived and died in Smyrna. This period ended after three hundred years when the city was attacked by the Lydians. The attacks of the Lydians ended with the devastation of the city and it ceased to exist for about three centuries.

In the 4th century B.C. Alexander the great ordered one of his generals, Lysimachus, to build a strong and beautiful city on this site, the most beautiful in Ionia. He succeeded and Smyrna became known as "The Flower of Ionia." The city prospered and grew into one of the greatest cities in the world at the time. They were allies to Rome and came under Roman control in 27 B.C. Strabo described Smyrna as "The Most Beautiful City in the World." It lies about 42 miles north of Ephesus and sported a double harbor, though the smaller half of this double harbor has since been silted in.

Over the centuries Smyrna was destroyed by earthquakes a number of times. So prosperous and productive was the region that the populace rebuilt the city following each catastrophe. Even today, this busy city, now called Izmir, is called "The Paris of the Levant."

Smyrna was literally full of temples and beautiful buildings. Indeed the collection of such fine architectural marvels surrounding Mount Pagos (recognize the root of the modern word *pagan*) caused it to be called "The Crown of Smyrna."

Speaking of temples and the pagan gods in evidence in Smyrna we should realize that the temple of Zeus, then called the father of the gods, was at the base of Mount Pagos. There were also temples and statues honoring other gods such as Apollo the sun-god, Aphrodite the god of love and beauty, Aesculapius the god of medicine, Cybele the Phrygian nature goddess, Poseidon the sea-god, and Demeter, the goddess of corn. In particular, the worship of Cybele was accompanied by ritual prostitution, drunkenness, and revelry and was accepted as common practice in Smyrna.

With this pantheon of gods the Smyrnans readily accepted Caesar worship. In 196 B.C. they erected a temple to Dea Roma, the goddess of Rome and subsequently built one to Tiberius. Worship of the Roman emperor was compulsory. Each year a Roman citizen had to burn a pinch of incense on the altar to acknowledge publicly that Caesar was the supreme lord. In return, the citizen received a formal certificate that he had done so. Originally this action was intended to simply prove one's political loyalty and unify the empire since citizens were free to worship whatever gods they desired so long as they acknowledged the emperor as number one. However, this test became a vital one for followers of Jesus Christ, many of whom refused to perform this ritual and were consequently burned at the stake or savagely torn apart by wild beasts in the arena.

About 160 years after the birth of Christ, the bishop of Smyrna, a man named Polycarp, refused to acknowledge the emperor as his lord. When he was offered the chance to recant his faith and deny Jesus Christ he said "Eighty and six years have I served Him, and he never did me wrong. How can I now speak evil of my King who has saved me?" The old man was burned at the stake on the Sabbath day.

Polycarp's death and suffering as well as that of many other believers who perished in similar circumstances could have been avoided had they simply put a pinch of incense on the altar acknowledging the Roman emperor as lord. Instead, they remained faithful to the King of the Universe.

There were, however, some so-called Christians, who did put a pinch of incense on the altar and received a certificate saying they did in fact recognize Caesar as lord. They rationalized this action by saying to themselves or perhaps even to God that they didn't really mean it. One can only imagine how the true Lord of all felt about this cowardly action on the part of these weak-kneed people. Actually, we don't need to wonder what Jesus thought about this. We can clearly see what he said when he walked the face of the earth in the following references.

Matthew 10:32–33

32 "Everyone who acknowledges me publicly here on earth, I will also acknowledge before my Father in heaven. 33 But everyone who denies me here on earth, I will also deny before my Father in heaven."

Matthew 10:28

"Don't be afraid of those who want to kill your body; they cannot touch your soul. Fear only God, who can destroy both soul and body in hell."

This is a life and death battle between good and evil. Believers are called to be in the arena of life doing their part for their Lord and King in whatever circumstance they find themselves. There are no obedient "armchair believers" sitting on the sidelines and blandly watching to see how things turn out. True believers must engage in this spiritual and cultural war on all fronts.

One almost hears echoes of Jesus' sentiment from Teddy Roosevelt, a former President of the United States of American when he said:

"It is not the critic who counts, nor the man who points out how the strong man stumbled, or where the doer of deeds could have done them better. The credit belongs to the man who is actually in the arena; whose face is marred by dust and sweat and blood; who strives valiantly; who errs and comes short again and again; who knows the great enthusiasms, the great devotions, and spends himself in a worthy cause; who, at best knows the triumph of high achievement; and who, at worst, if he fails, at least fails while daring greatly, so that his place shall never be with those cold and timid souls who know neither victory nor defeat."

However, unlike those who fail in a political or social cause, believers emerge victorious regardless of the short-term struggles, battles, set-backs, and suffering they endure.

We see this borne out in the following scriptural references. In fact, we even see God's Word providing a prescription for victory throughout the text going far beyond these few passages. We reviewed some of these in our previous lesson. Some are so important, however, that they bear reading again.

Hebrews 11:32-40

John 16:33

1 John 5:4-5

Revelation 17:14

Ephesians 6:10-14, 18

With that backdrop let's take a look at the passage from Revelation under consideration today.

Read: Revelation 2:8-11

The problem with Caesar worship was one of three great difficulties faced within the community of believers in the first century A.D. These three heresies, obstacles or weeds that needed to be dealt with were:

1. The Caesar worship herein described. If Jesus is Lord then Caesar is not. This denies the Lordship of Jesus Christ.

2. Gnosticism, which denies the humanity of Jesus Christ.

3. Legalism, which denies the efficacy of the completed work of Jesus Christ.

Strangely, these three obstacles still surface as stumbling blocks in the world today, although often under different cover.

What examples can you cite of these destructive and sometimes subtle heresies cropping up today?

Note: The word Gnostic is the root of the modern day term Agnostic. The Merriam Webster Dictionary defines an agnostic as a person who holds the view that any ultimate reality (as God) is unknown and probably unknowable; *broadly*: one who is not committed to believing in either the existence or the nonexistence of God or a god.

Agnostics generally regard themselves as intellectually superior to the rest of the human race. In what ways are they fooling themselves?

What are the destructive results of agnosticism in one's life when a person adheres to it?

Reread: Revelation 2:8

Who was addressing John?

How did the speaker in this passage, the One dictating the letter, identify Himself?

As we noted previously, the title used by Jesus Christ when addressing each church was significant in relationship to the situation faced by each specific group of believers. Why do you think Jesus referred to Himself as "The First and the Last, who was dead but is now alive" when writing to the believers in Smyrna who were living under the constant threat of death?

Why was it so important for these people to focus on the resurrection of Jesus as well as their own future resurrection?

Reread: Revelation 2:9

The word translated "tribulation" in some versions of the bible in this verse is *thlipsis*. This refers to a pressing together under pressure and infers great oppression, affliction, distress, and dire straits. It is not to be confused, however, with the Great Tribulation, with which we will deal later in the study of the book of Revelation.

There are two words for poverty in the Greek language.

Penia refers to the state of having nothing, but still being able to get by.

Ptocheia refers to the state of having nothing at all. Persons experiencing this type of poverty are spoken of as having been reduced to beggary. Chuck Missler says they have zero with the number rubbed out.

The poverty spoken of in this verse is ptocheia, that of the worst kind.

Why were many of the believers in Smyrna so poor?

Part of the answer to this question likely had to do with their refusal to day that "Caesar is Lord." They would have been excluded from the guilds and would have found it difficult if not impossible to find employment.

How do the following two verses relate to the question of riches and poverty?

2 Corinthians 6:10

2Corinthians 8:9

What does this definition of true riches and poverty mean to you?

Why did Jesus say the Smyrnans were rich when they were financially destitute?

Jesus also speaks of the blasphemy of a group opposing the believers in Smyrna. How does He identify this group?

This does, of course, beg the question of what a true Jew is as well as who are those who claim to be Jews but are not.

First, we need to realize that a true Jew, according to the Scriptures and as well understood by the apostle Paul, was an ethnic Jew who had accepted Jesus as his or her Messiah and Lord. Today such Jews are sometimes referred to as Completed Jews or Messianic Jews. Paul called them True Jews.

We can see this by reading Romans 2:17-29 in light of the whole of the scriptures as well as in the light of history.

We further see God's special relationship with the Jews in the following verses:

Matthew 10:5-6

John 4:22

Exodus 4:22

Deuteronomy 7:6

Genesis 12:3

We clearly see that through this small group of people God has:

1. Communicated His Word via the Scriptures. (The Bible is essentially a Jewish book written by Jews. These are Jewish scriptures and gentiles are privileged to benefit from them by the grace of God.

2. Brought the Messiah into the world.

God has amazingly referred to the Jews as "His People" and "The Apple of His eye" in His Word throughout history. The Jews have been given a pivotal role in all of human history from beginning to completion. God, in fact, promises to bless those who bless the Jews and curse those who curse them (Genesis 12:3). The Jews did nothing to deserve this. God chose this small and despised race to bring about His glorious purposes in the world. They are, quite appropriately, called "The Chosen People."

So who are the people claiming to be Jews who are not?

Many scholars believe the description of "those who claim to be Jews but are not" refers to ethnic Jews who have not trusted Jesus Christ as their Messiah. Such merely ethnic Jews often persecuted early Jewish believers and frequently continue to do so to this day.

Other scholars believe the epithet "those who claim to be Jews but are not" refers to those practicing what is sometimes called "Replacement Theology." This heresy claims that since the Jews rejected Jesus when he walked on the earth, the promises given to them have been transferred to Gentiles and most specifically to the Gentile church.

Such a claim ignores the fact that almost all of the first believers were, in fact, Jews. While there have been millions of Jewish believers over the centuries, the world has in some ways been turned upside down. For many years there have been far too few True Jews who have trusted in Jesus and far too many Gentiles who heretically claim that they are now true Jews or that the church has become the true Israel.

Holding to "Replacement Theology" ignores the facts of history, including the reestablishment of the nation of Israel exactly as and when foretold in the Old Testament thousands of years ago. It also ignores the fact that Israel reclaimed Jerusalem, again exactly as foretold by the Jewish prophets thousands of years ago. And, worse than that, this ignores the truth of God's Word by incorrectly allegorizing it, thus permitting the one doing the allegorizing to twist it to mean whatever they desire. (For help in correctly viewing God's Word see the appendix at the back of this study entitled "How to Avoid Error.")

The Scriptures cited below show quite clearly that God has remained faithful to His promises to the Jews. They also show quite clearly that Gentile believers are warned to not be arrogant about the grace that they have been shown in being privileged to be a part of God's family.

Leviticus 26:44-45

Jeremiah 33:24-26

Romans 11:1-2

Romans 11:13-18

Romans 11:18-20

And, one final possibility is that this reference has a double intent and refers to both non-believing Jews persecuting the believers as well as to heretical gentiles doing the same.

Again, a True Jew, according to the Scriptures and as well understood by the apostle Paul, was an ethnic Jew who had accepted Jesus as his or her Messiah and Lord.

Reread: Revelation 2:10

What does Jesus tell the believers in Smyrna is about to happen to them?

How does Jesus tell the believers in Smyrna they are to approach the suffering they are about to endure?

How long does Jesus tell the believers in Smyrna they are going to suffer?

Some bible scholars feel that the 10 days spoken of by Jesus in this verse meant more than ten literal days. They feel that the ten days of persecution spoken of refer to ten separate times of intense persecution. They do, of course, have the symbolic language of the scriptures as it relates to a more involved meaning of the term days when used in a prophetic sense on their side. (See Appendix 3) They also have the flow of the history and events that immediately followed this letter from Jesus on their side. There were, in fact, ten periods of intense persecution of believers in the Roman Empire extending over a course of 250 years. They are enumerated below.

Ten Days or Ten Periods of Roman Persecution

AD Years Involved   Emperor

1. 54-68   Nero (Paul beheaded; Peter crucified upside down.)
2. 95-96   Domitian (John exiled to Patmos.)
3. 104-117   Trajan (Ignatius burned at the stake.)
4. 161-180   Marcus Aurelius (Polycarp burned at the stake.)
5. 200-211   Septimus Severus (Irenaeus killed.)
6. 235-237   Maximinus (Killed Ursula and Hippolytus.)
7. 249-251   Decius
8. 257-260   Valerian
9. 270-275   Aurelian
10. 303-313   Diocletian (Worst of them all.)

_____

250 Years

During this long time of ten periods of Roman persecution, over 5 Million Jewish and Gentile believers were murdered for their faith. (This is according to Foxes Book of Martyrs). This was a terrible and bloody time. However, this was not the worst of times for believers.

The worst of times so far was actually the 20th century. In Russia alone Josef Stalin executed between 30 and 40 million people and it is estimated that at least half of them were Christians and Messianic Jews. In addition to this, believing Jews and Gentiles were slaughtered around the world during the past 114 years in Turkey, China, Germany, and elsewhere. Persecution in modern times has not died out. It has accelerated at an amazing pace.

Where do you think such persecution will it happen next?

Where is it happening now?

It is interesting to learn that the noted Christian scholar, author and preacher J. Vernon McGee predicted many years ago that he expected the church of real believers in the United States to someday go underground because of pressure upon it. (Especially in the case of home based Bible study groups.) He expected that the pressure upon believers and persecution of them would come partially from main line religious denominations.

What do you make of what J. Vernon said? Was he paranoid or prescient?

One must be careful that their view of the rapture (to soon be discussed in our study of Revelation) of believers does not distort their view of persecution and suffering. Sometimes believers living in countries that are currently not experiencing much persecution tend to think that God will remove them from the world at the time of the rapture so that they will not suffer hardship. Nothing could be further from the truth.

Believers must remember that they are told that persecution and trials will come. When the apostle Paul was in Mammertime Prison knowingly waiting for his execution, he wrote to Timothy to encourage him. See an excerpt from this letter below.

2 Timothy 3:12–13

12 In fact, everyone who wants to live a godly life in Christ Jesus will be persecuted, 13 while evil men and impostors will go from bad to worse, deceiving and being deceived. (NIV84)

The apostle Peter also had something interesting to say about persecution and suffering.

1 Peter 4:12

Dear friends, don't be surprised at the fiery trials you are going through, as if something strange were happening to you.

Why does God Permit believers to suffer and go through trials, suffering, and persecution if He loves them?

Is it more proper to say that God permits believers to go through trials, suffering and persecution specifically *because* He does love them?

Below you will find a list of eleven reasons believers go through trials with some corresponding references that help to give us some insight into this matter.

Eleven Reasons God Permits Believers to go Through Difficult Times

1. To glorify God.

    • Daniel 3:16-18

    • Daniel 3:24-25 (Be sure to see the NKJV)

2. As discipline for known sin.

    • Hebrews 12:5-11

    • James 4:17

    • Romans 14:23

    • I John 1:9

3. To prevent us from falling into sin.

    • 1 Peter 4:1-2

4. To protect us from problems with pride.

   - 2 Corinthians 12:7-10

   - Galatians 4:14

5. To build our faith.

   - 1 Peter 1:6-7

6. To cause us to grow.

   - Romans 5:3-5

7. To teach us obedience and discipline.

   - Acts 9:15-16

   - Philippians 4:11-13

8. To equip us to comfort others.

   - 2 Corinthians 1:3-4

9. To prove the reality of Christ in our lives.

   - 2 Corinthians 4:7-11

10. To give testimony to the angels.

    - Job 1:8

    - Ephesians 3:8-11

    - 1 Peter 1:12

11. To become more like Christ.

- 1 Peter 2:21

- Romans 8:17

James 1:2–4

2 Dear brothers and sisters, when troubles come your way, consider it an opportunity for great joy. 3 For you know that when your faith is tested, your endurance has a chance to grow. 4 So let it grow, for when your endurance is fully developed, you will be perfect and complete, needing nothing.

Reread: Revelation 2:10

What does Jesus promise believers who remain faithful to Him even unto death?

Crowns

The term used for crown in this verse is the Greek word *stephanos*. This is different that the crown one might find on royalty, referred to as a *diadem* in Greek. The priests of the various deities in Smyrna were termed *stephanophori* in reference to the laurel or golden crowns which they used to wear in public procession. They were awarded this honor at the end of their term in office. A *stephanos* was a crown of competed accomplishment. There are many crowns mentioned in Scripture and likely more than we are aware of.

Some of the crowns about which we are quite clear are listed below. Take a look at the scripture references to obtain an understanding of each. These crowns are rewards for works. They are awarded by Jesus Christ Himself at the "Bema" or judgment seat in the future. Be sure to identify who might receive each crown listed expanding upon what is summarized after each.

1. Crown of Life. See James 1:12 and Revelation 2:10.

   • For those who have suffered and endured for His sake.

2. Crown of Righteousness. See 2 timothy 4:7-8.

   • For those who have fought the good fight, remained faithful and look eagerly forward to His appearing.

3. Crown of Glory. See 1 Peter 5:2-4.

   • For those who care for and watch over His flock.

4. Crown of Incorruptibility. See 1 Corinthians 9:24-25.

   • For those who steadfastly press on.

5. Crown of Rejoicing. 1 Thessalonians 2:19-20.

   • For those who win souls.

Which of these crowns will you win?

Reread: Revelation 2:11

What did Jesus say that everyone reading this letter and who had ears to hear must do?

What great promise does Jesus make at the conclusion of the letter to the believers in Smyrna?

How does this promise apply to you?

Application Question

What steps can you take this week to build your strength and endurance in preparation to victoriously face the persecutions that will come your way?

Close in Prayer

LETTER TO PERGAMOS
REVELATION 2:12-17

Opening Prayer

Background

Pergamos, or Pergamum, was located about 48 miles north of Smyrna. Pergamos is the feminine form of this word and Pergamum is the neuter form. Both were used then and both can be used now. This city was the great religious center of the region. (Ephesus, which we encountered in Christ's first letter in Revelation, was the great political center. Smyrna, which we saw in the second letter, was the great commercial center.)

Pergamum's heritage as a religious center goes far back in history. In 539 B.C. it was captured as part of the dramatic conquest of the Babylonian Empire by Cyrus, the Persian king. This is detailed in the fifth chapter of the book of Daniel and is corroborated elsewhere by secular historians. At the time of this capture, Babylon was the occult capital of the world and the center of witchcraft and sorcery. When Pergamum was assimilated into the Persian Empire it became the new world-wide center of the occult where all manner of evil doctrines were rigorously taught.

The city itself did not have a port. It was about 18 miles inland. It was, however, a very large and booming city with a population of about 200,000. Today it is called Bergama and has declined in population to about 40,000.

Most notably, Zeus, chief among the pagan gods, is said to have been born there. It is in this city where the great temple and altar of Zeus stood. The altar itself rested on a foundation 125 feet by 115 feet and over 50 feet high in the midst of a colonnaded enclosure. This was possibly what was referred to as "the Seat of Satan."

It is also notable that a large temple was built to Aesculapius, the god of healing. The Caduceus, the symbol of a two headed snake on a pole (Hermes staff), was the official emblem of the city. We often see this symbol used today in the medical field.

Pergamos was also the first city to build a temple dedicated to Caesar worship in 27 B. C. and was rabidly devoted to the cult of imperial emperor worship. Many believers died in this city, as they also did around the empire, for refusing to acknowledge Caesar as lord by placing a pinch of incense on his altar as required as part of the annual attestation to one's loyalty to this false god.

Pergamum served as the capital and seat of imperial and judicial authority in Asia Minor until 6 B. C. when Ephesus succeeded the city in that role.

Pergamos also became the center of Hellenistic culture. As a center of fine arts and literature it sported a library with over 200,000 volumes that was built in 198 B.C. This library was so vast that it rivaled the famous one in Alexandria. Also serving as the home of many architects and philosophers the city was renowned as a center of learning, science and culture. As Gordon Haresign points out "it resembled a modern university town."

Group Warm-up Question

How do you conduct yourself when you find yourself in a group of people who hold religious views entirely different than yours?

Read: Revelation 2:12-17

Reread: Revelation 2:12

To whom was this letter written?

It is of some interest to learn that the name Pergamum seems to have some import. It literally means "mixed or objectionable marriage."

Realizing the meaning of the name of the city, what might it have had to do with the situation faced by the early believers who lived there?

How did the Speaker identify Himself in this letter?

With the background we now have on Pergamos and the prevailing culture, why was it important and significant that Jesus Christ identified Himself in this fashion?

Reread: Revelation 2:13

How did Jesus refer to Pergamum?

This would seem to be quite a derogatory way to refer to the city in which one lived. Let's take a look at some of the details.

First we must realize that Satan is real. He has a number of qualities of which we should be aware. He is:

1. A murderer. (Read John 8:44)

2. A deceiver without parallel. (Read Revelation 12:9 and 2 Corinthians 11:3)

3. A liar. (Reread John 8:44)

4. A habitual, willful sinner perpetually acting against God. (Read 1 John 3:8)

5. At the head of a vast and doomed demonic kingdom. (Read: Matthew 25:41 and Revelation 12:7-8)

6. At the head of the world system. (See 1 John 5:19)

7. Not omnipresent. (See Daniel 10) He and his angels have locality. His angels range far and wide extending his influence. (See Revelation 9:14)

This liar and deceiver is also referred to in a number of different ways in Scripture:

1. Our adversary. (See 1 Timothy 5:14 and 1 Peter 5:8)

2. The accuser of believers. (See Revelation 12:10)

3. The god of this world. (See 2 Corinthians 4:4)

4. The prince of the powers of the air. (Ephesians 2:2)

5. The spirit at work in those who refuse to obey God. (See Ephesians 2:2)

6. The enemy who sows distortions, heresies and discord. (Matthew 13:39)

7. The wicked one. (Please use your concordance and see how many times you can find that our adversary is mentioned in this way.)

Reread: Revelation 2:13

What happened to Antipas?

What did the believers in Pergamum do in spite of what happened to Antipas?

Will you remain faithful regardless of what happens to other believers? (Think of the answer Jesus Christ would like to hear and see having sacrificed His life just for you.)

Why do you think Jesus Christ singled out Antipas among the believers who had been murdered in this city?

It would seem, logically, that for the Lord of the Universe to single out the murder of one particular faithful servant, it must have somehow stood out. And, thinking further, if it was outstanding that the other believers in Pergamum remained faithful to Jesus, in spite of what happened to Antipas, it must have been a martyrdom of great impact. After all, believers at the time were constantly under threat of death and were often burned at the stake or otherwise executed. Something special and unique must have happened to Antipas to warrant such mention of his death as well as the specific mention of the unfailing loyalty of the believers who witnessed his death.

As we contemplate this question a review of history reveals more than is immediately obvious. Consider these facts:

1. Pergamos was the center of pagan religion at the time.

2. Zeus was the chief pagan god and a great temple was erected to him in Pergamum.

3. A great hollow bronze bull was erected on the altar of Zeus.

4. The pagan priests would reportedly bound and gag an infidel, someone opposing or not following their pagan religion, and place this person inside the bull.

5. The bull would then be heated from underneath during a pagan worship ceremony.

6. The person inside the bull would moan in pain as they were cooked and burned to death.

7. This practice was then regarded as evidence that Zeus had "given life" to the statue as one could actually hear the bull bellowing and making sounds.

8. Simeon Metaphrastes reported that Antipas, who according to tradition was appointed the Bishop or leader of the church in Pergamum by the apostle Paul, was similarly bound and placed in this bull as punishment for following Jesus Christ. (During the reign of Domitian.)

9. The plan to sacrifice Antipas to Zeus backfired in that he reportedly slipped his gag and ended up singing, praising God, and giving thanks even as he watched his body cook as he burned to death.

How do you think it impacted the pagan priests and those worshipping Zeus when the bull appeared to be praising God and giving witness to Jesus Christ?

How would it impact you if an important leader of the believers with whom you are associated was murdered in such a manner?

Let us, for a moment, take this one step further.

Today, all that remains of the great temple of Zeus is the foundation. What happened to it? Did it simply fall down and rot away over the centuries?

No. Something even more surprising occurred.

In the late 1800's the German engineer, Carl Humann, discovered the ruins and began to excavate them. He cataloged the artifacts and shipped them to Berlin by 1910 with the intention of reconstructing the temple of Zeus. World War I caused a delay in this process and it was not until 1930 that the "Throne of Satan," the reconstructed temple of Zeus, went on display.

Shortly thereafter Albert Speer, the Chief architect of the Third Reich appointed by Adolf Hitler himself, designed a great grandstand based upon the temple of Zeus, the "Throne of Satan." This grandstand was located in Nuremburg where millions of Germans swore an oath of loyalty before God to Adolf Hitler as he overlooked them from the temple's podium.

Let us now take another look at a few Greek words. The Greek word *holokauston* refers to the practice of sacrificing animals to a pagan deity. This word is constructed by combining the word *olo*, which refers to the whole animal, with the word *kaustos* which refers to a complete burning. In 1934 Adolf Hitler issued the Nuremburg laws, a portion of which stated that the Third Reich would solve the "Jewish Problem" with a "final solution." This appears to have been the genesis of the great holocaust in Germany when more than 6 Million victims were killed in the concentration camp ovens. Many people have said that this looks a lot like a sacrifice to Zeus (Satan) by Adolf Hitler.

The original reconstructed temple was badly damaged by allied bombings in World War II. Subsequent to the bombing it was looted by the Red army in the closing days of the conflict. Many of the stolen artifacts remain in the possession of the USSR to this day. Since that time, the temple was again reconstructed and renamed "The Museum of Pergamum" in Berlin. It was remodeled and expanded in 2010. It is now possible take a tour of the "seat of Satan" on line.

What do you make of these historical facts about the temple of Zeus, the "Seat of Satan?"

Reread: Revelation 2:14

What complaints did Jesus enumerate against some of the believers in Pergamum in this verse?

It would seem that some of these believers were compromising with the pagan religions of the city. How does this seem possible when many other believers, like Antipas, were faithful to the end?

In His letter Jesus is upset with the believers tolerating those who followed the teaching of Balaam. How did He characterize what Balaam did?

It is interesting to note that Balaam is mentioned many times throughout the New and Old Testament. He and his actions were so displeasing to God that Balaam was repeatedly used as a negative example to avoid. The believers at this time knew in greater depth just what Balaam did. Jesus told us all we need to know about it for our purposes today in Revelation 2:14. For more information about Balaam you may want to read the following references:

Joshua 13:22 to see that he was a soothsayer.

2 Peter 2:15 to see that Balaam loved to earn money by doing wrong and leading people astray.

Numbers 22 to see Balaam rebuked by his donkey for considering cursing Israel.

Numbers 23-24 to see Balaam refusing to curse Israel.

Numbers 31:16 to see that Balaam taught the enemies of Israel how to defeat them.

Numbers 25:1-3 and Deuteronomy 23:5 to see what Balaam influenced some of the Israelites to do.

Joshua 13:22 to remind ourselves of the consequences of Balaam's action for purposely causing God's people to compromise and rebel.

Jude 1:11 to see that Balaam sacrificed eternal riches for short-term monetary gain.

Reread: Revelation 2:15

What else was happening in Pergamum that displeased Jesus?

As a refresher, we might recall that the problem with the Nicolaitans was also beginning to surface in Ephesus. In short, this is what we learned:

The word "Nicolaitan" has its root in two Greek words;

Nicao which means to Conquer, overcome, or rule.

Laos which refers to the Laity (believers not part of the leadership), or the people.

The name actually means to conquer the people. This group claimed apostolic authority and is believed to have been a sect that "lorded it over" the believers thus attempting to rob them of their freedom in Christ. They also engaged in idolatry and sexual immorality. It was this group that brought into being the groups that we know today as clergy and laity.

What problems must the believers in Pergamum have faced having seen some people who attempted to rule over them as leaders influencing them to compromise their faith and participate in what they knew was overtly wrong?

Read:

Acts 17:11

2 Timothy 3:16-17

By what standard did the believers in Pergamum need to evaluate themselves as well as what they saw and heard from those who would be leaders among them.

By what standard must we evaluate our lives today?

Read: Galatians 5:22-23

What should the believers in Pergamos have been seeing from their leaders?

Reread: Revelation 2:16

What did Jesus tell the Pergamum believers that they must do?

We should be very clear on this topic. The specific problems in Pergamum that needed rectified were:

1. They were compromising with and participating in the pagan practices and religions around them.

2. They were committing sexual sin.

3. Even some of be their leaders were compromising with the pagan practices that surrounded them.

4. Some of their leaders were "lording it over" those who were not leaders in a very negative, condescending, and unscriptural fashion.

5. Some of these same leaders were guilty of sexual sin that was open enough to have been widely recognized.

Does Jesus expect anyone today who has fallen into these traps to also repent? (Repentance indicates a changing of one's ways.)

The believers in Pergamum had an even larger problem than a few errant members of their fellowship following into error. We see that the activities observed as problematic by Jesus were being engaged in by some of their leaders.

How did the fact that some of their leaders were involved with overt sin make the problems of the believers in Pergamum more difficult?

What must believers do today if leaders are caught in overt and open sinful behavior as defined by incongruence with the Word of God?

Must such leaders be openly and publicly rebuked and corrected as we see the apostle Paul doing with Peter in Galatians 2:11-12?

If a leader today is found to be involved in sinful behavior that is not yet public and is found out, how must that person and situation be handled? Read the following verses as you work through the construction of your answer.

James 5:19-20

Matthew 18:15

Matthew 18:16-17

1 John 5:16-17

Are there certain types of sin, such as those being indulged in by some of those in Pergamum, that are so destructive that they must be dealt with in an extremely firm manner?

Read 1 Corinthians 5:11 as you put together your answer.

Why is it necessary to deal with such people in a decidedly firm manner?

Read the following verses to help shed light upon this question.

1 Corinthians 15:33

Galatians 5:9

Reread: Revelation 2:16

What does Jesus say He will do to those in Pergamos who have been acting like Balaam and the Nicolaitans and refuse to change their ways?

Read Hebrews 4:12 as a reminder of what His two edged sword is comprised.

What does He mean by saying that He will *actually fight against them* with His sharp two edged sword?

Specifically, how do you think He would fight against them using His sword?

Read: Romans 8:28

For what purpose does Christ use His sword in the life of believers?

Does Jesus Christ use His sword, or His Word, in this fashion even today? How so?

Can you think of an example of when He used His sword in your life or that of someone you know to bring about His good purposes?

This is obviously a very serious issue.

What can believers do to live in such a way that they please God and avoid these pitfalls? Read the following verses for some insight into this matter:

1 Thessalonians 5:15-22

1 John 5:4-5

Hebrews 3:13

Ephesians 4:21-22

Colossians 2:8

Romans 8:9

1 Peter 1:5

Philippians 2:5-18

Reread: Revelation 2:17

What does Jesus say anyone with ears must do?

Why is it important for all believers to understand the situation in Pergamum and the solution to it?

What does Jesus say He will give to everyone who is victorious?

Read the following verses and discuss what manner of manna Jesus appears to be talking about in Revelation 2:17.

Exodus 16

Psalm 78:24

Psalm 105:40

John 6:51

What else besides manna does Jesus say those who are victorious will receive?

This white stone has several important characteristics. Please list them.

1.

2.

3.

4.

When completed, our list should include:

1. The stone is given to the victorious believer.

2. The stone is given personally by the Lord Jesus Christ.

3. A new name is engraved on the stone.

4. Only the one who receives the new stone and Jesus Christ know what the new name means.

Some people speculate that this new name has to do with what the recipient did in the cause of Jesus Christ. What do you think?

If it turns out to be true that this new name has to do with what you have done in the cause of Christ, what might your personal new name signify?

This reference to a white stone has puzzled many believers and even Bible scholars over the years. However, that need not be entirely so. A careful review of the customs and practices of the time this book was written sheds some helpful light on the subject. Some of the seemingly most relevant bits of information surrounding this white stone are listed below. As you read each one, discuss how it might relate to the engraved white stone Jesus will give to everyone who is victorious.

1. In ancient Greece, members of a jury would cast their vote by using either a black stone or a white stone. A black stone meant that they were voting for the condemnation of the defendant. A white stone signified acquittal.

2. In the ancient Roman world the victor in an athletic contest received a white stone with his name engraved upon it. This stone then served as his "ticket" to a special awards banquet.

3. A white stone was given to a person when he became a "freeman" of the city and thus became a symbol of citizenship.

4. In the period of time when this letter was written, a black stone was often displayed to symbolize sadness or calamity.

5. Conversely, a white stone was displayed to indicate joy and happiness.

6. A white stone called the *tessara hospitalis* was sometimes given to a close friend as a symbol of undying friendship. This stone was engraved with the name of the giver. The stone signified the assurance that the recipient would receive exemplary hospitality and a hearty welcome, even if presented to a friend of the donor.

7. At the time this letter was written a black stone symbolizing an Asian goddess of great wickedness was acquired by the city. The white stone offered by Jesus Christ would have symbolized purity and holiness.

8. Pagan worship at the time of the writing of this letter sometimes involved the worshipers of a heathen deity receiving a white stone with the name of the deity inscribed upon it. Victorious believers, of course, had no part in

this. Some feel that the white stone to be given to the victorious believing overcomers by Jesus may have acted as a counterpoint to the pagan practices, indicating faithfulness to the true Lord, Jesus Christ.

(These references to the white stone emanate from various historical sources including, but not limited to, Gordon Haresign's book, *Authentic Christianity*)

While I am attracted to the second definition, especially as it parallels other scriptural metaphors involving athletics, others might find different explanations helpful. When all is said and done, one can imagine ways in which each of these uses of a white stone at the time of this letter might apply to Jesus Christ and the victorious believer. Nothing in Scripture is there by chance. So perhaps it is by intention that this is a little bit unclear. By taking all of these definitions in concert one gains a greater understanding and appreciation for the privilege of having a personal relationship with Jesus Christ as a victorious believer.

Better yet, when the victorious believer meets Jesus Christ face to face I imagine this will all be crystal clear.

Application Questions

What can you do this week to encourage the leaders in your sphere of believers?

How can you help these leaders to remain humble and faithful at the same time that you encourage them?

Close in Prayer

LETTER TO THE CHURCH IN THYATIRA
REVELATION 2:18-29

Opening Prayer

Background

Thyatira was once an important military city. It was originally a Lydian town with several different names over time. It was conquered by the Persians and subsequently by one of Alexander the Great's four generals, Lysimachus. In 301 B.C. Lysimachus was defeated by his rival, Seleucids I (also called Nicator) and the city became part of Syria. He built the city into one of the most beautiful in the world and named it Thyatira, (*thygater* in Greek means daughter) on being informed that a daughter had been born to him. At that point it was converted into a frontier fortress to guard the way to Pergamos.

While Pergamos allied itself with Rome, Thyatira remained aligned with the Seleucids. They did not come under Roman influence until finally defeated by the Romans in 190 B.C. In New Testament times the city was at the junction of three main roads leading to Pergamos, Sardis, and Smyrna.

After their defeat by Rome Thyatira became an important center for artisans of all types. They boasted more trade guilds than any other city in Asia and included guilds comprised of potters, dyers, tanners, wool and linen makers, bakers, metal workers, bronze smiths, slave dealers, leather workers, and more. In the book of Acts we see one of the merchants from Thyatira becoming a believer when on a sales trip to Philippi. (Acts 16:13-15)

Each guild operated under the auspices of a pagan deity. Membership in the guild associated with one's trade was compulsory. All proceedings and feasts began with homage being paid to the patron god or goddess. This homage included sacrifices to the pagan deity and often also involved idolatrous rituals including drunkenness and sexual permissiveness.

Believers who were also craftsmen faced difficult decisions about how to ply their trade while also navigating their way through their own guild and remaining faithful to Christ. It was difficult for many believers to stand firm, with compromise being the path of least resistance on a temporal basis.

The biggest problems at Thyatira, however, did not arise primarily from Roman persecution or problems with unbelieving Jewish authorities. They were more dangerous and insidious than that. They arose from apostasy and disobedience within the body of believers itself.

Today the road from Istanbul to Izmir (formerly Smyrna) runs through the small and unattractive town of Akhisar with a population of 30,000 which occupies the spot where this once proud and important city stood.

Group Warm-up Question

What are the three best habits you have?

Read: Revelation 2:18-29

Reread: Revelation 2:18

How did Jesus refer to himself in the introduction to this letter?

This is the only place in Revelation that Jesus pointedly uses the title "Son of God." Why do you think he referred to himself in this fashion when communicating to a church with great internal problems?

Besides referring to Himself as the "Son of God," what else does Jesus say about Himself in this verse?

Fire and Brass are symbols of Judgment. Knowing this, why might Jesus have made sure he addressed the Thyatirans under the banner of this description?

Reread: Revelation 2:19

Jesus commended the believers in Thyatira for a number of things they were doing. Please list them.

    1.

    2.

    3.

    4.

    5.

Reread: Revelation 2:20

What great complaint did Jesus have against the believers in Thyatira?

What exactly was this woman doing?

This is not the first instance we find in the bible when someone encouraged others to do wrong in this fashion. Read the following verses to see other times when someone acted in this despicable manner and the serious way in which God regards this practice. As we progress through our lesson today, we will also see that these verses relate directly to the activities of Jezebel in the Old Testament.

Ezekiel 13:20-23

Ezekiel 44:10

Ezekiel 44:12

Jeremiah 23:13-15

Deuteronomy 13:5-10

Read: Acts 15:27-31

What few things did the Jewish believers in the book of Acts caution their new formerly pagan Gentile brothers and sisters to avoid?

Why was it so important that they avoid such practices?

Here, in Revelation 2:20, we see this woman doing exactly what the new believers were cautioned to not do.

What did Jesus call this woman?

The name Jezebel is has become synonymous with many bad traits and actions in modern day language. Off the cuff, what comes to mind when you hear someone refer to a woman as a Jezebel?

Let's take a look at the scriptures and history to see what Jesus meant when he called this woman a Jezebel.

Read 1 Kings 16:31 to see that Jezebel was the daughter of Eth-Baal, King of the Sidonians. Note the incorporation of the name of the pagan deity Baal into the name of the King who followed this terrible cult. This was a common practice at the time. Eth-Baal was already a priest of Astarte, the Phoenician equivalent of Aphrodite or Venus, the Greek and Roman goddess of love and beauty. His daughter grew up with this paganism as a part of her training.

Read 1 Kings 16:30-33 to see that Jezebel married Ahab and influenced him to greater evil than any king of Israel before him. Jezebel's religion, the pagan worship of Baal, was nothing more than depraved sex worship and prostitution. Jezebel and Ahab ushered in the worst period in Old Testament history by institutionalizing this pagan religion and bringing it into the very Temple of God.

Read the following verses to see the Israelites being corrupted by these pagan practices:

Judges 2:11-13

Judges 10:6

1 Samuel 31:7-10 (To see the pervasiveness in the culture at the time.)

1 Kings 11:1-5

1 Kings 11:33

Read Deuteronomy 16:21 to see God's command to be separate from these destructive pagan practices. (The groves referenced included phallic symbols and the pagan practices already mentioned that took place there.) Jezebel and Ahab acted in direct opposition to this command.

Read Jeremiah 7:18 to see God's anger at this corruption.

Read 2 Kings 23:1-7 to see King Josiah rectifying the abominable situation in the temple with these pagan religions.

However, if possible, Jezebel did even more evil than simply bringing in this corruption.

Read 1 Kings 18:4 to see that Jezebel murdered all of the Lord's prophets that she could find.

Read 1 Kings 18:19 to see that Jezebel supported 850 prophets of these debauched pagan deities.

Read 2 Kings 9:22 to see a reference to Jezebel's involvement in and encouragement of not only idolatry, but witchcraft.

Read 1 Kings 18:16-40 to see Elijah's famous confrontation with Jezebel's 850 prophets of Baal and Asherah and the effective destruction of their hold on Israel.

Read 1 Kings 19:1-2 to see Jezebel's vow to kill Elijah.

Read 1 Kings 21:1-16 to see Jezebel arranging the murder of Naboth, a righteous man.

Read 2 Kings 9:30-37 to see the end to which Jezebel came in fulfillment of Elijah's prophecy.

Based upon the Scriptures we just read and your personal study, please enumerate the despicable things Jezebel did in your own words.

1.

2.

3.

4.

5.

6.

7.

8.

9.

10.

Knowing what we do about Jezebel in the Old Testament, do you think that the woman compared to her by Jesus himself in the New Testament was actually a believer? Could she have been an unbeliever who somehow wormed her way into leadership in the community of people following Jesus Christ?

Read:

Revelation 2:21

2 Peter 3:9

How did Jesus show patience even to this destructive woman?

Read:

2 Peter 3:15

Romans 5:8

What do these verses tell us about the patience Jesus has shown toward us?

What encouragement should we take from the patience Jesus showed this woman?

How did this woman, this Jezebel, respond to the patience Jesus showed to her?

Reread: Revelation 2:22-23

What Judgments does Jesus pronounce upon this woman?

What judgments does Jesus say will come to those who joined this woman in her rebellion?

Read: Proverbs 5:3-6

How do you relate these verses to what was happening with the corrupt woman in the verses we are considering today?

What realistic and practical application do these verses have for us today?

The woman referred to as "that Jezebel" in Revelation 2:20 appears to have passed the point of no return. However, what attitude do we see Christ displaying to those she seems to have led into wrongdoing?

Although those who joined this woman are also subject to judgment, they are still being given a chance to repent. Why do you think Jesus is still giving them such an opportunity after all they have done?

Why does God still give people an opportunity to repent and turn toward Him today regardless of what they have done?

Read:

Jeremiah 17:10

Revelation 2:23

Psalm 64:3-7

1 Corinthians 4:5

What does God's Word tell us about thoughts and intentions? Please enumerate what we learn in these verses.

1.

2.

3.

4.

5.

What impact does it have on you to know that Jesus understands your motives and thoughts?

Why do people today still sometimes try to hide what is going on in them internally from an all-knowing God?

What comes of this practice?

What transgressions or sins do we tend to tolerate in our own lives and in the lives of fellow believers?

With what statement does Jesus end verse 23?

Note: This does not refer to one's final destination, which is assured if one has trusted Jesus Christ. (See Ephesians 2:8-9.) Revelation 2:23 refers to one's rewards.

How does it make you feel to know that *everyone* gets whatever they deserve?

How does it make you feel to know that *you* will get exactly what you deserve for what you have or have not done in the cause of Christ?

What dangers do we face if we refuse to respond to God or repent of something we are doing wrong?

Read: Hebrews 4:12

Based upon this verse, what can we do to be sure that our thoughts and intentions are pure and pleasing go God?

Dr. Wayne Dwyer tells a story about someone in the habit of doing something that was mildly harmful to them that is instructive. A woman came to see him with a terrible problem biting her nails. She bit them so much and so often that the tips of her fingers were a bloody mess. She wore gloves when she went out so no one would see her fingers.

When Wayne asked the woman why she didn't just stop, she said she had been to several specialists and not one of them could help her. She had tried hypnosis to no avail. One doctor had prescribed a foul tasting liquid to be applied to her nails so that when she bit them she would gag. She overcame the gags and kept on biting.

Others doctors told her to lose weight. Some told her she was lacking certain nutrients in her diet. Some said she was biting her nails as a psychological symbol of biting something else. One gave her some oral drugs to reduce her craving to bite her nails. Nothing worked.

Wayne said he would see the woman one more time and that was it. He was tired just listening to her excuses. She asked how he could solve her problem when so many other practitioners had failed over the years. He said he would do it in two sessions and told her to just not bite her nails. At that point she began to put her fingers in her mouth to bite them. Wayne slapped her fingers away from her mouth and said "Don't bite your nails." She said, "but I have to bite my nails." He said, "every time you try to bite your nails I am going to slap your hand." She said "Nobody ever explained it to me like that before." She was "cured" after one session.

This is obviously not a passage from Scripture; however, it does have practical applications.

In this true story how was Wayne Dwyer in at least one way acting as God does toward us?

How is the way the woman learned to think after Wayne "explained" things to her similar to the way God helps us learn to think?

Reread: Revelation 2:24-25

The "depths of Satan" spoken of in verse 24 are nothing more than the occult practices engaged in by Jezebel in the Old Testament and the woman referred to as "a Jezebel" in Revelation 2:20. This is in direct contrast to what the believer experiences as referenced in 1 Corinthians 2:7-12.

In your own words, what message does Jesus have in Revelation 2:24-25 for those who have remained faithful in Thyatira in spite of the activities of "this Jezebel?"

Are you in any way comforted or encouraged by these verses? How so?

Read: Philippians 4:8

Is there value in choosing to remain ignorant of certain evil ideas and practices? How so?

Who is responsible for any negative or out of place thoughts a person may have?

Wayne Dwyer tells another story about a person who was sent to him and who was having problems because of the evil thoughts they had about a former friend. Wayne told them to stop thinking such things. They said they couldn't. He told them to send the person putting such thoughts in their mind to him and he would treat them. He said he would simply tell the person giving them the evil thoughts to stop doing so. He knew, of course, that the person he was talking to was responsible for managing their own thought life.

Those who have trusted Jesus Christ in a personal way have an advantage in this endeavor. Read the following verses and comment on how they relate to a follower of Jesus Christ:

Hebrews 10:15-16

Philippians 4:6-8

Romans 8:5-7

Romans 12:2

If we find ourselves having been led into error by others, what process must we go through to correct our mistakes with both God and other people? What are the steps as you see them?

What have you been tolerating in your life that you need to change?

Reread: Revelation 2:25

This is the first instance in the book of Revelation of Jesus coming for believers; the event commonly called the Rapture. For other references to this event read the following verses.

1 Thessalonians 4:13-18

Revelation 3:3

Revelation 16:15

Revelation 22:7

Revelation 22:20

This is in contrast to the references in Revelation 1:7 and Revelation 19:11 that relate to Christ's return to earth in judgment, to defeat His enemies and establish His kingdom.

Reread: Revelation 2:26-28

Also Read:

1 Corinthians 6:2

Daniel 7:18

Daniel 7:27

Psalm 2:1-10

Psalm 110:2

Revelation 20:4

What promises does Jesus make to those who are victorious and who obey him to the end? Please make a list.

    1.

    2.

    3.

    4.

How would you differentiate these promises from one another?

What two conditions must be met by the people to whom Jesus is making special promises in these verses?

What does it mean to obey Jesus "until the end?"

Read:

1 John 5:4-5

John 16:33

Philippians 1:9-11

How do these verses help us remember what it means to be victorious?

What do these verses tell us about the role that Jesus Christ and the Holy Spirit play in a believer living victoriously?

How does this tie into the way Jesus refers to Himself in the letter to Thyatira in light of the situation there? Why is it significant?

In the last part of Revelation 2:28 we see Jesus referred to as "the morning star"

This is actually quite an amazing reference and is a fulfillment of a prophecy received some 3,500 years ago in Numbers 24:17.

We see its fulfillment in:

Revelation 22:16

2 Peter 1:19

Revelation 2:28

A morning star appears in the night sky in the east just before the dawn of a new day. It comes at the coldest and darkest part of the night, when the world appears to be at its bleakest point. What does it mean to you when Jesus is referred to as the "Morning Star?"

Reread: Revelation 2:29

In summary, what do you understand Jesus to be saying to all believers and churches in this letter?

Application Question

What specific steps can you take this week to monitor and control your thought life in a way that is pleasing to God?

Close in Prayer

WEEK 8

THE LETTER TO THE CHURCH IN SARDIS
REVELATION 3:1-6

Opening Prayer

Background

Sardis was one of the oldest cities in Asia. It was mentioned by a number of Greek writers including Aeschylus and Thucydides as a well-known city of importance. In fact, it was known as one of the greatest cities in the world 700 years before this letter was written.

Sardis served as the ancient capital of the Lydian empire about 1200 B.C. As such, it was the home of King Croesus, still renowned for his riches today, and mentioned in our introduction to the letter to Ephesus. Croesus, as you may recall, is credited with issuing the first coins used in commerce in the sixth century B.C. The geographic positioning of the city made it a center for trade as it lies between Pergamos, Smyrna, Ephesus, Philadelphia and Phrygia.

The patron deity of Sardis was the goddess Cybele, known as Diana in Ephesus. As in Ephesus, worship of this goddess was accompanied by pagan rituals involving temple harlots. At first glance, one might assume that this was all just like it was in Ephesus. However, if possible, it was much, much worse. Young single women often prostituted themselves in the temple for a few years to supplement their expected dowries. This was just a way of life in Sardis. No one thought ill of these girls for participating in this custom, even their future husbands. As their moral fiber rotted away the people became increasingly decadent and the men became effeminate. The Greek Historian, Herodotus, writing in the fifth century B.C. described them as "tender-footed Lydians who could only play on the cithara, strike the guitar, and sell by retail." (The cithara was a small stringed instrument that could be held in the lap and resembled a lyre.)

The son of the pagan goddess Diana was said to be the infamous Midas of Greek mythology. According to legend, Midas was king of Phrygia in Asia Minor. The story has it that because he had offered hospitality to a satyr by the name of Silenus, he was granted one wish by the god of wine, Dionysus. His wish, as one might recall from childhood stories, was that everything he touched would turn to gold. This worked out great until it was time for dinner. At that point he realized that his food and water turned to gold before he could consume them and that he would soon starve to death. Dionysus allegedly offered to free him from this problem if he would only take a bath in the Pactolus River. When he did wash in the river the sands were thereafter rife with gold.

Sardis was said to be impregnable. It was located on a hill 1000-1500 feet above the valley of Hermus at the foot of mount Tmolus. The steep cliffs bordering the city on 3 sides, however, were made of clay and suffered constant erosion. It was this erosion that made the conquest of the city possible when besieged by the Persians in 549 B.C.

The story goes that Croesus, then still king of Lydia and residing in Sardis, felt safe when besieged by Cyrus of Persia because he had mount Tmolus to his back and three cliffs to his front. For that reason he did not even post a guard along the three cliff sides of the city. Aware of this situation, Cyrus offered a reward to any man who could find a way of getting up and over these cliffs. One of his soldiers, a man by the name of Hyeroeades, happened to be staring at the unguarded battlements at the top of the cliffs when a passing Lydian soldier somehow dropped his helmet over the edge. Hyeroeades watched in wonder as this soldier clambered down and back up the cliff to retrieve his helmet, revealing a heretofore unknown path.

The next night Hyeroeades followed this path up the cliff accompanied by a Persian army, entered the city unopposed, and conquered it by surprise. Imagine the surprise of the Lydian townspeople and defenders when they turned around to find themselves surrounded by Persians who had seemingly materialized out of thin air.

Subsequent to this seizing of control by the Persians, the city was burned by the Ionians in 501 B.C. It was rebuilt and surrendered to Alexander the Great in 334 B.C. It was then taken by Antigonus in 322 B.C. The city was finally conquered by the Seleucids under Antiochus in 214 B.C. when he followed the example of the Persians that he had heard about and scaled the "impregnable "cliffs by way of a hidden path. Interestingly, this is where the saying "like a thief in the night" has its roots; a colloquialism alluded to by Jesus Himself when telling His followers to be ready for His return as well as by the apostle Paul. (See Matthew 24:43 and 1 Thessalonians 5:2.) In 190 B.C. Sardis was absorbed into the kingdom of Pergamum and later into the Roman Empire.

What an ignoble heritage. Hegel said that "history teaches that man learns nothing from history," and the Sardinians were quite a case in point. They were not watchful, they were not careful, and they were not wise. Unfortunately, this seems to be the lot of much of humanity. However, believers have a great advantage in that if they apply themselves to the Word of God they can in fact learn not only from history, but from the Creator of the world Himself.

This takes us to the situation we encounter with the believers in the sad city of Sardis at the time of Jesus' letter to them. By then the city had lost most of the dignity and splendor they had enjoyed under the Lydians. A major earthquake had caused extensive damage to the city in 17 A.D. So devastating was this quake that the Romans extended to them a five year moratorium on taxes as well as financial aid.

The city was ultimately destroyed by the Turkic conqueror Tamerlane in 1402. It was not until 1910 that archaeological excavations began in the area. However, the ruins of the city itself were not uncovered until 1958. Today, all that remains of this once proud city is the little town of Sart.

It is interesting to note that the believers in Sardis didn't seem to have been threatened by some of the problems plaguing other churches. No problem with Emperor worship is cited. No problem with opposition from Jews is spoken of. No overt scriptural or doctrinal heresy is mentioned. However, this may be the crux of the matter. While no overt heresy was mentioned, the believers in Sardis were in obstinate disobedience to the Word of God by virtue of their careless, complacent, uncaring, and unjustifiably confident (perhaps translated arrogant), approach to faith and life.

Group Warm-up Question

Which do you think is worse---wrongfully having a bad reputation or wrongfully having a good reputation? Why?

Read: Revelation 3:1-6

Reread: Revelation 3:1

How does Jesus refer to himself in the opening line of this letter?

Knowing that nothing is in Scripture by chance and understanding the problems in Sardis, why do you think He referred to himself in this fashion?

Is it possible that Jesus presented the believers in Sardis with the key to solving their problems even in the opening to their letter?

Read:

Revelation 4:5

Isaiah 11:1-2

Here we also see the Holy Spirit referenced as the Seven Fold Spirit and then described in seven ways. Please list the 7 facets of the Holy Spirit as described in Isaiah 11:1-2 below.

1.

2.

3.

4.

5.

6.

7.

Could the empowerment and filling of the Holy Spirit be what was lacking in the church in Sardis?

How could the believers in Sardis fix this problem?

Perhaps we can gain more insight into what the believers in Sardis needed by taking a look at the following verses.

John 7:37-39

John 14:15-17

John 14:26

Who receives the Holy Spirit?

Read: Galatians 5:22-23

Specifically what does the Holy Spirit produce in the lives of those indwelled by Him?

1 Thessalonians 5:16-22

Is it possible for a believer to overtly stifle the Holy Spirit?

Read:

Galatians 5:15-17

Ephesians 4:21-30

2 Timothy 2:14

Exactly what did the believers in Sardis need to let the Holy Spirit do in their lives?

What did they need to do to make this an ongoing reality?

It is interesting to note that the names of the churches involved with each of the seven letters from Jesus in Revelation 2 and 3 also seem to be significant. This is perhaps most interesting in the case of the church in Sardis. There was, in ancient times, a precious stone by the name of the sardius. There has been scholarly debate over what this stone actually was over the years and researchers have tried to nail down its identity without undisputed success. We find this stone mentioned several places in the Old Testament as a precious gemstone as you can in the following verses:

Exodus 28:15–20

15 And thou shalt make the breastplate of judgment with cunning work; after the work of the ephod thou shalt make it; *of* gold, *of* blue, and *of* purple, and *of* scarlet, and *of* fine twined linen, shalt thou make it. 16 Foursquare it shall be *being* doubled; a span *shall be* the length thereof, and a span *shall be* the breadth thereof. 17 And thou shalt set in it settings of stones, *even* four rows of stones: *the first* row *shall be* a sardius, a topaz, and a carbuncle: *this shall be* the first row. 18 And the second row *shall be* an emerald, a sapphire, and a diamond. 19 And the third row a ligure, an agate, and an amethyst. 20 And the fourth row a beryl, and an onyx, and a jasper: they shall be set in gold in their inclosings.

Exodus 39:8–12

8 And he made the breastplate *of* cunning work, like the work of the ephod; *of* gold, blue, and purple, and scarlet, and fine twined linen. 9 It was foursquare; they made the breastplate double: a span *was* the length thereof, and a span the breadth thereof, *being* doubled. 10 And they set in it four rows of stones: *the first* row *was* a sardius, a topaz, and a carbuncle: this *was* the first row. 11 And the second row, an emerald, a sapphire, and a diamond. 12 And the third row, a ligure, an agate, and an amethyst.

Ezekiel 28:13

13 Thou hast been in Eden the garden of God; every precious stone *was* thy covering, the sardius, topaz, and the diamond, the beryl, the onyx, and the jasper, the sapphire, the emerald, and the carbuncle, and gold: the workmanship of thy tabrets and of thy pipes was prepared in thee in the day that thou wast created.

Regardless of the correct identity of this stone, one thing is certain. It was once regarded as precious, but became common and was ultimately regarded no more highly than roadway gravel.

What symbolism and similarity do you see in the name of the city of Sardis and the state of the church in that locale?

What was the reputation of the church in Sardis?

What was the actual state of the group of believers in Sardis?

How could there have been such a wide divergence between reputation and reality in this fellowship?

Does such a divergence between reputation and reality exist in people and groups today?

How, in your experience, have you seen such a divergence develop? What seems to be the process?

What else did Jesus know about the believers in Sardis?

Why do you think Jesus hits the Sardinians right between the eyes with a strong accusation in the first verse? (It is hard to think of a stronger negative label than to have the very Lord refer to them as dead.)

What do you think is your reputation among your coworkers? Neighbors? People in your Small Group bible study? People at church? Clients?

Life-Cycle of Churches

There is a lifecycle that seems to be evident in many churches. This seems to generally be characterized as follows:

1. A church begins with a people-oriented pastor who is faithful to God's Word.

2. The church begins to be concerned more with what is coming from the pulpit than what is happening in the lives of the people.

3. The church begins to become quite concerned with their property and the use and maintenance of their property.

4. The church begins to become power oriented. Emphasis is on a group involved with leadership that "lords it over" the people much in the fashion of the Nicolaitans we have studied.

5. The church becomes politically driven from within. Leaders are concerned with their roles and their turf. They become out of touch with the purpose of the original fellowship.

And there you have it. At least from an organizational point of view, the church has had its teeth pulled. It is an institution more than it is the body of Christ or a body of believers.

Interestingly, this organizational decay seems to also be accompanied by doctrinal decay. It often seems to go like this:

1. The church is founded upon the Word of God and remains true to it.

2. Leadership begins to get soft and stray from the clear teaching of Scripture.

3. In its desire to be inclusive, leadership begins to allegorize Scripture, so that no one is "wrong" or left out.

4. The literal millennial reign of Christ is denied.

5. The prophetic destiny of Israel is denied and replaced with an allegorized church.

6. The personal biblically based devotional life of believers is ignored and disappears.

7. The emphasis on the Gospel of Christ disappears and is replaced with a system of works or a form of religious secular humanism at the worst.

8. Homosexuals and Lesbians are ordained.

9. Non-believers are welcomed as new members of what has become merely a religious club.

What can we do to prevent this decay in a church today?

Reread: Revelation 3:2

What does Jesus tell the believers in Sardis that they must do? (Be sure to read this in the KJV in addition to any other translation you are using.)

Read the following verses to get a flavor for what it means to wake up and be watchful in the biblical sense. Please comment on each reference.

Romans 13:11

1 Corinthians 16:13

1 Peter 5:8

Matthew 26:41

Matthew 24:43

Matthew 24:44

Mark 13:35-37

1 Thessalonians 5:1-6

What does Jesus say about what the believers in Sardis have?

What does Jesus say about the actions of the Sardinians?

What does Jesus mean when He says that He finds the actions of the believers in Sardis are not perfect before God?

What warning does Jesus give in Revelation 3:2?

This infers that one's actions can be such that they satisfy the requirements of God. How does one make sure that their actions are satisfying to God?

How can a church or group of believers appear to be alive but actually be almost dead?

Reread: Revelation 3:3

Question: Jesus tells the believers in Sardis that they must do five specific things. Please list them.

1.

2.

3.

4.

5.

Please read the following verses and list some of the key things the believers in Sardis heard, received, and believed at first.

1 Corinthians 15:1-4

Acts 4:12

Acts 15:11

Romans 10:9-13

2 Timothy 1:9-10

James 1:21

Ephesians 4:17-30

1.

2.

3.

4.

5.

6.

7.

8.

9.

10.

11.

12.

13.

14.

15.

16.

17.

18.

19.

20.

21.

22.

23.

24.

25.

26.

27.

28.

29.

30.

Why, particularly in light of their situation and culture, did the believers in Sardis need to be told to go back to these eternal truths and hold on to them firmly?

Were these believers perhaps being influenced by the pagan practices around them?

The believers in Sardis are being told to repent. What do you think they had to repent of given their city of residence and the culture in which they lived?

How do you think they got into such a mess that the Lord needed to tell them to repent?

Jesus tells the believers that after they have repented they need to turn to Him. Why do you think He tells them that they *must* turn Him *after* they have repented? Why is this necessary?

Do believers today ever find themselves in such a set of circumstances?

How and why do believers today sometimes fall into similar difficulties?

What does Jesus say He will do if the believers in Sardis do not wake up?

What does He mean when he tells them what He will do?

In what specific areas of devotion to our Lord have you become lazy this past month? (Bible reading, prayer, evangelism, helping those less fortunate?)

Reread: Revelation 3:4

What does Jesus say some of the believers in Sardis have not done?

If a small remnant of the believers has not soiled their garments with evil, what does this mean that the others have done?

In what ways might believers today "soil their clothes?"

What does Jesus say that those who have remained undefiled will do?

What do you think it means that they will "walk with Him in white?"

Jesus actually calls the believers who have not soiled their garments with evil "worthy." What does He mean that these few people are worthy?

What did this small group of people do to become worthy? (Hint: Think back to what they first heard, received, and believed.)

What advice might you give to a new believer who desires to live a life pleasing to God and keep from sinning?

Reread: Revelation 3:5

How will those who are victorious be clothed?

Why do you think Jesus mentions being clothed in white in two verses, one right after the other?

What do you think being clothed in white means symbolically?

Read: 1 John 5:3-5

What does it mean to be victorious, according to these verses?

What is the difference between the active trust or belief referenced in these verses and mere intellectual assent?

What two great promises does Jesus make to those who are victorious?

    1.

    2.

Reread: Romans 10:9-13

How can a person know if his or her name is written in the book of life and will never be erased? Please put this in your own words.

What does it mean in today's world for a believer to be "an overcomer?"

Reread: Revelation 3:6

What does Jesus say that anyone with ears must do?

To whom must anyone with an ear listen?

Why is this personage to whom we are to listen particularly important to the believers in Sardis?

Must we also listen to the Spirit?

This verse says we must "hear" what the Spirit is saying. What is the difference between listening and hearing? Please explain.

Is action expected of those who hear? How so?

The Church Today

There are many today who say that a number churches in the United States of America today are quite similar to the church in Sardis. As evidence of this fact they point out that:

1. The divorce rate among church goers is no different than that among those who do not attend.

2. Church members are defying the commandment to "not take Thy name in vain" by calling themselves Christians and not acting as such.

3. According to Charles Crismier writing in *Out of Egypt*, 52,000 people exit mainstream churches every week. 94% of those leaving were allegedly in some position of leadership.

4. Only 63% or less believe the Bible is true and literally the Word of God. (Statistics on this percentage vary depending upon how the survey is conducted and the group surveyed. It is, in any case, desperately low for an organization originally founded upon the Word of God.)

Consider this: The Early Church Grew and Prospered in Houses (They also met in the Temple and larger groups, but they were always in houses.)

Read the Following verses to see the early believers meeting regularly in houses:

Acts 2:1-2

Acts 2:46

Acts 5:42

Acts 8:3

Acts 9:11

Acts 12:12

Acts 16:40

Acts 18:7

Acts 20:20

Acts 21:8

Romans 16:5

1 Corinthians 16:19

Colossians 4:15

Philemon 1:1-3

I believe that a statistical study of churches today will reveal what has always been true. That is:

The Greatest Common Denominator of Growing Churches Today is the Involvement of Members in Small Group Bible Studies.

These groups typically meet in homes but can also be found gathering in schools, offices, and even churches.

They can be comprised of:

1. Members of a larger church who are serious about their faith.

2. Neighborhood groups.

3. Professional groups.

4. Residents of an extended care community.

5. Any other group.

These Groups have several advantages and characteristics, including:

1. There is, in effect, somewhat disciplined multiplication. As groups grow too large members that have benefited from their association in this structure can branch off and begin another group. (Some organizations who sponsor groups suggest that the ideal size for a group is between 12 and 20.)

2. The group is free of barriers to growth because of the ability to divide and multiply, much like the mitosis that occurs in a cell.

3. The participants in a group all tend to be much more "involved."

4. Group members hold each other accountable.

5. Group members experience personal growth and transformation.

6. This is a more effective way for new believers to grow.

7. Group members care for one another on a personal basis.

8. The leadership problems that one sometimes encounters in a larger organization are solved.

9. It is more along the line of the Biblical model.

10. It is more efficient.

11. It is lower in cost.

12. It provides a persecution-proof structure.

13. Group members "disciple each other" through the Word of God.

14. Group members assist each other in becoming more Christ like.

15. There is no bureaucratic problem.

16. There are no clerical mediators.

17. Groups grow by design and invitation.

18. The members struggle and grow together.

19. They share each other's burdens.

20. They are relational, not formal.

21. They flourish when members go through hard times.

22. They multiply under pressure.

23. They thrive in the midst of chaos.

24. Their only boast is in Jesus Christ.

Participation in such groups has:

1. Turned atheists into apostles.

2. Turned terrorists into teachers.

3. Turned plumbers into pastors.

4. Turned elders into evangelists.

Finding a group need not be difficult. Many Biblically oriented churches encourage and sponsor them. If you are not in such a group today I encourage you to either join or start one. Beginning and leading one is not hard. All one has to do is to stay one week ahead of the group itself if leading it. Resources for this abound and are almost too numerous to mention. They include:

1. Study series by organizations such as Koinonia House.

2. Study series by John MacArthur.

3. Study Series by Kay Arthur.

4. Material from Campus Crusade for Christ.

5. Studies prepared by the Navigators.

6. Series such as the Dynamic Bible Study series of which this study is a part.

7. Studies prepared by the Scripture Union.

These and other resources can be quite helpful in leading a Small Group. Many of them can be found at very low cost or free of charge. One need have only the desire and commitment to make it a success. God, through the power of His Spirit, will do the rest.

Application Questions

What can you do today to enhance your reputation in the world and with God at the same time?

What temptations do you know now that you will be facing this week? How can you prepare for them now?

Close in Prayer

WEEK 9

LETTER TO THE CHURCH IN PHILADELPHIA
REVELATION 3:7-13

Opening Prayer

Background

Philadelphia was the youngest city to which Jesus sent a personal letter. It was constructed in an area acquired by Pergamos in about 189 B.C. King Eumenes II of Pergamos had a younger brother, named Attalus II, who became his successor. The brotherly affection between these two was such that Attalus won the cognomen Philadelphus, which means "one who loves his brother." (A cognomen was a name in ancient Rome that often began as a nickname, but then became part of one's normal address.) He thus came to be called Attalus II Philadelphus in Greek. The city in question was named after this king in honor of his loyalty and affection for his brother Eumenes. Coins minted at the time showed the brothers completely alike in height, facial features, and garb.

Philadelphia was located on the imperial Roman road from Rome and Troas to Pergamos, Sardis and the interior of Phrygia and served as a gateway to the high central plain of Asian Minor. Because of its position it became a center for the spreading of Greek language and manners into the eastern parts of Lydia and Phrygia. Their principal deity was Dionysys, the god of wine, and they did produce this beverage in great quantity.

The area in which the city was located was referred to as *katakehaumene*, which means the burned land. It was a highly volcanic region that suffered from repeated earthquakes. Indeed, it was almost completely destroyed by the same earthquake that so devastated Sardis and other cities in the region in 17 A.D. Tremors were reportedly felt for years afterward and the economic disruption caused by the quakes lasted for more than twenty years.

The city never fully recovered from the destruction of the earthquakes. Such was the devastation that they were afforded assistance and tax relief by Tiberius in the same way that it was extended to Sardis.

The believers in the city suffered greatly at the hands of the "false Jews" mentioned in the body of the letter. It is of great note and to the credit of the church in Philadelphia that they persevered and prospered in the face of this persecution. Their victory in the face of these difficult times was so great that the bishop of Antioch, a man named Ignatius, wrote to the followers of Christ in Philadelphia several years after they received their letter directly from Jesus Christ Himself. Ignatius referred to the Jews, who had by then discovered that Jesus Christ was indeed their Messiah and were following Him, in very positive terms. These Jews had by then turned to the believers they had persecuted in complete and sincere remorse for the suffering they had caused and whom they now counted as dear brothers and sisters in faith. Those referred to as "false Jews" by Jesus had now become "True Jews" as referenced by the Apostle Paul.

Over the years the character of this small enclave radically changed. It is now called Alashehir. The city of friendship has become "Allah Shehu," the city of Allah. While the uninformed may say this effectively means "the city of God," it does not. Allah, the principal deity in Islam is diametrically opposed to the one true God of the Bible. How these poor people have fallen into deception over the centuries.

Group Warm-up Question

What is a nickname you had, or wish you had at some point during your lifetime?

Read: Revelation 3:7-13

Reread: Revelation 3:7

Jesus described Himself in a unique and special way in the opening line of this letter. Please list the component attributes He uses to describe Himself.

1.

2.

3.

4.

5.

Knowing the history of the situation in Philadelphia, why do you think Jesus referred to Himself in this fashion?

Merriam-Webster.com defines one who is holy as "exalted or worthy of complete devotion as one perfect in goodness and righteousness."

Read the following verses to gain a greater appreciation for what it means when Jesus is described as "holy" and how this holiness impacts His followers. Be sure to notice the Messianic implications and inferences from the Old Testament verses.

Leviticus 11:44

Leviticus 21:8

Isaiah 6:1-3

Isaiah 57:15

Luke 1:35

Acts 2:27

Hebrews 7:24-25

Luke 1:67-75

Revelation 6:10

Jesus also describes Himself as being "true" in Revelation 3:7. The Greek words used for truth are *alethinos* which means real and genuine and *alethes* which means truth in contrast to falsehood. Please read the following two verses to see this as it relates to both the Father and the Son. Please comment after reading.

John 17:3

John 5:20

Read Psalm 2 to see how holiness and truth relate to the character of God and Jesus Christ.

What does this passage tell us about those who do not trust in Jesus Christ in contrast to those who do? (See Especially Psalm 2:11-12)

What difference does it make to you personally that Jesus is "holy and true?"

Reread: Revelation 3:7

Jesus also refers to Himself as holding the "Key of David" in this verse. To understand this passage better we need to understand what is meant by the "Key of David." Going back to the Old Testament we see that Eliakim as referenced in the book of Isaiah was granted full administrative authority. He actually carried a heavy key on a loop that was slung over his shoulder, indicating his power to grant or deny others an audience with the king. He and he alone had the power to provide access to the presence of the king.

Read Isaiah 22:15-24 to see this concept at work in the Old Testament.

What prophetic allusions to Jesus Christ do you see in this passage?

Read the following verses to see the further implications of the full authority possessed by Jesus Christ as inferred by His holding the key of David.

Isaiah 9:6

Isaiah 9:7

Luke 1:32-33

Matthew 28:18

Revelation 1:18

This might also be a good time to deal with a related topic regarding keys in scripture.

Read: Matthew 16:13-20

When taken out of the context of the whole of scripture one might assume that Jesus was bequeathing the keys of heaven to Peter. However, upon closer examination we see that Jesus was speaking to his disciples as a group, and not to just Peter.

This then begs the question of whom or what is this rock upon which the church will be built and against which hell shall not prevail. This is very clear in scripture and can be found throughout the New and Old testaments. However, one can most effectively see what it means by reading the words of Peter himself:

1 Peter 2:4–9

4 You are coming to Christ, who is the living cornerstone of God's temple. He was rejected by people, but he was chosen by God for great honor. 5 And you are living stones that God is building into his spiritual temple. What's more, you are his holy priests. Through the mediation of Jesus Christ, you offer spiritual sacrifices that please God. 6 As the Scriptures say, "I am placing a cornerstone in Jerusalem, chosen for great honor, and anyone who trusts in him will never be disgraced." 7 Yes, you who trust him recognize the honor God has given him. But for those who reject him, "The stone that the builders rejected has now become the cornerstone." 8 And, "He is the stone that makes people stumble, the rock that makes them fall." They stumble because they do not obey God's word, and so they meet the fate that was planned for them. 9 But you are not like that, for you are a chosen people. You are royal priests, a holy nation, God's very own possession. As a result, you can show others the goodness of God, for he called you out of the darkness into his wonderful light. (NLT)

The rock is clearly Jesus Christ Himself and not a human being and his successors. Our purpose in pointing this out is not to disparage any group or individual. We simply wish to reiterate what we find in the Word of God. That is that the key to life for popes and paupers, rich and poor, high and low, is the same: Jesus Christ, a personal relationship with Him, a love and commitment to His Word, and the concurrent empowerment of the Holy Spirit.

Reread: Revelation 3:8

What did Jesus know about the fellowship of believers in Philadelphia?

How did he describe these believers?

For what two specific actions did Jesus commend these people?

What special thing did Jesus do for this group?

This imagery of the open or shut door finds its genesis in the same passage from the Old Testament that speaks about Keys in Revelation 3:7.

Review Isaiah 22:15-25 to see the first mention of the concept of an open door.

This passage has messianic implications and Eliakim is clearly a "type" of Christ. (A "type" is a representation or pre-figuring of something. We might think of it as a template or even a shadow.)

What observations do you make about this passage and how do you see it relating to Jesus Christ?

The Open Door Motif

The open door motif can be found throughout scripture. We see three primary ways in which it is used. (Gordon Haresign, in his book *Authentic Christianity*, deserves the credit for enumerating the symbolism of doors in this three-fold fashion.)

1. First and foremost Jesus Christ opens the door to the Father. He has opened the door to heaven, salvation, and a new life.

    Read:

    John 14:6

    John 10:1-10

2. Jesus Christ also opens the door for believers to share their faith and to serve.

    Read:

    1 Corinthians 16:9

    2 Corinthians 2:12

    Colossians 4:3

    Acts 14:23-27

    Matthew 28:18-19

3. In addition, Jesus opens the doors of deliverance.

    Read:

    Romans 7:25-8:3

    1 Corinthians 15:55-57

Nothing in scripture is there by accident. It is all by design. It might be said that the three-fold nature of the doors opened by Jesus has further significance in that it alludes to the triune nature of God. (Father, Son, and Holy Spirit)

Following this analogy, we can see the Father, Son, and Holy Spirit acting together in the opening and shutting of doors as referenced in the verses we have reviewed.

Questions About the Relationship Between the Father, the Son and the Holy Spirit:

1. How do they act together in salvation, one's entrance to heaven, and a new life?

2. How do they act together in providing opportunities to serve others and share one's faith?

3. How do they act together in opening the doors of deliverance?

How can we obey Christ and stand up for Him even when we are physically exhausted as the believers in Philadelphia seem to have been?

What examples can you cite of persons or groups standing up and enduring for Christ in the face of such exhaustion? Please list at least seven below.

1.

2.

3.

4.

5.

6.

7.

Reread: Revelation 3:9

How did Jesus identify the people who were giving the believers such a hard time in Philadelphia?

We might recall from our study of the church in Smyrna that the people in that group of believers were also suffering from "false Jews from the Synagogue of Satan." As we learned in that session, a true Jew, according to the Scriptures and as well understood by the apostle Paul, was an ethnic Jew who had accepted Jesus as his or her Messiah and Lord.

Any other iteration of a Jew, whether a Gentile claiming to have replaced Jews in the plan of God or Jews who were legalists replacing God's grace with a system of works, might be called a "false Jew." They are not "true Jews" as we see in Romans 2:17-29 and elsewhere in Scripture. Each of these groups created problems for the Jewish and Gentile believers both at the time this letter was written and continue to do so up until this very day. In the case of Revelation 3:9 and in the face of the history mentioned at the introduction to this session, the false Jews mentioned seem to have primarily been the type of legalists with whom Paul dealt in Galatians.

What two things did Jesus say he would force these "false Jews" to do?

When do you think He was planning to do this? (Refer back to the introduction to this letter in thinking about your answer.)

In Revelation 3:8 Jesus commended the believers in Philadelphia for what they were doing, but they were still under attack.

Read: 1 Peter 2:13-17

How and why should we rejoice today when we are attacked and persecuted for our faith or for doing right?

What does it show when believers who are endeavoring to be faithful to Christ are attacked today?

What form might such attacks take in your life?

What can we do to remain faithful and victorious in the face of such attacks?

Read: Revelation 3:10

This has been a difficult verse for many believing theologians. There is not consistent agreement on the timing of what is called the Rapture in relationship to the Great Tribulation that seems to be referenced in this reading. This is no reason for divisiveness in the fellowship of believers. One day in the future this will be clear to everyone. For the time being all believers need to be able to say with the Apostle Paul:

2 Timothy 1:12

"…, for I know the one in whom I trust, and I am sure that he is able to guard what I have entrusted to him until the day of his return."

This important point being made, we can now turn to the other practical things we can learn from this verse.

What world-wide event did Jesus speak of in Revelation 3:10?

What did Jesus promise to do for the believers in Philadelphia in relationship to this event?

Why did Jesus extend this special privilege to the fellowship in Philadelphia?

Why did Jesus infer this hour of trial would come upon the earth?

What do you think about the idea that the world today is getting better and better? What evidences can you cite for such a position?

What do you think about the idea that the world is generally in a state of spiritual and moral decay. What evidences might one cite for this position?

Reread: Revelation 3:11

When did Jesus say He is coming?

Note: The Greek word here implies that this return will occur "suddenly."

How do you see this tying in with John 14:3?

What did He tell the Philadelphian believers to do?

Jesus mentions a crown in the possession of these people. What crown do you think they had?

It is instructive to note that the only other church for which Jesus had no overt criticism was the fellowship in Smyrna. They also were promised a crown. Read Revelation 2:10 to see this promise and the condition upon which it is based.

What did Jesus say would be the result of the believers in Philadelphia holding on to what they have?

What do you think Jesus meant by telling these people to "hold on to what you have?"

What does this infer would happen to the believers in Philadelphia if they did not hold on to what they had?

How does this concept of holding on apply to believers today?

Can believers today lose their crowns?

What impact does it have upon someone today if they somehow lose their crown?

How can believers today be sure to hold on to their crowns and rewards?

What is the relationship between one's crown and one's salvation? How are they alike and how are they different? Please make a list.

Ways that Crowns/Rewards and Salvation are Alike

1.

2.

3.

4.

5.

Ways that Crowns/Rewards and Salvation are Different

1.

2.

3.

4.

5.

The subject of crowns will come to the fore in Revelation 4 where we discuss them further.

How can believers today best prepare for the return of Jesus Christ?

Revelation 3:12

To whom did Jesus make the promises in this verse?

Why is it that some believers seem better equipped to live victoriously and patiently endure more so than others? What has happened in their lives to make them this way?

Read the following verses as you contemplate your answer.

Isaiah 55:10-11

Ephesians 6:10-18

Jesus made a number of specific promises to those who are victorious in this Revelation 3:12. Please list them.

1.

2.

3.

4.

5.

What does it mean that those who are victorious will become "pillars?"

Read: 2 Corinthians 6:14-7:1

Just what is this "Temple of God" in modern day terms?

Read: Galatians 2:9

Who are some members of your community of believers who might be considered "pillars?" (Those who are faithful and godly members who wholeheartedly support the cause of Christ in your organization, whatever it may be.)

According to Revelation 3:12, just who might be considered a pillar?

If you are living a victorious life as a follower of Jesus Christ, might you not also be considered to be a "Pillar?"

What responsibilities come along with being a "pillar" in the Temple of God?"

Revelation 3:12 also mentions the New Jerusalem. This is a topic of importance that will receive great attention later in this unique book. Read Revelation 21:1-8 to get an idea what this New Jerusalem will be like.

Specifically who will NOT have citizenship in the New Jerusalem?

Specifically who WILL be citizens in the New Jerusalem?

Reread: Revelation 3:13

Who did Jesus say those with ears must listen to?

Who might be included in this group of people who "MUST" listen to the Holy Spirit?

What might be the consequences of not listening to the Holy Spirit and understanding what he is saying to the seven specific churches mentioned in Revelation?

Application Question

How can you share what you have learned so far in the book of Revelation with non-believing and spiritually seeking friends in such a way to effectively help them find what they are looking for?

Close in Prayer

THE EMETIC CHURCH IN LAODICEA
REVELATION 3:14-22

Opening Prayer

Background

Laodicea was a large and prosperous city located south of Philadelphia on the river Lycus, a tributary of the river Meander. (It is from the name of this river and its winding course that we derive the modern term "meander" which means to slowly wind one's way through a situation or life.) It was thought of as the twin city to Hieropolis, a city six miles away which was well known for its hot springs. Laodicea stood midway between Hieropolis and the cold waters of the city of Colossae. Laodicea received its fresh water supply via an aqueduct from Hieropolis. By the time the hot waters of Hieropolis reached Laodicea it was lukewarm. These people knew about the unpalatable nature of lukewarm water first hand. On an interesting side note, the hot springs at Hieropolis still exist and the Turkish government is attempting to harness the geothermal source of these hot waters.

The city of Laodicea was an old one. It was founded by the Ionians about 2000 B.C. as the relatively small town of Diospolis. Because of its geographic location it was indefensible and consequently adopted the posture of compromise when threatened. By the 19th century B.C. the Hittites added it to their growing empire. About a thousand years later it was captured by the Phrygians and soon after by the Lydians. It was renamed Rhoas, but in 250 B.C. was taken by the Syrians and Antiochus II rebuilt the town and named it after his wife Laodice. It then became part of the Kingdom of Pergamos in 190 B.C. and ultimately became part of the Roman Empire. The famous historian Josephus reported that a large Jewish enclave existed in the city.

This was a very rich city. It was home to a number of bankers, gold refiners, and merchants. It stood at the junction of roads leading from Ephesus and Smyrna. Because of this favorable location they handled caravan trade from as far away as the Yellow River in Punjab by the China Sea. Cicero, of old world fame, held court there and did his banking in the city. Marcus Tullius Cicero, who lived from January 3, 106 B.C. until December 7, 43 B.C., was a Roman philosopher, politician, lawyer, orator, political theorist, consul and constitutionalist. He came from a wealthy family and is widely considered one of Rome's greatest orators and prose stylists. The influence of Cicero upon the history of European literature and ideas greatly exceeds that of any other writer. Cicero introduced the Romans to the chief schools of Greek philosophy.

Laodicea was also known for a particular species of black sheep bred in the Lycus Valley and renowned for their unusually soft and glossy black wool. This wool was the basis for a thriving textile and garment industry.

In addition to the production of the aforementioned special wool as well as of its concomitant products, Laodicea was also home to a famous medical college. It was at this college that they developed a famous eye ointment made of oil and collyrium powder. People from far and wide came for this ointment or traded for it via the caravans visiting the city. Aristotle himself, the great Greek philosopher, made reference to this salve and called it "Phyrgian Powder."

The people of this city had become rich from their various economic and business activities. It is said, in fact, that they had become arrogant and proudly self-sufficient. When their city was devastated by an earthquake in 62 A.D. they proudly rebuilt the city using their own wealth and without any assistance from Rome. (This is unlike the cities of Sardis and Philadelphia who were able to survive the earthquakes of 17 A.D. only because of the assistance and tax relief provided by the Roman Emperor, Tiberius.) The remains of this prosperous commercial and financial center can still be seen today. One can see the ruins of a great theater, aqueducts, public baths, a gymnasium and an impressive stadium; all reminders of its former wealth and luxury.

The fellowship of believers in Laodicea seems to have fallen under the spell of the temporal riches that abounded therein. It is felt that the church there was likely founded by Epapras. When the letter to the Colossians was written Paul had not yet visited Laodicea.

Colossians 2:1

1 I want you to know how much I have agonized for you and for the church at Laodicea, and for many other friends who have never known me personally.

A separate circular letter seems to have been written to the Laodiceans. This letter is referenced in Colossians 4:16.

Colossians 4:16

16 After you have read this letter, pass it on to the church at Laodicea so they can read it, too. And you should read the letter I wrote to them.

In Colossians we also see that Paul was with Epaphras, who is said to have founded the church in Laodicea, at the time he wrote to the Colossians. We see that many people including Paul, Epaphras, Luke and Demas were concerned for and praying for the believers in Laodicea. (We see this concern in Colossians 2:1 and the involvement of the other believers later in the letter.)

Colossians 4:12–14

12 Epaphras, a member of your own fellowship and a servant of Christ Jesus, sends you his greetings. He always prays earnestly for you, asking God to make you strong and perfect, fully confident that you are following the whole will of God. 13 I can assure you that he prays hard for you and also for the believers in Laodicea and Hierapolis. 14 Luke, the beloved doctor, sends his greetings, and so does Demas.

Tradition has it that Archippus became the bishop of Laodicea after Epaphras left and his weak leadership contributed to the problems they were having. This seems to be borne out in Paul's admonition to him in Colossians 4:17.

Colossians 4:17

17 And say to Archippus, "Be sure to carry out the work the Lord gave you."

Some say that the Apostle Paul later visited Laodicea and wrote the first letter to Timothy from there. This seems to make great sense since Paul is thought to have suffered from an eye malady and would likely have made his way to the city to seek treatment and their famous eye salve.

Group Warm-up Question

What is the nastiest food or drink you have ever tasted?

Read: Revelation 3:14-22

There is an inscription on a cathedral in Lubeck, Germany that is brought to mind by the letter to Laodicea. See if it does the same for you.

Thus speaketh Christ our Lord to us:

Ye call Me Master, and obey Me not.

Ye Call Me Light and see Me not.

Ye call Me Way and walk Me not.

Ye call Me Life and choose Me not.

Ye call Me Fair, and love Me not.

Ye call Me Rich and ask Me not.

Ye call Me Eternal and seek Me not.

Ye call Me Noble and serve Me not.

Ye call Me Gracious and trust Me not.

Ye call Me Might, and honor Me not.

Ye call Me Just, and fear Me not.

If I condemn you, blame Me not.

Some say that this inscription as well as the letter to Laodicea reminds them of the general condition of the church in the 21st century. What do you think of this comment?

Reread: Revelation 3:14

In all of Jesus' letters to the seven churches, He describes Himself in a way significant to the problems each fellowship was having. How did he describe Himself when writing the letter to the Laodicean believers? Please list the component parts of this description below.

1.

2.

3.

4.

5.

Knowing a little bit about the state of things in Laodicea, why do you think Jesus Christ described Himself in this fashion?

Let's take a moment and see what we know about some of the component parts of the way Jesus described Himself from our scriptural resources.

Jesus refers to himself as the "Amen." This term initially sounds strange to modern ears. In our culture we are probably most familiar with amen as a sort of a benediction at the conclusion of a prayer. However, in the New Testament we see that it means more. It is sometimes used interchangeably with the old English term "verily." In this context it refers to the truth of a matter. When someone says "amen" after a statement has been made it implies not only agreement, but that the statement was absolutely true. Read the following verses to see this in action.

Revelation 1:6

Revelation 1:7

Revelation 3:14

Revelation 7:12

Revelation 22:20

This concept of truth also extends to give us insight into the very character of God. Read the following verses to see this:

Isaiah 65:16

John 14:6

1 Corinthians 1:18-22

It is also interesting to note that the real nature of truth cannot be perceived apart from the One who is The Truth. Many colleges and universities quote a verse from the bible on their seal. One most often sees John 8:32.

John 8:32

"Then you will know the truth, and the truth will set you free."

However, the use of this verse alone is somewhat disingenuous. When it is quoted by many institutions of higher learning they take this verse out of context, even including it on their seal, and saying "you will know the truth, and the truth will set you free." They thus imply that it is they who will teach you the truth. This is, of course, incorrect. By dropping the word "then" at the beginning of the sentence they obscure that fact that knowing the truth is tied to something else. If we read the verse in context and include the preceding verse to which it refers we find:

John 8:31–32

31 To the Jews who had believed him, Jesus said, "If you hold to my teaching, you are really my disciples. 32 Then you will know the truth, and the truth will set you free." NIV 84

Seeing this verse in context allows us to more properly answer the following questions?

Who is the Truth?

How can we know the Truth?

How then does the Truth set us free?

Jesus also refers to Himself as the "faithful and true witness." Read the following verses to get a flavor for what is implied by this approbation.

Revelation 1:4-5

Psalm 89:34-37

Isaiah 55:3-5

John 18:37

Finally, in Revelation 3:14 Jesus refers to Himself as the "beginning of creation." The Greek used here means beginning, first origin, cause; ruling power, authority, ruler.

We see this same concept in:

Revelation 1:8

Isaiah 41:4

However, the concept is stated in a fashion that is somewhat unique in Revelation 3:14 and also appears in:

John 1:3

Colossians 1:15

Colossians 1:18

What do you think Jesus is driving home from the very start of His letter to these people by telling them the following?

1. He is the Truth.

2. He is the true and faithful witness.

3. He is the beginning of all creation, the Alpha and the Omega.

Reread: Revelation 3:15

How much did Jesus know about what the Laodiceans were doing?

Question: How did Jesus characterize the way these people were living?

Read:

1 Kings 18:21

2 Kings 17:41

Ezekiel 20:39

Matthew 6:24

2 Timothy 3:1-5

Is it possible for a person to have enough religion to dull their conscience, but not enough to save them?

When and where do you see this playing itself out in the world today?

Reread: Revelation 3:16

Knowing the geography and culture of the time we see that Jesus was using the nature of the hot and cold springs in the area to make His point. By the time water reached Laodicea in the aqueduct from Hierapolis it was a sickening lukewarm. It was an emetic. It made you want to throw up.

How would it make you feel if the ruler of the Universe said you made Him want to throw up?

What one thing could Jesus say to the people in Laodiciea that would be worse than telling them they make Him want to regurgitate?

Jesus obviously does not want believers to be lukewarm. Having said this, how do you think a lukewarm believer acts in today's world?

What should we do today to be the kind of "hot" believer that Jesus desires?

Read: Matthew 7:21-23

How do you relate this to what Jesus is saying in Revelation 3:16?

How can it be that some people who do many good works do not really know God?

What can you do to be sure you are on the right side of this equation?

Reread: Revelation 3:17

In what ways was the Laodicean church deceived?

When all is said and done, what seems have been the root of the sickening lives of the believers in Laodicea?

Read:

1 Timothy 6:10

1 John 2:16

How does these verses relate to the problems in Laodicea?

The writer of Ecclesiastes had much to say about the futility of loving money and the impact of such misplaced love. Read the following verses and comment as you do so:

Ecclesiastes 2:16

Ecclesiastes 2:11

Ecclesiastes 2:18-19

Ecclesiastes 9:5-10

Ecclesiastes 1:9

These scriptural concepts about the fleeting nature of wealth have been borne out in practice through the centuries. Most recently we might consider the following:

1. "Commodore" Cornelius Vanderbilt, who lived from 1794 until 1877 built a huge fortune in Railroads and Shipping. It is estimated that his fortune was valued at over $100 Billion in today's dollars. The Commodore's heirs enjoyed his hard earned money. They built huge estates and indulged their every whim. One of their most famous projects was the Biltmore, a 250 room French-Style chateau in North Carolina. In fact, the name Biltmore became synonymous with wealth and the impression of wealth. One can still purchase Biltmore hats, so named for their supposed elegance and the impression of wealth they hope to bestow upon their wearers. In

1973 a reunion was held of 120 of the descendants of the Commodore. Arithmetically, if they had simply divided his fortune between themselves and invested modestly to keep up with inflation they should have each been worth somewhere in the neighborhood of $833,000,000. However, a canvasing of the celebrants revealed that not one of them had even $1 Million.

2. Most people in the United States have heard of or shopped at an A&P grocery store. Huntington Hartford II was heir to the fortune that emanated from this chain of stores and his net inheritance was worth hundreds of millions of dollars. He built an art Museum in Manhattan for about $7.4 million and established a 145 acre artist colony in California. One of his favorite projects was the development of a Bahamian resort, estimated to cost between $20 and $30 Million, replete with an imported medieval cloister and gold-plated bathroom fixtures. One of the most famous photographs of him shows HHII locking lips with a woman who appears to be young enough to be his great-great granddaughter. By the time he died at the age of 97 his fortune had vanished.

3. Most people in the United States are also familiar with the old Woolworth five and ten cent stores. The heir to the Woolworth fortune, estimated to have been $500 Million, was Barbara Woolworth Hutton. She blew through art, jewelry and seven husbands. By the time of her death she had a net worth of $3,500.

Besides loving their money, the Laodiceans seem to have been proud and arrogant about their wealth. Read the following verses to see what God's Word has to day about pride, arrogance, and humility.

Psalm 101:5

Psalm 138:6

Proverbs 16:5

Luke 1:42-52

Psalm 18:25-28

Psalm 40:4

Isaiah 66:2

1 Peter 5:5-6

Colossians 3:10-15

Reread: Revelation 3:18

What solution does Jesus give the believers in Laodicea for their deadly problems?

A simple mapping of the problems these people had and the solution offered by Jesus might look like this.

1. They thought they were rich and in fact they rebuilt their devastated city without any outside financial help. Jesus said they were actually poor and needed to buy true riches from Jesus. Read the following verses and discuss what Jesus seems to have meant.

   • Psalm 19:7-11

   • Psalm 12:6

   • 1 Timothy 6:17-19

2. They thought they could see and in fact were home to the renowned medical school with a world famous eye salve. Jesus said they were blind and needed to buy ointment from Jesus so they could see.

- Read 1 Thessalonians 5:16-20 to see what the Laodecians had apparently neglected and done to cause their blindness.

- Read John 14:26 to see the power available to these people if they were to truly "see" again.

3. They arrayed themselves in fine garments and in fact produced a unique soft and glossy wool from a species of sheep found nowhere else. Jesus said they were actually naked and needed to buy white garments from Jesus. Read the following verses and discuss what this seems to mean.

- Revelation 19:7-9

- Revelation 6:10-11

- Revelation 7:9-16

- Revelation 19:12-15

Jesus' Action Plan for Success in Laodicea

Successful businesses, churches and organizations of all kinds generally have some sort of action plan detailing the specific things they do that will lead to success. Jesus Christ has given the people in Laodicea just such a plan. In your own words, please enumerate the action steps he provided to them.

1.

2.

3.

4.

5.

6.

7.

Is this action plan also for us today?

Reread: Revelation 3:19

Also Read:

Hebrews 12:5-8

Hebrews 12:9-11

Proverbs 3:11-12

Despite the fact that the Laodiceans made Jesus want to throw up, did He still love them?

Reread: Revelation 3:20

Read: John 15:5

In a real sense Jesus's statement that He "stands at the door" is further indictment of the people in Laodicea. He is standing outside and not inside with them where He should be. (Apply John 15:5)

What great opportunity does Jesus afford the Laeodiceans in spite of their sickening actions?

Does Jesus still make this offer to people today?

What does it mean to you to know that Jesus makes this offer to you personally?

What must one do to take advantage of this offer and privilege?

Reread: Revelation 3:21

Read:

1 John 5:4-5

Hebrews 1:3

1 Corinthians 6:3

2 Timothy 2:11-12

What surprising information do we find in these verses?

Note: We will learn more about this topic as we continue in our study of Revelation.

Jesus reiterates the phrase about being "victorious" or an "overcomer" one way or another to all the churches in Revelation. He then tells the churches that each letter is to be circulated among the others. Each group of believers then hears this again and again. It is obviously very important to Him that we "get it."

Who is an "overcomer?"

How can you personally be sure of your position as a victorious overcomer?

Reread: Revelation 3:22

Who must listen to the Spirit?

What must these people do?

Application Question

What steps do you need to take this week to be sure you have implemented Jesus' action plan for success in your life?

Close in Prayer

WEEK 11

WORSHIP IN THE
THRONE ROOM
REVELATION 4:1-11

Opening Prayer

Group Warm-up Question

When and where was your most meaningful worship experience?

Read: Revelation 4:1-11

Reread: Revelation 4:1

What did John see after having received the messages for the seven churches?

What kind of voice did John hear?

What did the voice tell him?

Note: It is at this point that many scholars believe the event known as the *Harpazo* or the Rapture takes place. While we will deal with this event here in brief, we will deal with it as it relates to a Road Map of End Times Prophecy in Part Two of today's material.

We might also note that there are committed and very competent Bible scholars who differ in their view of the timing of the Rapture. Internationally known Bible scholar Chuck Missler believes it will occur at this point in the book of Revelation. One of Dr. Missler's favorite authors is Dr. Arnold Fruchtenbaum, who is among the most accomplished Messianic Jewish scholars. Dr. Fruchtenbaum believes that the rapture will take place mid-way through the seven year period known as the Tribulation. These committed brothers in Jesus Christ have a profound respect for the scholarship and scripturally based research of the other while differing on the timing of this particular event.

Dr. Fruchtenbuam might point to Psalm 83, Ezekiel 37-39, the book of Obadiah or other Old Testament references to wars to come as preconditions of the Rapture. Chuck might see these as obviously occurring, but not as preconditions to the *Harpazo*. And, a minority of committed believers feels that the Rapture that takes place after the Great Tribulation.

So, who is right?

The ones who are correct are those who live their lives in the daily expectation of the Rapture and Second Coming of Jesus Christ. Their lives are in order and they desire to bring as many people as possible along with them into the kingdom of God.

Each of us then, must be ready. We must be strong and realize that regardless of when the Rapture occurs we may suffer for our faith. We must trust God, study the Scriptures and be ready at all times to answer anyone who asks us to explain the certainty and hope we have within us. When these events do take place all believers will know for sure just exactly how all of the Old Testament prophecies about them fit together.

Read 1 Thessalonians 4:16 to see the similarity of terms and imagery and why many believe Revelation 4:1 pinpoints the time of the Rapture.

Read Isaiah 26:19 to see this foretold in the Old Testament.

Read 1 Thessalonians 4:13-17 for a fuller description of this event.

Read Luke 24:39 to see that transformed heavenly bodies are real and still possess physical dimensionality.

Read 1 Corinthians 15:50 to see that the bodies of believers must be transformed.

Read 1 John 3:2 to see that our transformed bodies will be like Jesus's transformed body.

Read 1 Corinthians 15:50-53 to see the instantaneous process whereby this takes place. (It takes 10_{-43} seconds (That is 10 to the minus 43 seconds.) for an eye to twinkle. According to physics this is the digital limit to the shortest period of time that is measurable.)

To illustrate this I suggest that everyone in the group snap their fingers simultaneously. Do this several times. A "twinkling of an eye" by comparison is much, much faster.

Read Job 19:25-27 for an Old Testament reference to this event and process.

Reread: Revelation 4:2

What was the first thing that John saw in heaven?

Reread: Revelation 4:3

How did John describe the One sitting on the throne?

What did John see encircling the throne?

What impression does this give you of God the Father?

The jasper herein referenced is a clear stone as we see in Revelation 21:11. Most researchers believe this is the way in which diamonds were referred at the time this book was written. The other stone referred to is the sardine or carnelian, a beautiful red gemstone from the area of the city and church of Sardis. As we see in Exodus 28:17-21 both of these precious and brilliant stones were found in the breastplate of the high priest.

In Revelation 4:3 we see that God is robed in light. This is corroborated in Psalm 104:2 and 1 Timothy 6:16.

In addition to being robed in light, we see that God is encircled by a glow like a rainbow in the color of an emerald. The Greek word for rainbow is *iris*, which can also mean "halo."

Reread: Revelation 4:4

Who or what else did John see encircling the throne?

How were the twenty-four elders dressed?

This then begs the question of the identity of these elders.

Read Revelation 7:13-14. Here we see one of the elders being asked about the group of believers that has been killed during the Tribulation and is now wearing white robes. Since an elder is being asked to identify this other group we can clearly see that the elders are not Tribulation believers.

Read Revelation 7:11 to see that they are not angels.

See Revelation chapters 7 and 12 to see that they cannot be representative of Israel. (Israel has still other parts to play in the plan of God.)

What then are the distinguishing characteristics of these elders?

1. They sit on thrones. Read Revelation 3:21 for a clue as to what this means.

2. They are clothed in white. Read Revelation 3:5 for another clue to their identity.

3. They are wearing crowns. The Greek word used for crown is *stephanos*, the victor's crown. Read the following verses to see other places where the victor's crown is referenced for a further clue.

   • Revelation 2:10

   • Revelation 3:11

   • 1 Corinthians 9:25

   • 1 Thessalonians 2:19

   • 2 Timothy 4:8

   • James 1:12

   • 1 Peter 5:4

4. They sing the song of the redeemed. Read Revelation 5:8-10 and see what this seems to reveal about these elders.

5. They are called "Elders." They are crowned like kings and serve God like priests. They might be thought of as "Kings and Priests." Elders in the New Testament (*presbuteros* in the Greek) are the highest officials in the church and as such are representatives of the church as a whole. Read the following verses to learn more about elders, kings and priests as well as for clues as to how this all fits together and what it might mean.

   • Revelation 5:10

   • Titus 1:5

   • Acts 15:6

   • Acts 20:28

   • 1 Peter 2:5

   • 1 Peter 2:9

   • Revelation 1:6

6. There are 24 Elders. The only other place we see the number 24 in scripture is in relationship to the priests serving in the Jewish Temple. They served twice each year in 24 lots. We can see this in:

    - 1 Chronicles 24:3-5, 18

    - Luke 1:5-9 (Zechariah was serving as a priest as part of his group that was chosen by lot.)

7. Daniel seems to have seen thrones put in place in front of God in the Old Testament. However, at that point they were empty (Daniel 7:9) unlike their full occupancy in Revelation.

After considering all of this, who do you think these elders are?

Many people think they are representatives of the whole believing church. Do you think this holds water?

Other people think that in addition to acting as representatives of the whole church they symbolize the people of God in heaven, enthroned and rewarded. Does this make sense to you?

Is it possible that these two explanations might be true simultaneously?

My friends Ron Jones and Jim McCarthy suggested that they might actually be the 12 apostles and the final 12 leaders of the tribes of Israel, thus showing the unity of the Old and New Testaments. What are your thoughts about this?

Reread: Revelation 4:5-6

What did John see coming from the throne?

What was in front of the throne?

With the backdrop of all of Scripture, what seems to be the significance of what we see before the throne?

In your opinion, what is the significance of the lightning and thunder coming from the throne?

Reread: Revelation 4:6-7

What different kinds of creatures were in the center around the throne? Please list and describe them:

    1.

    2.

    3.

    4.

Reread: Revelation 4:8

How were the four living creatures around the throne similar?

What attribute of God did the four living creatures praise three times in succession?

Why do you think they did this three times?

Could this somehow relate to the very nature of God?

As with so much in the book of Revelation, there is even more at work here than we can see on the surface. However, when we relate what we see to whole of scripture the Word of God becomes even more amazing. With this in mind, let us investigate the four living creatures or beings around the throne of God. If you are like me, you have wondered just what these creatures are.

Who Are These Guys?

As we are learning, the book of Revelation is very rich and contains lessons for us on many levels.

Many people wonder about the identities of the beings mentioned in Revelation 4:6-11.

Revelation 4:6-11

6 In front of the throne was a shiny sea of glass, sparkling like crystal. In the center and around the throne were four living beings, each covered with eyes, front and back.

7 The first of these living beings had the form of a lion; the second looked like an ox; the third had a human face; and the fourth had the form of an eagle with wings spread out as though in flight.

8 Each of these living beings had six wings, and their wings were covered with eyes, inside and out. Day after day and night after night they keep on saying, "Holy, holy, holy is the Lord God Almighty— the one who always was, who is, and who is still to come."

9 Whenever the living beings give glory and honor and thanks to the one sitting on the throne, the one who lives forever and ever,

10 the twenty-four elders fall down and worship the one who lives forever and ever. And they lay their crowns before the throne and say,

11 "You are worthy, O Lord our God, to receive glory and honor and power. For you created everything, and it is for your pleasure that they exist and were created."(NLT)

We know that every detail of Scripture is there by design.

This leads us to ask "Why does the Holy Spirit want us to know about these four creatures? Of what possible significance can they be?"

Many scholars have equated the four creatures with the four gospels. They would correctly point out that:

1. Matthew presents Jesus as the Messiah, the Lion of the Tribe of Judah, and this relates to the creature that has the form of a lion. (The lion is a symbol of strength and majesty.)

2. Mark presents Jesus as a Servant and this relates to the creature that looks like an Ox, a traditional symbol of humble service.

3. Luke presents Jesus as the Son of Man and this relates to the creature with a human face. (This is a symbol of a rational being.)

4. John presents Jesus as the Son of God and this relates to the creature with the form of an eagle. (When something is accomplished with power, confidence, competence, and timeliness it is sometimes said to be accomplished "with the swiftness of eagle's wings.")

These observations all have merit. It is certainly true that the complimentary descriptions of Jesus in the four Gospels help us to better understand our Lord.

Other scholars think that these creatures are the Seraphim or Cherubim found elsewhere in the Scriptures, most notably in the Old Testament. This also has merit and we can see such creatures in Genesis 3:24, Exodus 25, Exodus 26, Exodus 36-37, Numbers 7, I Samuel 4, II Samuel 6, I Kings 6-8, II Kings 19, I Chronicles 13 and 28, II Chronicles 3, 5, and 8, Psalm 80 and 99, Isaiah 6 and 37, Ezekiel 1, 9 through 11 and 41.

Moving in this direction helps us to again realize the Jewishness of the New Testament. As we do this and realize that John was a Jew writing to many who were Jews we may have a further clue as to yet another significant insight to be found in this passage.

Realizing the Old Testament roots of this passage can then lead us back even further to the Torah, the Five Books of Moses.

One of these books, the Book of Numbers, has been enigmatic to many people over the ages. In fact my guess is that many of us have often too quickly read through this book and inwardly wondered "Why in the world did God put this here? Of what possible significance can this be and why would the Holy Spirit want us to know these things with such precision?"

We can gain some insight into one possible answer by diagramming the camp of the Israelites in the Sinai desert.

Read: Numbers 2:1-2

1 Then the Lord gave these instructions to Moses and Aaron:

2 "Each tribe will be assigned its own area in the camp, and the various groups will camp beneath their family banners. The Tabernacle will be located at the center of these tribal compounds. (NLT)

This area can be represented in the center of the diagram by a square. In actuality this encompassed about 12 square miles. For our purposes today let's represent this with a square in the middle of the board with 9 inches on each side.

The directions for the four camps around the Tabernacle were very specific. These camps were to be to the North, South, East, and West, but apparently not to the NW, SE, etc...

Read: Numbers 2:3-9

4 "The divisions of Judah, Issachar, and Zebulun are to camp toward the sunrise on the east side of the Tabernacle, beneath their family banners. These are the names of the tribes, their leaders, and the number of their available troops:

Tribe	Leader	Number
Judah	Nahshon son of Amminadab	74,600
Issachar	Nethanel son of Zuar	54,400
Zebulun	Eliab son of Helon	57,400

9 So the total of all the troops on Judah's side of the camp is 186,400. These three tribes are to lead the way whenever the Israelites travel to a new campsite." (NLT)

The first camp mentioned after the camp of the Levites around the tabernacle is the camp of Judah, which was to the east and encompassed 186,400 able bodied warriors. For our purposes we will represent this by drawing two lines directly down from the Tabernacle in the direction we will designate and label as East. In order to attempt to draw this to scale, we will extend it downward 17 inches.

At this point we should all be aware that the ensign on the banner of the tribe of Judah is a Lion. (Note on diagram)

Now Read: Numbers 2:10-16

11 "The divisions of Reuben, Simeon, and Gad are to camp on the south side of the Tabernacle, beneath their family banners. These are the names of the tribes, their leaders, and the number of their available troops:

Tribe	Leader	Number
Reuben	Elizur son of Shedeur	46,500
Simeon	Shelumiel son of Zurishaddai	59,300
Gad	Eliasaph son of Deuel	45,650

16 So the total of all the troops on Reuben's side of the camp is 151,450. These three tribes will be second in line whenever the Israelites travel." (NLT)

Next we find that the camp of Reuben is to be to the south and it encompasses 151,450 warriors. We will represent this by drawing lines directly out from the left of the Tabernacle a distance of 14 inches.

We should also note that the ensign on the family banner of Reuben was that of the face of a man and note this on the diagram.

Now Read: Numbers 2:18-24

19 "The divisions of Ephraim, Manasseh, and Benjamin are to camp on the west side of the Tabernacle, beneath their family banners. These are the names of the tribes, their leaders, and the number of their available troops:

Tribe	Leader	Number
Ephraim	Elishama son of Ammihud	40,500
Manasseh	Gamaliel son of Pedahzur	32,200
Benjamin	Abidan son of Gideoni	35,400

24 So the total of all the troops on Ephraim's side of the camp is 108,100, and they will follow the Levites in the line of march." (NLT)

In this instance, we will show the camp of Eprahim extending to the west by drawing lines up from the camp of the Levites a distance of 9 inches. Here we will also note that the ensign of the Camp of Ephraim was the Ox.

Read: Numbers 2:25-31

26 "The divisions of Dan, Asher, and Naphtali are to camp on the north side of the Tabernacle, beneath their family banners. These are the names of the tribes, their leaders, and the number of their available troops:

Tribe	Leader	Number
Dan	Ahiezer son of Ammishaddai	62,700
Asher	Pagiel son of Ocran	41,500
Naphtali	Ahira son of Enan	53,400

31 So the total of all the troops on Dan's side of the camp is 157,600. They are to bring up the rear whenever the Israelites move to a new campsite."(NLT)

To illustrate this we will draw lines out from tabernacle to the right for a distance of 13.5 inches. It is important to realize and note on the diagram that the ensign of the Tribe of Dan was the Eagle.

For forty years this symbol was seen every day and every night in the Sinai desert.

The four creatures in revelation 4 seem to point back toward this symbol when we realize how the forms of the creatures correspond to the Camps of Israel in the Sinai desert.

The very form of the camp seems to point toward Yeshua Ha-Maschiach, The Jewish Messiah, Jesus Christ, our Lord and Savior.

To further illustrate the symbolism of the camp of the Israelites in the wilderness we have diagrammed it on the following page.

And finally, when we put all of these references together we find these same four creatures in the Book of Numbers, the four Gospels, and the Book of Revelation. They all point to Jesus Christ.

Note: Source of Tribal Standards of Ancient Israel is Dr. Charles Missler.

W

Ephraim-Ox

108,100

S   Levi   N

Dan-Eagle   Ruben-Man

151,450   157,600

Judah-Lion

186,400

E

Numbers----------------------------Gospels-------------------------Revelation

As we can see, the longest part of this cross is symbolized by Judah, whose symbol is a lion. What significance might there be for us to see as we contemplate this and think about the Lion of Judah Himself?

Reread: Revelation 4:9-11

How did the twenty-four elders worship God?

What do you think it means when we see the elders laying their crowns before the throne?

How should this action relate to you and me today?

Reread: Revelation 4:11

Read: Revelation 5:12

To worship means to ascribe worth. It involves using all that we are and have to praise God for all that He is and does.

Why did the elders say God was worthy of their worship?

Warren Wiersbe says "Heaven is a place of worship. What can you do to get in practice now?" How would you answer his question?

Application Questions

What changes do you feel inspired to make when you reflect upon the holiness and power of God?

How can you make praise and worship more of a regular part of your life?

Close in Prayer

REVELATION 4-PART II
ROADMAP TO END-TIMES PROPHECY

Opening Prayer

Group Warm-up Questions

Do you prefer to take a long trip by automobile with our without a road map? Why?

If you were to take a tour of another country for two weeks, would you prefer to know the daily itinerary (where you would go and what you would do) in advance? Why or why not?

For some time many people approached Ron Jones and me about doing a study on the book of Revelation. This was not, I believe, been based upon a desire to learn principles and practices that will help one in their daily life. It was, I think, been based upon the desire that so many people have to know what comes next on God's timetable.

Believers and non-believers alike are fascinated with the "end times." They want to know what the future holds for them, those around them, and the world at large. Hopefully, having reviewed the Biblical groundwork for the future, those studying it can make the proper personal preparations for the times ahead.

While these times to come are important, they are no less important than the information God imparts to us in the first three chapters of Revelation. In the letters that Christ wrote to the seven churches in Asia Minor we find not only history, but practical and imperative guidelines for successfully navigating our lives now and in the years to come. If one is able to incorporate the lessons in the first three chapters of Revelation with the rest of the book they can come away truly better equipped to face and victoriously overcome the events to come in both the short and long term.

The Map

In order to make this discussion and inquiry more effective we will take a look at the end-times one step at a time. Most maps and charts about the things to come seem to start with a complex chart that must then be torn apart and explained. This makes the whole subject somewhat more difficult to understand and tends to shroud it in mystery.

By taking things one step at a time and gradually building our roadmap or chart, we hope to make things much more easily understood. This is the approach that was taken by Dr. Michael McCormick, Jr. at the Bible Chapel in McMurray, Pa. when making just such a presentation. His summary was so clear and so helpful to the audience that with his permission I am incorporating some of the examples he used as well as the simple progressive charts he developed for the lesson at the end of this chapter. Following Dr. McCormick's progressive material you will also find a chart that is slightly more in depth for those who might find it helpful. This second chart comes to us by way of Dr. David Hurtado which he compiled from the teaching he received from his professors when studying at the Master's College in California. This school was founded and at this writing is still led by John MacArthur, a supremely intelligent and competent scholar and theologian. (These charts are included at the back of this chapter.)

Whether we realize it or not, the approach we are taking is the same one taken by a good lawyer in a court of law. The case for this view of the end-times is presented by God in His Word both in Revelation and the rest of the Judeo Christian scriptures in a similar fashion. One building block rests upon another until the structure is complete. Like a high-quality and complete building, everything fits together just right. While we can examine the various parts of scripture involved and see how they fit into the whole, there are still parts of the construct that are not quite clear. Like the plumbing in a building that cannot be seen when viewing, understanding and appreciating the working structure from the outside, we cannot, with 100 percent accuracy, know the timing of certain events to come, even though we know and appreciate how things all fit together.

Let's take this in steps and relate them to scripture and Dr. McCormick's chart along the way.

1. As we begin in the Old Testament we see a short Summary of God's long-term plan in Genesis 12:1-3

Genesis 12:1–3

1 The LORD said to Abram, "Leave your country, your relatives, and your father's home, and go to a land that I am going to show you. 2 I will give you many descendants, and they will become a great nation. I will bless you and make your name famous, so that you will be a blessing. 3 I will bless those who bless you, But I will curse those who curse you. And through you I will bless all the nations."

Here we learn that:

1. God has chosen Abraham and his Jewish descendants to bless all humankind.

2. Those who bless Israel and the Jews will be blessed and those that curse them will be cursed.

3. God has used the Jews to communicate His Word to us.

4. The Old Testament, from the start, points forward to the way in which God will bless the world.

    We see this represented in the timeline on the first of Mike's charts where we see Israel and the Old Testament at the beginning.

2. Next we might look at Dr. McCormick's second chart where we see Jesus Christ and the cross. Here we learn that:

    1. The whole of the Old Testament points forward to Jesus Christ.

    2. The first coming of Jesus is predicted in over 300 prophecies in the Old Testament. One of the most poignant groupings of such prophecies is Isaiah 53.

3. While the first coming of the Jewish Messiah was undeniably fulfilled in Jesus Christ, His second coming was also referenced throughout the Old Testament. We see this referenced in:

    1. Mike's third chart where we see an arrow representing the second coming of Christ.

    2. Hebrews 9:28 where we see both the first and second coming mentioned.

    3. Daniel 7:13-14

    4. Revelation 19:11-16

4. Dr. McCormick's fourth chart includes the Final Judgment. At this time:

1. The whole world will be judged as we see in Matthew 25:31-33, 46.

2. The first to be judged will be Satan as we see in Revelation 20:10.

3. Death itself will be judged and eliminated as we see in Revelation 20:14 and I Corinthians 15:25-26.

5. Mike's fifth chart includes the coming New Heaven, New Earth, and New Jerusalem. We can see this in:

    •   Revelation 21:1-5

From this point we will examine three specific future prophetic events. These events are generally referred to as the Rapture, the Great Tribulation, and the Millennium. While there is some disagreement among scholars as to the timing of these three events in relationship to the ones already mentioned, all biblically based churches agree that the Scriptures clearly teach that they will occur. The Bible Chapel, where Dr. Michael McCormick, Jr. made this presentation, holds to what would be called a "Pre-millennial, Pre-tribulation Rapture."

While every believer and Bible scholar needs to be sure that their view of coming events is grounded in the scriptures themselves we must also each approach the subject of timing with humility. Since there are divergent views on the timing of these events it is obvious that some people are wrong about exactly where these three events fit in; particularly the order and timing of the Rapture and Tribulation. We must each evidence the same relative confidence and humility evidenced by internationally known Bible Scholar Dr. Charles Missler. In speaking to other believers who hold a view different than his about the timing of the rapture in particular he says "If you hold a different view than me on the timing of the rapture, that's ok. We'll explain it to you on the way up." And he is also humble enough to say "and if I am somehow wrong, that's ok, too. You can explain it to me." (Dr. Missler also adheres to a "Pre-millennial, Pre-tribulation rapture.")

The point here is that the timing of these events is not an essential point of faith. The important thing is that each of us has a personal relationship with Jesus Christ and that we are counted among His followers who will be "on the way up" as referenced by Dr. Missler. One must not be so attached to their view of timing that they become overly insistent about it or discouraged if the rapture happens at a different time than they expect. These events will all occur at the perfect time and we are privileged to have the opportunity to be among the followers of Christ both now and at that time.

6. Mike's sixth chart adds the Millennium, which is a period of 1000 years of Christ's reign on earth. The chart shows this occurring directly after the second coming of Jesus Christ. We can see this in:

   • Revelation 20:1-6

7. The seventh chart adds the Tribulation, a time of great suffering on the earth. This is shown directly prior to the second coming.

   1. We see a reference to at least part of this time period in Matthew 24:3-8 and in much greater detail in Revelation 6-19.

   2. We see a reference to both the tribulation and the rapture in Daniel 12:1-2

8. The Rapture, the event about which there is so much anticipation and controversy regarding timing is added on Mike's final chart. (This is the black arrow in the middle of the time line.) We see this referenced in:

   • 1 Thessalonians 4:13-18.

The important thing for each of us is to participate in this event, whether it happens when we expect it or not. As they used to say in American culture when some big activity was planned "Be There or Be Square" We just need to be there. Not being there is a whole lot worse than being "square."

Following Dr. McCormick's final chart we find an additional chart which we have available due to the courtesy of Dr. David Hurtado. This fleshes things out a little further.

So what do we do in the meantime, prior to the occurrence of these events? In popular culture there was once a saying that one ought to live each day as if it were the rest of one's life. However, we as believers might more correctly strive to live each day as if it were our last.

Which of these ways of living on a daily basis makes the most sense to you in light of the Word of God? Why?

If we are living with the end in mind we ought to follow the scriptural admonitions so clear to us in the Old end New Testament. Read the following verses and discuss what believers can do today to make each a reality in their day by day experience:

1. Be generous. See Matthew 6:19-21 and Matthew 6:33.
2. Be pure. See Titus 2:11-14 and Ephesians 5:3-6
3. Be just. See Amos 5:24.
4. Be ambitious for Christ. See 1 Corinthians 15:30-32 and 1 Corinthians 15:58.
5. Keep the Goal in Mind. See Colossians 3:23-24.
6. Be wise. See Colossians 4:5-6.
7. Be joyful. See 1 Thessalonians 5:16.

8. Pray. See 1 Thessalonians 5:17.

9. Be thankful. See 1 Thessalonians 5:18.

10. Be filled with the Holy Spirit. See 1 Thessalonians 5:19.

11. Listen to the Word of God. See 1 Thessalonians 5:20.

Read: Revelation 22:20

What was John's attitude about the return of Jesus Christ?

We are to live our lives in the positive expectancy of the return of Jesus Christ. In theological terms this is referred to as the "Doctrine of Imminancy." This can be seen throughout the New Testament. There are several components of this expectation.

1. We are to live as if we expect His return at any moment. Read the following verses to see this:

    Philippians 3:20

    Titus 2:11-13

    Hebrews 9:27-28

    1 Thessalonians 1:10

    1 Thessalonians 4:15-18

    1 Thessalonians 5:1-6

2. We are to look forward to His return with a feeling of warm expectancy.

    Reread: 1 Thessalonians 1:10

3. This daily expectancy should result in a victorious and pure life.

   Read: 1 John 3:2-3

We should also note that:

1. Paul included himself among those who eagerly and daily looked forward to Christ's return. We can see this in:

   1 Thessalonians 4:15

   1 Thessalonians 4:17

   2 Thessalonians 2:1

2. Timothy was admonished to live obediently until the return of Jesus.

   Read: 1 Timothy 6:13-14

3. Jewish believers were reminded that He was coming back soon.

   Read: Hebrews 10:36-37

4. Jesus instructed believers to live productive lives in the expectation of His return.

   See: Luke 19:13-27

5. Some believers throughout history have become so caught up in the expectation of Christ's return that they ceased to be of any earthly good. By getting this confused and acting in an unscriptural manner they actually ceased serving Him here and needed to be reminded to get back to work and have patience.

Read:

2 Thessalonians 3:10-12

James 5:8

The New Testament is replete with references to the event we call the Rapture. This is not some obscure idea. Following you will find a list of a number of these verses, some of which we have referred to in our study already. In some cases the reference is quite direct and in some it is in passing. In all cases it is incorporated into the whole of the knowledge and experience of believers.

John 14:1-3

Romans 8:19

1 Corinthians 1:7-8

1 Corinthians 15:1-53

1 Corinthians 16:22

Philippians 3:20-21

Colossians 3:4

1 Thessalonians 1:8-10

1 Thessalonians 2:19

1 Thessalonians 4:13-18

1 Thessalonians 5:9

1 Thessalonians 5:23

2 Thessalonians 2:1-3

1 Timothy 6:13-14

2 Timothy 4:1-2 (These verses are of particular interest since they mention three of the events we have reviewed so far today in one place. Take a look at the final chart from Mike McCormick to remind ourselves of how these things fit together.)

2 Timothy 2:12-13

Titus 2:12-13

Hebrews 9:28

James 5:7-9

1 Peter 1:7

1 Peter 1:13

1 John 2:28-3:2

Jude 21

Revelation 2:25

Revelation 3:10

So what about the Second Coming? Is this also well attested to? We know that the first coming of Jesus Christ is referred about 300 times in the Old Testament. We and any honest scholar and mathematician also know that each of these predictions was undeniably fulfilled in Him. As in the case of the Rapture, the Second Coming is referred to throughout the Bible. A smattering of the myriad verses regarding this event and the other events surrounding it can be found below.

Daniel 2:44-45

Daniel 7:9-14

Daniel 12:1-3

Zechariah 14:1-15

Matthew 13:41

Matthew 24:15-31

Matthew 26:64

Mark 13:14-27

Mark 14:62

Luke 21:25-28

Acts 1:9-11

Acts 3:19-21

1 Thessalonians 3:13

2 Thessalonians 1:6-10

2 Thessalonians 2:8

2 Peter 3:1-14

Jude 14-15

Revelation 1:7

Revelation 19:11-20:6

Revelation 22:7 (This verse is also sometimes applied to the Rapture.)

Revelation 22:12

Revelation 22:20 (Like Revelation 22:7, this verse is also sometimes applied to the Rapture.)

Perhaps it might be helpful to delineate dome of the differences we seem to see in Scripture between the Rapture and the Second Coming.

Rapture	Second Coming
Translation of All Believers.	No Translation.
Those translated go to heaven.	Translated Believers return to earth.
Earth not Judged.	Earth Judged: righteousness established.
Imminent, any moment.	Follows definite predicted signs.
Signless—no warning.	Follows the tribulation.
Hard to find in Old Testament.	Found often in Old Testament.
Believers only.	Impacts everyone.
Before the day of wrath.	Concludes the day of wrath.
No reference to Satan.	Satan is bound.
Christ comes for his own.	Christ comes with His own.
Christ claims His bride.	Christ comes with His bride.
Only His own see Him.	Every eye shall see him.
Tribulation begins (primary view).	Millennium Kingdom begins.

How do you feel when you realize that the flow of history yet to come is mapped out before us?

Application Questions

How should you live each day knowing what is coming and that your future is secure?

How should you relate to any of your family and friends whose future is not yet secure?

Close in Prayer

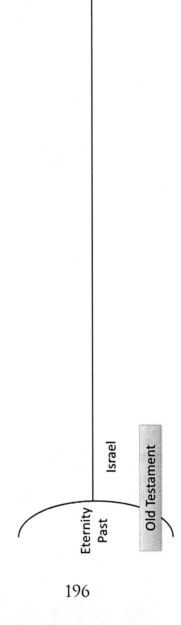

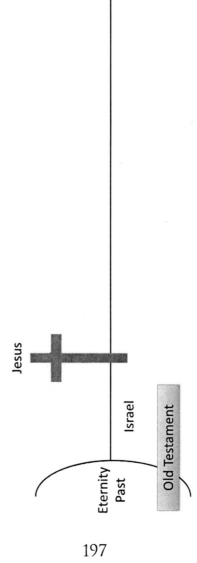

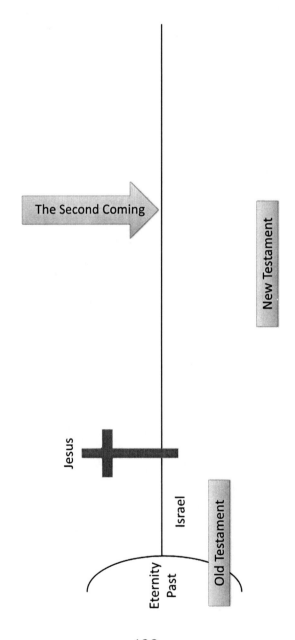

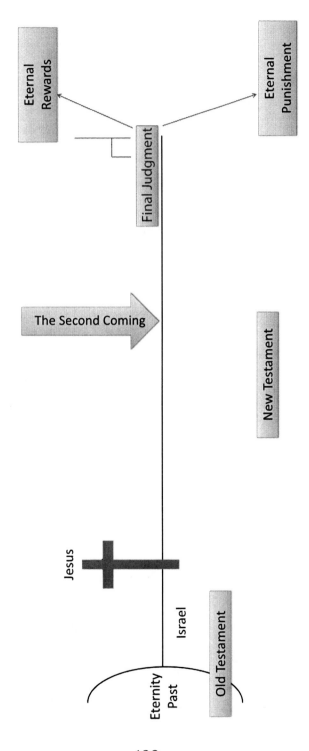

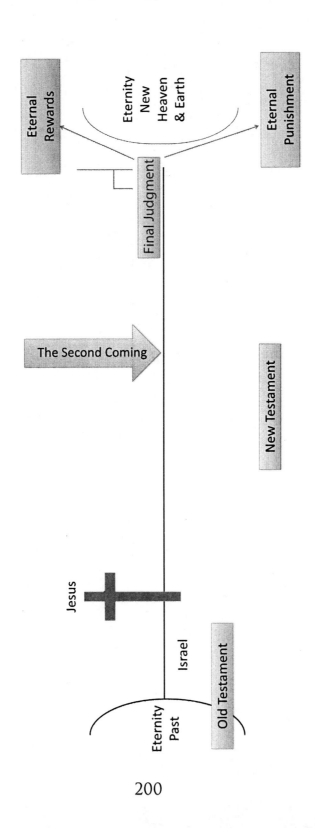

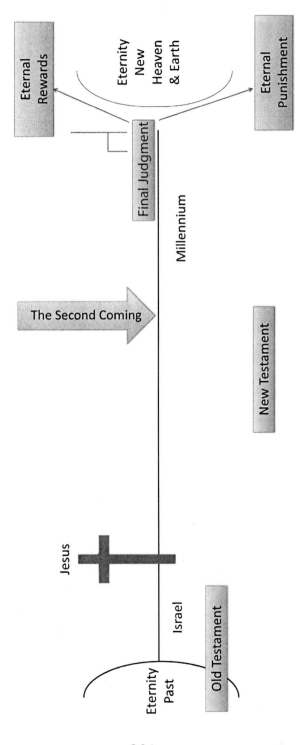

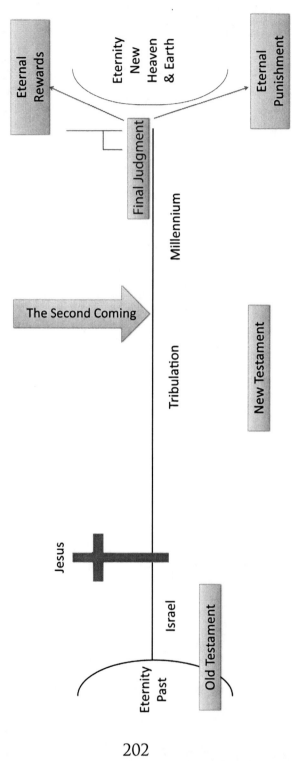

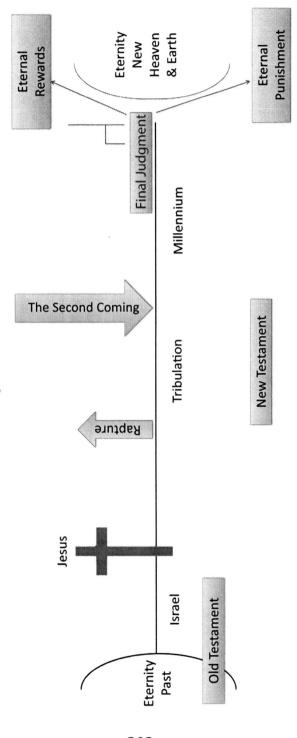

203

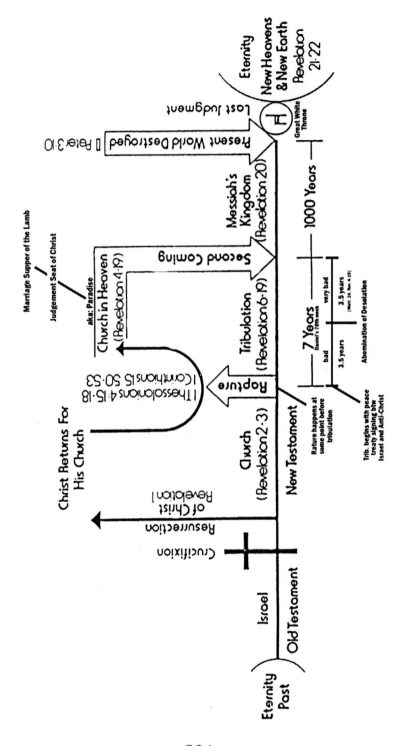

REVELATION 5:1-14
THE SCROLL AND THE LAMB

Opening Prayer

Group Warm-up Question

What steps do people take today to keep their wills and important papers secure?

Read: Revelation 5:1-14

Reread: Revelation 5:1

What was in the right hand of the one sitting on the throne?

Is it significant that He held the scroll in His right hand? How so?

Scrolls were made of papyrus, which was made from bulrushes. These bulrushes grew to a height of 15 feet, with six feet of that height often under water, and were as thick as a man's wrist. The pith of these plants was extracted and cut into thin strips with a sharp knife. Rows of these strips were laid out vertically and then horizontally crossing each other. They were then moistened with water and glue, pressed together, beaten with a mallet, and smoothed with a pumice stone.

The front side of these scrolls was called the *Recto*. It had a horizontal grain and a relatively smooth surface. This is the side on which writing was normally done. If the scroll in question was a contract, this is the side that would contain the details of the agreement.

The back side of these scrolls was called the *Verso* and had a vertical grain. This side was rougher and more uneven than the front. On this side, the outside of the scroll, one would find a summary of what was contained in the document itself.

A sheet of papyrus with writing on the back was called an *opisthograph,* which means a sheet "written behind." This was unusual because of the aforementioned rough and uneven surface of the back.

The papyrus was made into 8 by 10 inch sheets which were then joined together horizontally and put on wooden rollers. Writing on these scrolls was done in narrow (3 inch) columns. The top and bottom margins were 2.5 inches and there was a space of ¾ inch between the columns.

The books of the New Testament penned on such scrolls could be quite lengthy. Shorter books such as Jude, First and Second John, and Philemon could fit on one sheet. However longer books could extend on a roll or Scroll several feet long. Romans was in fact 11 ½ feet long, Mark was 19 feet long, Matthew extended to 30 feet, Luke and Acts were 32 feet each, and the book of Revelation was 15 feet.

It is significant that the scroll in Revelation 5 was rolled up and sealed with seven seals. This is exactly how a Roman will was sealed. Furthermore, we should note that John saw writing on both sides of this scroll. Writing on the back of a scroll of this nature normally contained the requirements that had to be met for the scroll to be opened. This also means that like the Word of God, nothing could be added to it. What was written was complete and final.

This particular scroll represented Christ's title deed to the earth. We can see this alluded to in Psalm 2:1-8. We also see Jesus Christ spoken of as "the heir to all things" in Hebrews 1:1-2.

Reread: Revelation 5:2

What proclamation did the strong angel make?

Was this angel asking a question, making a request, or making a statement?

Is it possible that the angel was making a statement, asking a question, and making a request all at the same time? How so?

Reread: Revelation 5:3

What areas were searched to find a person capable of opening the scroll?

Who came forward to open the scroll?

Reread: Revelation 5:4

What requirement could no person meet that would have enabled them to open the scroll?

How did John react when no man was found who was worthy to open the scroll?

What does this infer about the nature of all men and women? (See Ephesians 2:8-9)

Note: A Roman will or title deed could be opened only by the appointed heir. For the scroll in Revelation 5:4 to be opened someone worthy and qualified as the appointed heir had to be found.

We should also realize that as a Jew steeped in the Old Testament Scriptures, John was quite familiar with the concept of a "Kinsman-Redeemer." This can be seen quite clearly in the book of Ruth. We also see it operating in Leviticus 25:23-25 in relationship to land. In addition, the Kinsman Redeemer was "the avenger of blood." To act in the role of the Goel (Kinsman-Redeemer) one had to:

1. Be a Kinsman.

2. Have the ability to actually effect the redemption.

3. Assume all of the obligations of the beneficiary.

4. Be willing to serve in this position

A man, that is a kinsman of Adam, had to be found to open the scroll. John knew that Jesus was the only one capable of acting as our Kinsman-Redeemer.

Read Romans 8:32-33 and discuss how Jesus is able to meet the four necessary qualifications listed above in order to act as our worthy Kinsman-Redeemer.

Reread: Revelation 5:5

Who spoke to John as he was weeping?

What did he say to John?

Why did the elder say that the lamb was able and worthy to break the seven seals?

Reread: Revelation 5:5-6

Notice that when the elder told John to look he saw the Lion of the Tribe of Judah. However, when John looked he saw the Lamb of God. This seems to be important. What do you think it means?

What did the lamb look like?

According to the text, what is the symbolism of the seven horns and seven eyes?

(We also see horns used symbolically in Scripture to indicate power, honor, strength, dominion, glory, and fierceness.)

What additional insight do you gain from the symbolic use of horns in scripture, including the fact that there are seven of them, as they relate to Revelation 5:6?

Who was surrounding the lamb?

We should note that 24 different titles were used for Jesus Christ in the first three chapters of Revelation. These titles apply to Him in His present role in relationship to the body of believers known as the church.

We have now transcended to Jewish titles for Jesus. These titles are specifically not used in the letters to the seven churches in Revelation. Many scholars take this transition to mean that the "church" has been Raptured by this time.

In any case, from this point on we will see Jewish titles emphasized. We will see Israel moving back to center stage as we approach the end of the age. All of the history of the earth is moving toward a climax. As Chuck Missler says, if you want to know where we are on God's time clock, take a look at Israel." Accordingly, as we proceed through Revelation we will continue to see God's promises to Israel fulfilled.

In general, when we see Jesus referred to as the "Lamb of God" it is in relationship to His first coming and sacrificial death for all humankind. Read the following verses to see this:

John 1:29

John 1:36

Acts 8:32

Isaiah 53 7

1 Peter 1:19

Jesus is generally spoken of as the "Lion of the tribe of Judah" in relationship to His second coming. He is to reign from Jerusalem. This can be seen in the following references:

Genesis 49:8-10

Hosea 5:14-15

Revelation 5:5

Psalm 2:6

Psalm 2:7-8

Luke 1:33

Jesus is also both the source of David and the heir to David's Throne. (Interestingly this seems to confound some translators. Jesus is spoken of as "the root of David" in the KJV and the "descendant of David" in the NLT in Revelation 5:5. The root of David is the correct translation; however He is also his descendant.)

Read Matthew 22:41-46 to see Jesus using this same conundrum to confound the Pharisees.

We can also see this prophetically in prediction and fulfillment in the following verses:

Isaiah 11:1

Isaiah 11:10

Jeremiah 23:5

Romans 15:12

Revelation 22:16

Jesus Christ is, of course, both the Lamb of God and the Lion of the tribe of Judah at the same time. How do you see these two titles working together to help us understand the character of Christ?

What problems arise when one focuses only on Jesus as the Lamb of God?

What problems arise when one focuses only on Jesus as the Lion of Judah?

What can we do to be sure we understand and communicate the character of the Father and the Son correctly?

Before we leave Revelation 5:6, we should also note that the word used to indicate that the Lamb was killed means He was violently slain. When we first read the whole of today's study we also saw a reference to His death in Revelation 5:9.

As you may recall from our earlier sessions we read the following in Revelation 1:5-6

…Unto him that loved us, and washed us from our sins in his own blood, 6 And hath made us kings and priests unto God and his Father; to him *be* glory and dominion for ever and ever. Amen. (KJV)

Also read:

Leviticus 17:11

Hebrews 9:22

Why is the shed blood of Jesus Christ so important?

Warren Wiersbe said "In heaven they sing about the cross and the blood. I read about a denomination that revised its official hymnal and removed all songs about the blood of Christ. That hymnal could never be used in heaven, because there they glorify the Lamb slain for the sins of the world."

J. Vernon McGee took this a step further when he said "Some churches tend to delete "by thy blood" from their hymnals (and sermons.) Perhaps that's why the Lord isn't going to embarrass them by taking them into heaven because they would have to sing about the blood up there."

Reread: Revelation 5:7

What did the lamb do?

Reread: Revelation 5:8-10

Also read:

Psalm 141:2

Luke 1:10

What two things did the elders and living creatures around the throne do when the lamb took the scroll from the One on the throne?

What were the elders and creatures each holding?

Reread: Revelation 5:8

Also Read: Revelation 8:3-4

Why do you think the prayers of God's people appeared as incense from golden bowls?

What do we learn about the impact of the prayers of believers from this imagery?

What were the chief components of the new song we see in Revelation 5:9-10? (For what did they praise the Lamb?) Please list the specifics.

1.

2.

3.

4.

5.

6.

7.

8.

9.

10.

What was the significance of the bowls filled with incense?

How did the prayers of God's people relate to the new song?

Reread: Revelation: 5:11-12

Who next joined the elders and creatures in their worship?

How many worshippers were now singing?

What did this group sing?

What two main characteristics of the Lamb did this large group praise? (See the first line of the song in verse 12.)

What seven specific things did the worshippers sing that the Lamb was worthy to receive? Please list them below.

    1.

    2.

    3.

    4.

    5.

6.

7.

Having made our list, now read the following verses in relationship to each of the things the Lamb is worthy to receive and discuss what is meant.

1. Power

   • Matthew 28:18

   • Colossians 1:16-17

   • Hebrews 1:3

2. Riches

   • 2 Corinthians 8:9

   • Ephesians 3:8

3. Wisdom

   • 1 Corinthians 1:20-24

4. Strength

   • Psalm 24:8

5. Honor

   • Hebrews 2:9

   • Philippians 2:9-11

6. Glory

- John 1:14
- John 2:11
- John 11:4
- John 11:40
- John 17:5
- John 17:24

7. Praise

- Psalm 103:1-2

Reread: Revelation 5:13

Who made up this even larger group singing and praising the lamb? Please list them.

1.

2.

3.

4.

5.

6.

7.

8.

9.

What races or ethnic groups do we see delineated from others in this group?

How does God appear to value people of all groups in this throng of worshipers in respect to one another?

Note: This does not in any way diminish the role of Israel and the Jews in the plan of God. We see this from the first books of the Bible through the whole of God's Word to Revelation.

Deuteronomy 7:6

For you are a people holy to the LORD your God. The LORD your God has chosen you out of all the peoples on the face of the earth to be his people, his treasured possession.

Genesis 12:1–3

1 The LORD had said to Abram, "Leave your country, your people and your father's household and go to the land I will show you. 2 "I will make you into a great nation and I will bless you; I will make your name great, and you will be a blessing. 3 I will bless those who bless you, and whoever curses you I will curse; and all peoples on earth will be blessed through you."

To whom was this huge group specifically singing?

    1.

    2.

What four things did this group say belonged to the Father and the Son in their song?

    1.

    2.

    3.

    4.

For how long did these worshippers say these things belonged to the Father and the Son?

Where was the Holy Spirit in all of this activity?

Was He (The Holy Spirit) filling the worshippers, inspiring the writer, or some sort of combination?

Reread: Revelation 5:14

What did the four living creatures say to the throng singing to the One on the throne and to the Lamb?

What did the twenty-four elders do at the conclusion of this great song?

In the KJV this verse concludes with the words "him that liveth forever and ever." What impact does this phrase have on you?

Why do you think the Holy Spirit includes the words "forever and ever" at the end of each of the two verses concluding this chapter?

What is the benefit of bowing one's head or bowing down when worshipping God?

Application Question

How can you develop an attitude of praise and thanksgiving to God as you go about your daily life?

Close in Prayer

REVELATION 6:1-17
THE SEALS ARE BROKEN

Opening Prayer

Overview

When we read Daniel 9:27 we see:

1. A period of seven years is prophetically referenced both there and now beginning in Revelation.

2. This period of seven years begins with a person acting as a peacemaker and enforcing a treaty with Israel and their enemies.

3. After three and a half years this peacemaker will show his true colors. He will end the sacrifices and offerings in the temple and will also desecrate the temple with a sacrilegious act. (This is also referenced in Matthew 24:15,

Daniel 11:31, Daniel 12:11, and Mark 13:14.) The second half of the seven year Tribulation period is referred to as the Great Tribulation.

Warm up Question

What is one natural disaster that stands out in your mind?

Read: Revelation 6:1-17

Preparatory to delving into this chapter in greater depth we should realize that in Scripture horses are associated with judgment. We see this in:

2 Kings 6:15-18

Jeremiah 46:9-10

Joel 2:3-11

Nahum 3:1-7

Zechariah 1:8-11

Zechariah 6:1-7

Reread: Revelation 6:1

Note: Modern readers might wonder how the Lamb, Jesus Christ, could break one seal at a time and partially reveal what is on the scroll. We ask such a question today because we don't typically use scrolls. However, a quick look at the history of scrolls reveals that they were sometimes sealed not just on the edge, but throughout the scroll. Thus, someone could break open one seal, unroll the scroll to see what was there, and then arrive at the next seal, which would also need to be broken to reveal more of the document.

Who do we see at the opening of this chapter and what is He doing?

Drawing upon our discussion from our last session, why is this significant?

How does one of the living beings respond when the first seal is broken?

What is meant by the way in which these beings (Angels) respond to the Lamb?

Reread: Revelation 6:2

What was the nature and appearance of the first rider?

Many readers, upon a cursory reading, have thought that this first rider is Jesus Christ. In fact, this is the first conclusion most people jump to upon an initial reading of the verse. This is an easy mistake to make.

However, when one puts this together with the whole of scripture, the situation becomes clear.

Please take a moment and Read Revelation 19:11-16.

There are obviously some similarities between the Rider in Revelation 6:2 and Jesus Christ as we see Him in Revelation 19:11-16.

The similarities include:

1. Both personages are on white horses.
2. Both of them carry a weapon.
3. Both of them wear a crown.

Years ago when I read Revelation 6:2 for the first time I too saw these similarities, but something about it bothered me. I knew that something was amiss with this picture. After careful study on my own, prayer, and consulting the works of great Biblical scholars I realized that something is indeed amiss if one identifies this rider as Jesus Christ.

To flesh this out we need to put it together with a few other references to see that something else is going on:

Please read:

Matthew 24:15-16

2 Thessalonians 2:1-12

How would you put these warnings into your own words?

The rider on the white horse Revelation 6:2 cannot be the Christ because:

1. Jesus Christ Himself is the Lamb who breaks the seal and releases the rider.

2. The rider on the horse in Revelation 6:2 carries a bow, but no arrows. The weapon carried by Jesus Christ in Revelation 19 is a sword.

3. When we tie in the fact that the rider in Revelation 6:2 goes forth to conquer without actually using his weapon, this becomes more interesting. Somehow he conquers, at least in this portion of his attack, through treaty or diplomacy. This is exactly what we see from the antichrist as he is clearly defined in the book of Daniel. In fact, Daniel 9:27, shows that he will make a treaty with Israel for three and a half years. This treaty will be violently violated, but he does appear to begin with deception. We can also see this in Daniel 8:25.

4. Further examination of the "bow" held by this rider reveals that the same word used to describe this implement is used in the Septuagint when referring to the covenant God made after the flood of Noah. He sealed this covenant with a bow, which we know as a rainbow. This seems to further indicate that the rider in this passage will use a covenant or a treaty as a weapon.

5. The rider in this passage is wearing a crown. The Greek word for this crown is *stephanos*. This is a victor's crown and the particular rider is in some sense victorious. However, the crown worn by Jesus Christ in Revelation 19 is a *diadema* in the Greek. This is a kingly crown of a ruler. The two types of crowns are distinctly different.

6. This rider is called forth by one of the living creatures that serve the Lord. This is obviously not a position in which one might find the Lord Himself.

7. We might also note that 2 Thessalonians 2:6-9 is often pointed to in order to show the Rapture. Concomitantly this is then thought to also show that the restraining power exerted by Bible believing and Spirit-filled followers of Christ has been removed, with this occurring prior to the time the antichrist is revealed.

Conversely, the rider in Revelation 19:11-16 evidences a long list of characteristics that identify him clearly as Jesus Christ Himself. Please enumerate these characteristics to make this as clear as possible.

1.

2.

3.

4.

5.

6.

7.

8.

9.

10.

11.

12.

13.

14.

These characteristics are corroborated elsewhere in scripture and one might profit from an in-depth review of them. However, at this point, we have been able to clearly see that the Rider in Revelation 19 is Jesus Christ. The rider in Revelation 6:2 is the Antichrist.

Let us digress for a moment and deal with a hypothesis inferred by some scholars. This group believes that 2 Thessalonians 2:9-12 indicates that if a person has had the opportunity to accept Christ prior to the Rapture and doesn't do it, he or she will not have a second chance. These verses, could, indeed indicate just that. However, the situation is somewhat confounded when we realize that there are great multitudes of people who do come to trust in Jesus during the course of the tribulation as we will see in the succeeding chapters of Revelation.

Examining this further we see that many of those turning to Jesus later in Revelation are Jews, just as foretold throughout the New and Old Testaments. We also see, however, that many gentiles come to Him.

While we are at it, we should also mention that there are people who say they will wait until the Rapture occurs so that they are sure the Bible is true to make a decision for Christ.

If it is true that people who reject Christ prior to the Rapture will not have a chance to accept Him afterwards, what should they do now?

If it is true that people who reject Christ now might possibly have a chance to do so after the Rapture, what should they do now?

Is there any rational reason for waiting? Please explain.

In the end, history, prophecy, experience, and even composite probability theory all prove that Christ is who He claimed to be. Waiting to begin a relationship with Him based upon some ill-conceived intellectual games one might play has a great statistical possibility of leading to disaster.

Is there any downside to accepting the invitation oftentimes summarized as in Revelation 3:20? How so?

Do you think that the Antichrist, the man of lawlessness, might be alive today?

This evil man is referenced throughout the scriptures. While we tend to refer to him as the Antichrist, we see him called by many other names. So that we better understand what the world should expect from him let's take a brief look at a few of the Biblical references that tell us more about him.

At your convenience you may want to look up the following verses and discuss how they allude or point to this personage. You may get even more out of this exercise by including the KJV as one of the Bible translations you utilize to review these references.

Old Testament

- Genesis 3:13-15 (The Seed of the Serpent)
- Zechariah 11:16-17 (Idol Shepherd)
- Daniel 7:8-11 (Little Horn)
- Daniel 7:21-26 (Little Horn)
- Daniel 8:9-12 (Little Horn)

- Daniel 8:23-25 (Fierce King and Master of Intrigue)

- Daniel 9:26 (Prince that Shall Come, *KJV*)

- Daniel 11:36 (Willful King)

New Testament

- Revelation 11:7 (The Beast)

- 1 John 2:22 (Antichrist)

- 2 Thessalonians 2:3 (Man of Sin)

- 2 Thessalonians 2:3 (Son of Perdition)

- John 5:43 (One coming in his own name)

- 2 Thessalonians 2:8 (Man of Lawlessness)

Personal Characteristics

- An intellectual genius (Daniel 8:23, Ezekiel 28:3)

- A persuasive Speaker (Daniel 7:20, Revelation 13:2)

- A crafty politician (Daniel 11:21, Daniel 8:25)

- A financial genius (Revelation 13:16-17)

- A forceful military leader empowered by Satan (Daniel 8:24, Revelation 6:2, Revelation 13:4)

- A deceptive and ingenious religious leader (2 Thessalonians 2:4, Revelation 13:3, Revelation 13:13-14)

Physical Description

- Zechariah 11:17

Reread: Revelation 6:3-4

How are the second horse and rider described?

We often see the color of this horse, red, associated with terror, bloodshed, death and evil as in Revelation 12:3 and Revelation 17:3.

What happened when the second horse and rider were released?

Remember, Jesus Christ foretold these wars in:

- Matthew 24:6

- Matthew 24:7

- Mark 13:7-8

- Luke 21:9-10

Since the beginning of recorded history there have been about 14,500 wars. In the course of those wars it is estimated that 4 billion people have been killed. In pre-modern history the worst conflict likely occurred in India where Moslems killed 50 million people who refused to convert to Islam. World War II killed at least 66 million people around the Globe. World War I, however, was even deadlier if you count the people who died from the flu pandemic as a result of the close-quarters situations emanating from the war. (Some estimate that this number was 115 million.) The first 128 armed conflicts since 1989 resulted in at least 250,000 deaths each year. And, if this all seems bad, Jesus tells us it will get worse during the tribulation.

After an initial period of peace, how do you think the Antichrist might be involved in these wars?

Reread: Revelation 6:5-6

What happened at the opening of the third seal?

What explanation was offered that helps us to understand what this means? Please describe this situation in your own words.

Note: The color of this horse, black, is often connected with famine. Read the following verses to see this:

Lamentations 4:4-8

Lamentations 5:10

Read:

Leviticus 26:26

Matthew 20:2

These verses aid our understanding of Revelation 6:5-6. To "eat bread by weight" as mentioned in Leviticus 26:26 is a Jewish phrase indicating that food is scarce. Matthew 20:2 shows us that a penny or denarius was the standard day wage for a laborer. Food will be so scarce at the time that one will need to engage in hard labor all day just for a day's ration of food. (A measure of wheat would provide the minimum daily nourishment for one person. The barley mentioned was normally fodder for livestock at the time and was therefore cheaper. In "normal" times a laborer would receive eight to twelve measures of wheat for a penny.

As we reread Revelation 6:6 we see that wine and oil will still be available to those who can afford them. However, they will be tremendously expensive. This brings to mind the hyper-inflation seen in the days of the Weimar Republic in Germany after World War I during which time it required a wheel barrel full of German marks to buy a loaf of bread.

It is interesting to see that this famine does not extend to all levels of society or all people. As we mentioned, there are those who still have access to the luxuries of oil and wine as noted in the text. It is of further interest to realize history teaches us that most famines are not caused by the vagaries of weather. They are implemented by governments and politicians to control the populace or even to eliminate certain groups within the populace.

Read: Revelation 13:16-17

Do you think it might be possible that the Antichrist will use food and famine as a weapon during the tribulation period?

How much power do you think a corrupt ruler is able to wield over a populace by controlling the food supply?

Reread: Revelation 6:7-8

Who is riding the fourth horse?

Who is following the rider of the fourth horse?

As we think about this passage we should delineate between death and hades or hell.

Physical death merely claims the body.

Hades or hell, however, claims the soul. This is a grievous, serious, eternal, mournful and irreversible event. It could be accurately stated that losing one's soul in hades is absolutely the worst thing that can happen to a person. Nothing else is more terrifying, painful, or permanent (in italics for emphasis).

Unbelievers, when they die, go to Hades, the unseen world, the (temporary) realm of the dead. Believers go immediately into the presence of the Lord. (Philippians 1:19-23; 2 Corinthians 5:6-8). Hades will be emptied of its dead in Revelation 20:13. (The Greek equivalent of Hades is Sheol.)

It would do us well to remember a few of the things that the Word of God says about our bodies and soul.

Read and discuss:

Matthew 10:28

Matthew 16:26

Mark 8:37

Matthew 11:29

1 Peter 2:11

James 1:21

1 Peter 1:9

Matthew 22:35-37

Luke 10:26-28

How might it benefit those going through the tribulation if they were to read and take seriously the verses we just read?

How might we benefit from reading these same verses, taking them seriously, and applying them to our lives?

Reread: Revelation 6:7-8

How do these verses say that so many people will be killed?

From this passage, how many people appear destined to die from these terrible things?

Read: Ezekiel 14:21 to see these same judgments in the Old Testament.

Besides speaking about the time in which this verse was written in Ezekiel do you think it might also have prophetic application? How so?

In our supposedly modern society it is not uncommon for people living safe in their homes to doubt that these things could actually occur. However, we should realize:

1. As we noted earlier, over 4 billion people have been killed in wars since the beginning of recorded history.

2. Even now, Action Against Hunger tells us that between 3 and 5 million people each year starve to death.

3. The Merriam Webster dictionary defines the word correctly translated in verse 8 as pestilence as: a contagious or infectious epidemic disease that is virulent and devastating; *especially*: BUBONIC PLAGUE.

   - In the 14th century this disease, called the "black death," killed 30-60% of the adult population in Europe. In addition, we have seen the various swine flu viruses spoken of as the possible beginning of pandemics for several years.

   - In addition, we are currently seeing a firestorm of death from the deadly AIDs virus, which many researchers now claim can be transmitted without intimate contact or the sharing of blood and needles. (Some claim this can be accomplished through simple touch or even airborne infection.) At the end of 2011, an estimated 34 million people were living with HIV worldwide, with two-thirds of them living in sub-Saharan Africa. In the United States alone the CDC tells us that more than 1.1 million people in the United States are living with HIV infection, and almost 1 in 5 (18.1%) are unaware of their infection. While they tell us that AIDS related deaths have now dropped below 2 million people per year, this ignores the problem that exists when people die of other diseases they have contracted as a result of the AIDS infection. These deaths may be categorized as being from some other source when the root cause was the HIV virus. Whatever the real numbers might be, they are huge and frightening to many.

4. For some it seems difficult to think that so many people might be killed by wild animals. While in North America we are currently seeing a great resurgence in the populations of animals that were formerly decimated (mountain lions, coyotes, bears, wolves, poisonous snakes), it hardly seems likely to most people that this could account for the reference in Revelation 6:8. However:

- Rats, a wild animal carrying the bubonic plaque as mentioned above, are certainly a wild animal. Dr. Julian Whitaker and others are quoted as saying that "Rats multiply so quickly that in 18 months two rats can have over a million descendants." Not only do these animals carry many different diseases, attack the food supply and occasionally humans, but they are amazingly prolific.

- Speaking of amazing statistics, the most lethal animal in the world is the mosquito. While estimates differ, many researchers claim that about 2 Million people die each year from mosquito borne illnesses. These include malaria, dengue fever, yellow fever, encephalitis, and west Nile virus among others. Malaria alone, supposedly the greatest killer of the mosquito borne diseases, kills one child every thirty seconds.

What commonalities do we see between all of the judgments brought about by the four horsemen of the apocalypse? Please list as many as you can.

1.

2.

3.

4.

5.

6.

Reread: Revelation 6:9-11

What did John see when the fifth seal was broken?

What question did the Martyrs ask?

Read Revelation 19:2 to see this request finally answered.

What do we learn about the character of the Lord from the way in which the martyrs address Him?

What do we learn about the attitude of the martyrs toward Jesus by the way in which they address Him?

Reread: Revelation 6:9

Here we see the souls of those slain for the Word of God, a synonym for Christ, under the altar. The Greek word used in this instance is *martus*, which gives us our English word martyr. It simply means "a witness."

It is important to tie the imagery in this verse to the rest of Scripture.

Read Leviticus 17:11 to see that in Old Testament imagery blood represents life.

Read the following verses regarding the blood of sacrificial animals poured out at the base of the altar:

Leviticus 4:7

Leviticus 4:18

Leviticus 4:25

Leviticus 4:30

Read Hebrews 9:11-12 to see that it is the shed blood of Christ that effectively takes away sin.

Read Philippians 2:17 and 2 Timothy 4:6 to see the apostle Paul writing about his death as a martyr being like a drink offering poured out.

Read: Revelation 12:9-11

How does this tie into Revelation 6:9 as well as all the other verses we just read?

How does Revelation 12:9-11 relate to believers today?

Reread: Revelation 6:10

In this verse we see that those whose souls are under that altar seem to have been murdered between the time of the Rapture and this point in the Tribulation. This seems to be apparent since their murders still "dwell upon the earth."

Here we also see further clues showing that the rider on the horse in Revelation 6:2 is the Antichrist and not Jesus.

1. Jesus is referred to as the Sovereign Lord. This definitively identifies Him as the Rider in Revelation 19 who is wearing the *diadema* crown. (The crown of a ruler.) In contrast to this, the Antichrist in Revelation 6:2 wears the *stephanos*, the crown of one winning a victory.

2. Jesus is also spoken of as holy and true. Read Revelation 19:11 to see Him referred to in a similar fashion.

Finally, this verse (Revelation 6:10) has also been disquieting to some who have mistakenly equated being a follower of Christ with being a pacifist or being one who does not hold others to account for their behavior. These mistaken people, who have concentrated only on a portion of God's Word, have done more to contribute to the problems of the world today than one might imagine. They have permitted abortion to spread like a cancer, and dishonesty and corruption to consume society. In what has become their mistaken self-righteousness or view of God they have even accused the martyrs in Revelation 6:10 of making a request that is "not Christian." This is absolutely incorrect.

The martyrs in Revelation 6:10 are not calling out for personal revenge, but for justice. "How long, O Lord?" has been the cry of God's suffering people through the ages. We see this in:

*   Psalm 74:9-10

- Psalm 79:1-7

- Psalm 94:1-3

- Habakkuk 1 and 2

God's suffering people have always cried out for Him to call the wicked to account. See:

- 2 Chronicles 24:22

- Deuteronomy 32:43

The Scriptures teach us that God is just, something we cannot possibly miss in the book of Revelation.

However, they also tell us that we have a responsibility to bring about justice in our time on earth. Read the following verses to see the kind of justice that God demands of His followers:

Proverbs 21:15

Proverbs 31:8-9

Isaiah 1:17

Jeremiah 9:24

Amos 5:14-15

Amos 5:24

Reread: Revelation 6:11

How did Jesus answer the murdered martyrs?

Why do you think He gives them a white robe? What does this symbolize to you?

Soul Sleep

Revelation 6:9-11 also puts to rest the notion of "soul sleep."

In the Scriptures we see that souls are conscious.

Read 1 Thessalonians 4:14-16 to see that the souls of those believers who have died are with Jesus and that these people will return with Him.

The notion of soul sleep comes from a failure to see scripture as a whole and relate it to itself. In John 11:11-14 we see Jesus Himself using the term "fallen asleep" to indicate that Lazarus had died.

Read 2 Corinthians 5:8 and Philippians 121-23 to see that the dead in Christ are with Him right now.

Read Luke 16:19-31 to see that both the ungodly and godly are conscious after death.

Reread: Revelation 6:12-14

Please list the things that happen when the Lamb breaks the sixth seal:

    1.

    2.

    3.

    4.

5.

6.

7.

This is the first of the three great earthquakes. We also see other cosmic changes during the Tribulation. We find some of the references to these events in:

Revelation 6:12

- Isaiah 13:9-10 (Alluded to beforehand.)

- Matthew 24:29 (Alluded to beforehand.)

- Mark 13:24 (Alluded to beforehand.)

- Joel 2:30-31 (Alluded to beforehand.)

- Joel 3:15 (Alluded to beforehand.)

Revelation 6:13

- Matthew 24:29 (Alluded to beforehand.)

- Mark 13:25 (Alluded to beforehand.)

- Luke 21:25 (Alluded to beforehand.)

- Hebrews 12:26 (Alluded to beforehand.)

Revelation 11:13

Revelation 16:18-20

- Jeremiah 4:23-24 (Alluded to beforehand.)

- Haggai 2:6 (Alluded to beforehand.)

Revelation 6:14

- Isaiah 34:4 (Alluded to beforehand.)

Reread: Revelation 6:15-17

Also read:

Isaiah 24:1-4

Isaiah 2:10-19

What did everyone do when the sixth seal was broken?

How was the response of the "common" people different than that of those who felt they were "important?"

What did these people say?

What did these people most pointedly not do?

Why do you think these people did not turn to God, accept Jesus, and repent?

Reread: Revelation 6:17

What day has now come at this point in prophecy and history?

At this time, after the passage of three and one half years, we are half way through the tribulation period and about to enter what is known as "the Great Tribulation."

Jesus spoke of this time in Matthew 24:21-22

As mentioned before, there are some believers who feel that this is the point at which the Rapture occurs.

Some of these people point to 2 Thessalonians 2:3 with the thought that the verse is addressed to believers mid-way through the tribulation period and before the Great Tribulation and that no Rapture has yet occurred.

To be fair, we must also say that those holding to a Pre-Tribulation Rapture position feel this is addressed to those becoming believers after the Rapture and prior to the Great Tribulation.

Those holding to such a Mid-Tribulation position also point to:

1 Thessalonians 5:9 and Revelation 3:20.

Here we see that believers will not experience the wrath of God. The remainder of the judgments detailed in Revelation are easily identified as exactly that; the wrath of God.

Therefore, both those who believe in a Pre-Tribulation Rapture and those who feel it is a Mid-Tribulation event agree that at this point they will be watching things unfold during the Great Tribulation from "the mezzanine."

Side Note: Some readers, upon a surface examination, point to Matthew 24:14 as a precondition to the Rapture. This verse says

"And this gospel of the kingdom will be preached in the whole world as a testimony to all nations, and then the end will come."

Lest anyone be confused, this verse relates to the second coming, which at this point in the text is still a future event. In chapter 7 we will see many people still turning to Christ even at this late juncture in human history. This is obviously prior to the second coming of Jesus and seemingly after the Rapture. Even those holding to a Post-Tribulation Rapture can still see that this event refers to the second coming and not the Rapture.

How long do you think God will wait before visiting judgment upon the earth?

Groups of Signs

We have seen that there are a number of signs of the times in this Chapter. They all seem to point to the beginning of the seven year-long period of time known as the Tribulation. (The Great Tribulation refers to the last three and a half years of the overall Tribulation period.) Jesus Christ warned us about them and now we see them coming to fruition.

In summary, they are:

1. False Christs.

   • Matthew 24:4-5

   • Luke 21:8

   • Revelation 6:1-2

2. Wars.

   • Matthew 24:6

   • Luke 21:9-10

   • Revelation 6:3-4

3. Famines.

- Matthew 24:7
- Luke 21:11
- Revelation 6:5-6

4. Death.

- Matthew 24:7-8
- Luke 21:11
- Revelation 6:7-8

5. Martyrs.

- Matthew 24:9
- Luke 21:12
- Revelation 6:9-11

6. Global Upheaval.

- Matthew 24:29
- Luke 21:25
- Revelation 6:12-17

Application Questions

How can you help a non-believing friend or relative see their need for Jesus Christ?

How can you encourage a faithful believer who is being persecuted for following Jesus?

What can you do to make Amos 5:24 a reality in your world?

Amos 5:24

But let justice roll on like a river, righteousness like a never-failing stream!

Close in Prayer

REVELATION 7:1-8
144,000 SEALED JEWS

Opening Prayer

Group Warm-up Question

How do you prove ownership of your most valuable possessions?

Writing in his commentary on the New Testament Warren Wiersbe reminds us about God's divine purposes and we would do well to remember his insight. He says "The center of His program is Israel, particularly the city of Jerusalem. God has a covenant purpose for Israel, and that purpose will be fulfilled just as He promised."

Gentile believers are admonished by the Apostle Paul, a Jewish believer himself, to see this plan properly. He first reiterates the wonderful commonality shared by Jews and Gentiles alike:

Romans 10:9–13

9 That if you confess with your mouth, "Jesus is Lord," and believe in your heart that God raised him from the dead, you will be saved. 10 For it is with your heart that you believe and are justified, and it is with your mouth that you confess and are saved. 11 As the Scripture says, "Anyone who trusts in him will never be put to shame." 12 For there is no difference between Jew and Gentile—the same Lord is Lord of all and richly blesses all who call on him, 13 for, "Everyone who calls on the name of the Lord will be saved."

Unfortunately for the Jews and just as fortunately for the Gentiles, most of the Jews turned away from their own Messiah for two centuries. A few, however, did find their Messiah in Yeshua Ha-Maschiach, who we know as Jesus Christ. We see this in Romans 11:5.

Romans 11:5 "It is the same today, for not all the Jews have turned away from God. A few are being saved as a result of God's kindness in choosing them."

During the two thousand years when most Jews missed their Messiah, many Gentiles truly found Him. (We are not referring to those who found solace in some sort of religious group or denomination, but to those who found God through a personal relationship with Jesus Christ and the empowerment of the Holy Spirit.) In some cases Gentiles seemed to forget their Hebraic roots and are reminded in Romans 11:18 to not become arrogant about their privilege.

Romans 11:18

But you must not brag about being grafted in to replace the branches that were broken off. You are just a branch, not the root."

So, most appropriately, we will begin this session by reading Romans 11:11-25. You may wish to read this passage in several translations to get the full measure of it. Following is a recent rendering from the NLT.

Romans 11:11–25

11 Did God's people stumble and fall beyond recovery? Of course not! They were disobedient, so God made salvation available to the Gentiles. But he wanted his own people to become jealous and claim it for themselves. 12 Now if the Gentiles were enriched because the people of Israel turned down God's offer of salvation, think how much greater a blessing the world will share when they finally accept it. 13 I am saying all this especially for you Gentiles. God has appointed me as the apostle to the Gentiles. I stress this, 14 for I want somehow to make the people of Israel jealous of what you Gentiles have, so I might save some of them. 15 For since their rejection meant that God offered salvation to the rest of the world, their acceptance will be even more wonderful. It will be life for those who were dead! 16 And since Abraham and the other patriarchs were holy, their descendants will also be holy—just as the entire batch of dough is holy because the portion given as an offering is holy. For if the roots of the tree are holy, the branches will be, too. 17 But some of these branches from Abraham's tree—some of the people of Israel—have been broken off. And you Gentiles, who were branches from a wild olive tree, have been grafted in. So now you also receive the blessing God has promised Abraham and his children, sharing in the rich nourishment from the root of God's special olive tree. 18 But you must not brag about being grafted in to replace the branches that were broken off. You are just a branch, not the root. 19 "Well," you may say, "those branches were broken off to make room for me." 20 Yes, but remember—those branches were broken off because they didn't believe in Christ, and you are there because you do believe. So don't think highly of yourself, but fear what could happen. 21 For if God did not spare the original branches, he won't spare you either. 22 Notice how God is both kind and severe. He is severe toward those who disobeyed, but kind to you if you continue to trust in his kindness. But if you stop trusting, you also will be cut off. 23 And if the people of Israel turn from their unbelief, they will be grafted in again, for God has

the power to graft them back into the tree. 24 You, by nature, were a branch cut from a wild olive tree. So if God was willing to do something contrary to nature by grafting you into his cultivated tree, he will be far more eager to graft the original branches back into the tree where they belong. 25 I want you to understand this mystery, dear brothers and sisters, so that you will not feel proud about yourselves. Some of the people of Israel have hard hearts, but this will last only until the full number of Gentiles comes to Christ.

This is the point in history at which we find ourselves in Revelation 7:1-8. The "full number of Gentiles" have apparently found the Jewish Messiah and now God is beginning to use His "Chosen People"(referred to as The apple of His eye in Zechariah 2:8) to accomplish what He said he would do before His second coming. We see this in Matthew 24:14.

Matthew 24:14

And the Good News about the Kingdom will be preached throughout the whole world, so that all nations will hear it; and then the end will come.

Read: Revelation 7:1-8

Reread: Revelation 7:1

Who did John see after the breaking of the sixth seal?

Where were the four angels John saw located?

What were these four angels doing and why were they doing it?

In your own words, how would you describe the power and authority of these four angels?

Note: Do not allow anyone to mislead you by saying that the expression "the four corners of the earth" is an unscientific statement evidencing that the Bible is an outdated collection of fairy tales. First of all, this expression is one in common usage today and one can find it in newspapers, magazines and books with regularity denoting the full expanse of the earth to the uttermost extremes. This figure of speech has been in use for thousands of years as we see in Isaiah 11:12, which was written about 2700 years ago.

When we continue in the book of Isaiah to Isaiah 40:22 it is obvious that God's Word incorporates the literal truth of science and nature in this case (as in all others).

While some people make a point of saying that the Bible is not a textbook of science, history, archaeology, biology, astronomy, geography, or mathematics they oftentimes take the point too far. While the purpose of God providing us with His Word goes far beyond the particulars of these various fields of academia, we need to be fully cognizant of one overriding discovery.

That discovery is the fact that God's Word is a truly integrated message system communicating to us not only the Words of life, but truth in all regards. Whenever God's Word speaks of any field of human endeavor it always speaks accurately. Indeed, all of the branches of academia in existence simply corroborate the truth of God's Word when one takes the time to see what the Bible says in comparison to what we humans have so far figured out about the world and universe. Sometimes it takes our "modern" science years to catch up to the eternal truth of all sorts revealed in the Bible.

However, human discoveries, when taken to their end, always validate scripture. If there are any areas where we are not yet aware of that fact, it is simply a matter of time until we see the corroborating data come to the fore. This does, of course, require a degree of intellectual honesty not always seen in those who oppose the principles of the Judeo Christian Scriptures. Those in opposition to the ways of God as revealed in the Bible have a vested interest in skewing their results and interpretations since giving assent to the incontrovertible truth of God's Word would require them to somehow respond to it.

Reread: Revelation 7:2-3

What did John see coming from the east?

What did the angel coming from the east have in his possession?

What power and authority did the angel coming from the east possess?

At what point did the first four angels receive permission to wreak God's judgment by their use of the land and the seas?

Why do you think it is important for us to know that the 144,000 servants will be sealed before the coming judgments that will impact the land and seas?

What are some ways angels are at work in the world today?

Reread: Revelation 7:4

How many people received God's seal?

How were these people marked?

Of what race were these people?

Reread: Revelation 7:4-8

How many people were sealed from each of the twelve tribes of Israel?

Read: Revelation 14:1

How were the 144,000 Jewish believers sealed?

It is of interest that the followers of the Antichrist, the "beast," are also "sealed." Their sealing, however, is quite different from the sealing of the servants of God. Read the following verses and jot down the ways the people following the Antichrist are sealed and the impact it has upon them.

Revelation 13:17

Revelation 14:11

Revelation 16:2

Revelation 19:20

Revelation 14:9-10

Read: Revelation 9:1-4

What further impact does the seal of God have upon the 144,000 Jewish believers we see in Revelation?

Throughout the ages God has always had His faithful remnant.

Read 1 Kings 19:18 to see that when Elijah thought he was alone, God had yet preserved 7,000 who were faithful to Him.

Read Ezekiel 9:1-7 to see the faithful being sealed before God's judgment took place.

The 144,000 Jewish believers we see in Revelation are sealed for the service of God.

Have you had the privilege of meeting and getting to know Jews who have discovered that the Messiah, their Messiah, is none other than Yeshua Ha-Maschiach, or Jesus Christ? These blessed people are on fire for God like no others. They have found the Messiah, He is theirs, and they want everyone else in the world to have the same wonderful experience.

One can only imagine the tremendous impact that such a group of what are essentially Jewish Evangelists will have upon the earth. There will be a revival like never before and the cost of following Christ for many of those who make that decision will be death. We will see more about this in the coming sessions on Revelation.

We see hints of this already in the world today as more Jews are coming to a personal relationship with Jesus Christ than any time since the first century A.D. Great numbers of the Chosen People are beginning to find Him in the old Soviet

Union and South America. Many are even coming to this knowledge in the State of Israel. And, of course, in the United States we see Chosen People Ministries and Jews For Jesus gradually, albeit slowly, gaining steam. For more information on this topic you may find the book *A Rabbi Looks at the Last Days* by Jonathan Bernis to be illuminating.

So what about 144,000? What is the significance of this number? There are 12 tribes of Israel and there were 12 apostles. 144 is thought of as signifying completeness and perfection. For an interesting study one may wish to investigate the use of the number 12 in Scripture. If one has further interest in the significance of numbers in Scripture they may want to read and digest the book *Number in Scripture: It's Supernatural Design and Spiritual Significance* by E. W. Bullinger. In their description of this book Amazon.com says:

"This classic reference book on biblical numerology is one of the most famous and helpful reference books on numerology ever written. E. W. [Ethelbert William] Bullinger (1837-1913) was a Vicar of the Church of England, a Biblical scholar, and dispensationalist theologian. Educated at King's College, London, he was a recognized scholar in the field of biblical languages. In 1881, the Archbishop of Canterbury granted him an honorary Doctor of Divinity degree in recognition of his biblical scholarship. Bullinger also wrote the notes and appendixes of The Companion Bible and is the author of numerous other works including Commentary on Revelation, Great Cloud of Witnesses, and How to Enjoy the Bible."

Reading this book and digesting the contents simply makes the Scriptures more amazing as we realize their supernatural design. There is a related discipline known as Gamatria in which one analyzes the text of the Scriptures in the original tongue. This is based upon the knowledge that Hebrew is an alpha numeric language and properly used can provide surprising insights. The key with this is proper usage. The overt and clear words of the text itself are simply validated by this endeavor. Any other usage is counter-productive as is a concentration on this field of knowledge to the exclusion of the power of the Word itself. (This is not dissimilar to a concentration on theology without a personal knowledge of the Author of Life.) One can study theology or Gamatria without knowing God. To do so is pointless unless it leads one to Him.

The Myth of the Ten Lost Tribes

So what about the ten lost tribes of Israel that one hears about in movies like *The Raiders of the Lost Ark*? While this movie is entertaining and enjoyable to many, it is not exactly scripturally accurate.

There has arisen a popular myth in our culture that ten of the tribes of Israel are "lost." This myth derives from a misreading of passages such as 2 Kings 17:7-23. Accompanying some of these legends are aspersions on the present state of Israel and the people being regathered there in fulfillment of prophecy. These various theories even include "British Israelism." This is a crazy doctrine that surprisingly still has adherents based on the hypothesis that people of Western European descent, particularly those in Great Britain, are the direct lineal descendants of the Ten Lost Tribes of Israel. The doctrine often includes the tenet that the British Royal Family is directly descended from the line of King David. The central tenets of British Israelism have been refuted by evidence from modern genetic, linguistic, archaeological and philological research. They are by their nature anti-Semitic and blasphemous because they deny the Jewish people and their proper place in the plan of God.

Besides being at their heart anti-Semitic, the theories about the ten lost tribes are also unscholarly. They derive from a misunderstanding of history and the way in which the tribes are referred to in the biblical text. At times in the Old Testament different tribes are listed in different ways. Sometimes two smaller tribes are listed under the same banner, but all the tribes are always there. For a more detailed study on this subject one might take a look at the scholarly review of this topic from Koinonia House incorporated into their commentary on the book of Revelation.

However, for most of us we can simply put the topic to rest with an understanding of how it is treated in Scripture. Here we see:

1. References to the whole of the tribes as a unity in the Old Testament.

    •   After the Babylonian captivity the terms "Jews" and "Israelite" are used interchangeably.

    •   In 2 Chronicles 11:3 we see the Jews of all tribes referred to as "all of the Israelites."

    •   In Ezra 2:70, 3:11, 8:35 and many other instances we see him referring to the returning remnant as a unity. In fact we see the twelve tribes referred to as "Jews" 8 times and as "Israel" 40 times.

    •   In Nehemiah 12:47 we see Nehemiah referring to "all of Israel" being back in the land. In this book of the Bible we see the members of the 12 tribes referred to as "Jews" 11 times and "Israel" 22 times.

    •   In Malachi 11 we see the 12 tribes again addressed as the unity of "Israel." (Here we must stop since time is limited and the references in the Old Testament are so many.)

2. References to the 12 tribes as well as to the unity of the tribes in the New Testament.

    •   In Matthew 19:28 we see that if there were any lost tribes, the Lord Jesus Christ didn't know about it. (Excuse the humor.)

    •   In Acts 26:7 we see that the apostle Paul, the most learned man of his time didn't know there were any lost tribes.

- In James 1:1 we see that the brother of Jesus knew that there were no lost tribes.

- In Matthew 10:5-6 we see that Jesus Christ spoke of the twelve tribes of Israel as a unity and simply called them "Israel."

- In Matthew 15:24 we see Jesus again referring to the twelve tribes as the unity of "Israel."

- In Romans 11:1, 2 Corinthians 11:22, and in Philippians 3:4-5 we see Paul referring to one the tribes (Benjamin) individually and to all of them as a unity.

- In Acts 2:36 Paul referred all of the tribes as "Israel." (Here we must again stop. Time does not permit us to examine each of the 75 times "Israel" is spoken of or the 174 times "Jews" are mentioned as a whole in the New Testament.)

3. All of the tribes regathered as one.

- In Ezekiel 37:16-17, 21-22 we see all of the tribes referred to as "Israelites."

- In Romans 9:3-5 we see all the tribes again referred to as "The People of Israel."

The cult of Jehovah's Witnesses deserves at least passing mention. They believe that those of their number found observing the Sabbath when Christ returns are those referenced as the 144,000. They used to say that the number represented all Jehovah's Witnesses until they realized they had more than 144,000 members and contributors so they changed their rules. There is so much wrong with their unscholarly and biblically illiterate assumptions that we will not waste our time by beginning to address the subject in any depth here. One can quickly help them move in the direction of the truth by asking which tribe they are from and from there going into the truth of the Scriptures. For more help in understanding the difficulties with this cult and having a productive discussion with those entrapped in it there are many wonderful resources available. Rose Publishing, for one, has some helpful pamphlets, books, and DVD based material.

Read: Ephesians 1:13-14

How else has God marked or sealed His people?

Read: Ephesians 4:29-32

What are some of the concrete ways believers can reflect God's mark of ownership upon them?

Read: Galatians 5:22-23

What should be evident in the lives of believers if they have been sealed with the Holy Spirit?

Read: Galatians 5:24-25

What can believers do today to make this a minute by minute reality in their lives?

In summary of Galatians 5:24 and 25 we might say our old nature must be overcome by:

1. Walking in the Spirit. (Galatians 5:16)

2. Being led by the Spirit. (Galatians 5:18)

3. Living in the Spirit. (Galatians 5:25)

Application Questions

What marks of ownership can others see in your life to indicate that you belong to God?

Are there any additional marks of ownership that you feel should be evident in your life and life-style to be a beacon to others leading them toward the life available in Jesus Christ?

How can you incorporate these additional marks of ownership into your daily routine?

Close in Prayer

THE MULTITUDE OF MARTYRS
REVELATION 7:9-17

Opening Prayer

Group Warm-up Question

What are some of the things about earth that you won't miss in heaven?

Read: Revelation 7:9-17

Reread: Revelation 7:9

How large was the group of people John saw?

What was the makeup of this multitude?

What were these people wearing?

These people were also waving palm branches. We see these branches being used in the Old Testament in relationship to the Feast of Tabernacles or Booths as well as in the New Testament when Jesus entered Jerusalem. As you go through the following verses, bear in mind what we read in Colossians 2:17.

Colossians 2:17

These are a shadow of the things that were to come; the reality, however, is found in Christ.

Read:

Leviticus 23:33-44

Ezra 3:11-12 (Note the singing and shouting at the Feast of Tabernacles)

Nehemiah 8:14-17

John 12:12-13

How would you tie all of these verses together?

Why do you think the multitude is holding palm branches in Revelation 7:9?

Reread: Revelation 7:10

What was this great crowd crying out?

Why do you think they were crying out these particular things?

Reread: Revelation 7:11

The multitude was standing before the throne. Who was standing around it?

Why do you think this other group was standing around the throne while the Multitude was standing in front of it?

What was the group standing around the throne doing?

Reread: Revelation 7:12

What were the angels, elders, and four creatures saying as they worshipped God?

What is the significance of what this group was saying as they worshipped Him?

Drawing upon what we learned in earlier sessions, what is the significance of the fact that this group preceded and followed what they said about God with "Amen?"

Hint: In the session on Revelation 3:14-22 we discussed the word amen. This term initially sounds strange to modern ears. In our culture we are probably most familiar with amen as a sort of a benediction at the conclusion of a prayer. However, in the New Testament we see that it means more. It is sometimes used interchangeably with the old English term "Verily." In this context is refers to the truth of a matter. When someone says "amen" after a statement has been made it implies not only agreement, but that the statement was absolutely true.

Should we be saying things like those being said by the elders, angels and four creatures as we worship and praise God today? Why or why not?

Reread: Revelation 7:13

Who asked John a question?

Exactly what did this elder ask him?

Reread: Revelation 7:14

It appears that the elder asked John a rhetorical question. Why do you think God uses such a linguistic device in this instance?

How did the elder answer John about this great multitude?

What does it mean that they "washed their robes and made them clean in the blood of the lamb?"

This group is obviously made up of believers who have died during the Great Tribulation (They are in heaven so they are dead.) Do you have any hint as of yet as to how they died?

This event appears to be occurring after the rapture and is obviously prior to the second coming of Christ. That being said, a great many people will come to know the Messiah during this difficult time. What people, resources or experiences might help this come about? Please list them below.

1.

2.

3.

4.

5.

6.

7.

8.

9.

10.

11.

12.

After Jesus died and rose from the dead there were 12 Messianic Jews in his core group. (The Jewish disciples, excluding Luke who was a gentile doctor, but including the apostle Paul comprised the 12.) This group, with the empowerment of the Holy Spirit turned the world upside down. In our previous session we discussed the fact that God had, at this point in Revelation, turned 144,000 Jewish believers loose. This is 12,000 more times than the number that He started with in the first century A.D.

How much more rapid an impact might this group of Messianic Jews in Revelation have upon the world than the original 12?

If we try to analyze this mathematically we can attempt to do so by representing the impact over time that the first disciples had by dividing 12 by 2000, assuming that the rapture occurs sometime prior to 2033. (If it occurs afterwards, this number can easily be adjusted by dividing 12 by the current year minus 33.) Doing this and using our hypothetical 2000 we come up with .0060.

If we try to do the same thing with the 144,000 Jewish evangelists we divide 144,000 years by 3.5 (the time of the Great tribulation in the second half of the tribulation period). Here we get a result of 41,142.857.

If we then divide 41,142.857 by .0060 we get 6,857,142.857. This means that the impact as measured by the time available to the Jewish evangelists taking into account their number will be staggering. The impact in a time and temporal sense will seem to be almost 7 Million times greater in the daily life of the residents of the world than over the last 2000 years.

If these calculations are anywhere near correct no living person on the face of the earth will fail to hear the truth of Jesus Christ. It does appear that our Lord will use this great group of Messianic Jews to spark the greatest revival in the history of the world. This will be a spiritual explosion like no other. As we read at the beginning of this chapter John said "I looked and there before me was a great multitude that no one could count, from every nation, tribe, people and language."

As we discussed in our prior session:

God is beginning to use His "Chosen People"(referred to as "The apple of His eye" in Zechariah 2:8) to accomplish what He said he would do before His second coming. We see this in Matthew 24:14.

Matthew 24:14

"And the Good News about the Kingdom will be preached throughout the whole world, so that all nations will hear it; and then the end will come."

We are seeing the ultimate fulfillment of Jesus' command in Mark 16:15

Mark 16:15

He said to them, "Go into all the world and preach the good news to all creation."

Read: Acts 2:16-21 to see that the early believers looked forward to this time with positive expectation.

Read the following excerpts to see that the Old Testament prophets also looked forward to this great time of people coming to God.

Isaiah 49:10–12

10 "They will neither hunger nor thirst, nor will the desert heat or the sun beat upon them. He who has compassion on them will guide them and lead them beside springs of water. 11 I will turn all my mountains into roads, and my highways will be raised up. 12 See, they will come from afar— some from the north, some from the west, some from the region of Aswan."

Isaiah 60:1–3

1 "Arise, shine, for your light has come, and the glory of the LORD rises upon you. 2 See, darkness covers the earth and thick darkness is over the peoples, but the LORD rises upon you and his glory appears over you. 3 Nations will come to your light, and kings to the brightness of your dawn."

Joel 2:28–32

28 "And afterward, I will pour out my Spirit on all people. Your sons and daughters will prophesy, your old men will dream dreams, your young men will see visions. 29 Even on my servants, both men and women, I will pour out my Spirit in those days. 30 I will show wonders in the heavens and on the earth, blood and fire and billows of smoke. 31 The sun will be turned to darkness and the moon to blood before the coming of the great and dreadful day of the LORD. 32 And everyone who calls on the name of the LORD will be saved; for on Mount Zion and in Jerusalem there will be deliverance, as the LORD has said, among the survivors whom the LORD calls."

Question: Why will these Messianic Jews need to have such a rapid and explosive impact?

Having said so much about this great revival, let us not forget about the titanic struggle going on at this point in Revelation and human history. Unnumbered people will come to trust in the Jewish Messiah. And, unnumbered people will also die horribly painful deaths as a direct result of that decision. This is both a glorious and unspeakably terrible time on the face of the earth.

Read: Revelation 20:4-6

The people we see in Revelation 7:14 are part of this group. What do we learn about them, death, and resurrection in this passage?

You may have heard it said that non-believers live once and die twice while believers die once and live twice. How would you explain this to someone?

Reread: Revelation 7:15

How will these so called "tribulation believers or tribulation saints" be spending their time while they are in heaven?

What do you think it means that "He who sits on the throne will spread his tent over them?"

Read: Revelation 7:16

What statement of fact do we find here about the relief these believers will find?

Does this privilege extend to what believers today can expect?

Read: Revelation 7:17

What do you think it means that "the Lamb at the center of the throne will be their shepherd?"

Read Revelation 7:17 again.

Also Read:

John 4:7-14

John 7:38-39

Revelation 22:17

What does it mean that "the Lamb will lead them to springs of living water?"

How does it make you feel to know that God will wipe away every tear from their eyes?

Does this apply to those who have trusted Christ today?

Read Revelation 7:17 once again.

Also Read:

Isaiah 49:8-10

Revelation 21:1-4

The fact that God will wipe away every tear from their eyes indicates that there must be something they might cry about in heaven as well as in the New Jerusalem. What might one possibly cry about in heaven?

Read: Luke 16:19-31

What might the rich man in this story have cried about?

What might he have cried about if he had been in heaven?

Perhaps even more amazing than the great number of people coming to Jesus in this chapter is the fact that everyone will not respond to the call and grace of God in these final days. As we work through Revelation we will see that although the God of the Universe sacrificed his only Son for the world and did everything He could to bring all people to Him, many will still not make such a decision. We certainly understand that every person has free will in this matter and that God knows what they will do.

Given God's grace and effort to reach every human being, why do you think some will still choose to reject Him?

Do you think that this might possibly be part of what one might cry about in heaven? How so?

Application Questions

What steps can you take to incorporate the type of praise and worship practiced by the martyred multitudes that we see in this passage in your life?

What can you do in your life now to minimize any tears you might shed in heaven?

Close in Prayer

THE CALM BEFORE THE STORM
REVELATION 8:1-5

Opening Prayer

Quick Introduction

By this time you may have noticed the importance of certain recurring themes and numbers in the book of Revelation. This is certainly evident with what is referred to as the major series of seven's in the book. This is also called the heptadic structure of Revelation.

One place we can see this is in the series of three 7 fold events beginning in Revelation 6. We start off with the 7-Sealed scroll. This is followed by the seven trumpet judgments which are contained in the seventh seal judgment. The seven trumpet judgments then lead to the seven bowl judgments, which are contained in the seventh trumpet judgment. In each case, there is a pause between the sixth and seventh event in the series. This apparent pause or parenthesis has a purpose. Merriam Webster's dictionary defines a parenthesis as "an amplifying or explanatory word, phrase, or sentence inserted in a passage."

In this session we see that there has been such an insertion or pause between the sixth and seventh seal. We also see that the seventh judgment in each series then leads directly to the first event in the next. To understand all of this as fully as possible we need to realize that Israel is the centerpiece of the Old Testament and therein we see them used to communicate God's Word and message to us. (It is also necessary to understand the Hebraic roots of the New Testament and our faith to fully comprehend it.) We now see Israel reemerging as the centerpiece of God's plan as it comes to fruition in the book of Revelation.

Group Warm-up Questions

In what ways can silence be good or helpful?

When might a silence of 30 minutes seem like an eternity?

When might a silence of half an hour seem like a mere moment in time?

Read: Revelation 8:1-5

Reread: Revelation 8:1

Who do we see opening the seventh seal?

What happened when the seventh seal was opened?

For how long was there silence in heaven after this seal was opened?

Why is it significant and dramatic that there was silence in heaven?

Why do you think there was silence in heaven at this time?

Do you think that the gravity of the events to come somehow influenced this silence?

Read:

Zephaniah 1:7

Zechariah 2:13

Habakkuk 2:20

What do these verses infer about silence?

Do we need to be talking all the time as we engage in our relationship with God?

Should silence be part of our worship of God? How so and why?

J. Vernon McGee tells a humorous story about a young boy and heaven. J. Vernon had been invited to be the guest speaker at a summer youth camp. When he arrived he was immediately engulfed by an uproarious group of young girls all seemingly at odds with one young boy. When he asked what the problem might be the girls told him that the young boy had told them that there were no girls in heaven.

Of course, J. Vernon then asked the young boy if he had any Scripture to back up his assertion. The boy pointed to Revelation 8:1 and said he thought no girl could be silent for half an hour and that therefore there will be no girls in heaven. Obviously, this young Bible scholar made an illogical jump, took one verse out of context, didn't relate it to the whole of Scripture, and made a mistake. He did, however, attract the attention of a large group of girls, which may have been his intention in the first place.

Reread: Revelation 8:2

Who did John see after the half hour of silence in heaven?

What was given to each of these angels?

John was Jewish, an apostle, and a student of the Scriptures. As such he was familiar with the role of trumpets in God's Word and in the life of Israel. In the book of Numbers we see three specific ways in which trumpets are used.

The Use of Trumpets in Scripture

1. To Call His people together.

    • See Numbers 10:1-8

2. To call His people to battle.

    • See Numbers 10:9

3. To announce special times.

    • See Numbers 10:10

Read the following passages to see specific examples of the use of trumpets in God's Word. As you read them, please jot down the specific way God used them in each instance.

1 Kings 1:34

1 Kings 1:39

Exodus 19:16-19

Joshua 6:13-16

1 Thessalonians 4:13-18

Knowing the way in which trumpets are seen in the Word of God, what might one expect when we see them handed out to seven angels during the tribulation period?

Warren Wiersbe said "Sounding seven trumpets certainly would announce a declaration of war, as well as the fact that God's anointed King was enthroned in glory and about to judge His enemies." (See Psalm 2:1-6)

What do you think about what Warren Wiersbe said and how he tied it into Psalm 2:1-6?

Reread: Revelation 8:3

Who did John then see?

What did the angel have in his possession?

The Merriam Webster dictionary says that a censer is a vessel for burning incense; *especially*: a covered incense burner swung on chains in a religious ritual.

This is not to be confused with the word censor, which means a person who supervises conduct and morals: as an official who examines materials (as in publications or films) for objectionable matter.

What was this angel supposed to do?

Reread: Revelation 8:4

Also Read: Psalm 141:2

What did John see going up before God?

What is significant about the fact that incense accompanies the prayers of God's people in Revelation 8:4?

Does this apply to the prayers of believers today? How so?

How do you see the purpose of prayer?

a. To get our will done in heaven?

b. To get our will done on earth?

c. To achieve God's purpose on earth?

d. To achieve God's purpose through space, time, and eternity?

e. To enhance and expand one's relationship with God?

f. C, D, and E above?

We should note that the term "saints" mentioned in Revelation 8:4 is a reference to all of God's people who have entered into a personal relationship with Him through Jesus Christ. We can see this throughout God's Word. A few of these many places include:

2 Corinthians 1:1

2 Corinthians 9:1

2 Corinthians 9:12

2 Corinthians 13:13

"Sainthood" is conferred by God as one comes to Him through Jesus Christ and is filled with the Holy Spirit.

Some religious organizations have mistakenly thought that it is like knighthood granted by a King and that they somehow have the authority to make someone a saint. This is counter to what we find in the Bible.

Reread: Revelation 8:5

With what did the angel fill the censor?

Why do you think the censor being filled with incense and the prayers of the saints led to it immediately thereafter being filled with fire from the altar?

What did the angel do with the censor after it was filled with fire from the altar?

Why do you think the censor was so violently hurled at the earth?

What happened when the censor filled with fire from the altar hit the earth?

Why do you think these things occurred when the censor and fire from the altar hit the earth?

We see similar imagery to Revelation 8:5 in other places in this great book. Take a look at:

Revelation 4:5

Revelation 11:19

Revelation 16:18

How can one read these words without knowing that a great storm of events is beginning to take place?

Application Questions

How can you incorporate silent meditation on the Word of God as part of your daily life?

All of God's servants have specific God-given tasks or areas of responsibility, including the angels we read about today. What specific God-given responsibility do you need to fulfill today?

Close in Prayer

WEEK 18

THE TRUMPET JUDGMENTS BEGIN
REVELATION 8:6-9:21

Opening Prayer

Group Warm-up Question

What one characteristic of wildfires, earthquakes, floods, hurricanes, and tornadoes impacts you the most? Why?

Read: Revelation 8:6-9:21

Reread: Revelation 8:6-7

What kind of a storm came upon the earth when the first trumpet was sounded?

The text says that this storm was "hurled upon the earth." What does that make you think about the ferocity of this event?

Read: Exodus 9:18-26

In what ways does the hailstorm in Exodus remind you of the storm in Revelation 8:7?

Which one do you think was worse? Why?

Read: Joel 2:30

Do you think this verse prophetically alludes to Revelation 8:6-7? How so?

This first trumpet judgment in Revelation 8:7 had three specific effects upon the earth. Please list them below.

1.

2.

3.

Note: The Greek word used for "trees" in this verse usually refers to fruit trees.

How would a storm of this magnitude impact the food supply for humans and livestock alike?

What would be the economic impact of this event?

Might this event cripple the world economy?

Reread: Revelation 8:8-9

What went into the sea as a result of the sounding of the second trumpet?

Note that the text says that this object was "like a mountain." What do you think it was?

The grammatical tool used by God in this instance is a simile. That means that the object was not a flaming mountain, but was in some significant respects like it.

What does the verbiage that says this object was "thrown" into the seas infer to you about the magnitude of the force upon impact?

Read: Exodus 7:19-21

In what ways does the event in Exodus remind you of the event in Revelation 8:8-9?

Which was worse and why? (Remember that oceans cover three fourths of the surface of the earth.)

There were three specific results of this object being thrown into the sea. Please list them below.

1.

2.

3.

Do you think an event of this enormity could cause tidal waves around the world?

How do you think the three results of this huge flaming object going into the sea are brought about? (Capsizing of ships, superheating the water, etc..?)

How would the death of one third of all sea creatures impact the balance of life in the ocean's ecosystems?

How would this event impact the world's food supply?

How would this event impact the world economically?

For those unfamiliar with shipping we should realize that there is an awful lot going on in the sea.

The Marine Knowledge Center tells us that there are 104,304 ships on the seas including cargo ships, fishing boats and small craft.

In July of 2012 Shipping Intelligence Weekly said that there were 58,900 cargo ships around the world.

The World Fleet Monitor tells us that there are 87,483 ships on the seas of the world, not including cargo ships, fishing boats, or naval vessels.

Wikipedia claims there were 3,074 naval vessels as of 2011.

How do we make sense of this data? If we take the number from the Marine Knowledge center and add in an estimate for naval vessels (with the naval vessel number multiplied by a factor of at least two since we really don't expect any sovereign state to provide accurate data on this intelligence secret) we are probably somewhere near to the truth.

For our purposes let's assume the following numbers are somewhat close to being accurate.

104,304   Approximate Number of Non-naval vessels.

6,148   Approximate Number of Naval vessels.

110,452   Approximate number of ships on the seas.

One can only imagine the tremendous loss of life, cargo, and capital if 36,817 of these ships were to suffer sudden destruction. (One third as referenced in Revelation 8:8-9.)

Might this event alone cripple the world economy?

How might this event in concert with the results of the sounding of the first trumpet impact the world?

Reread: Revelation 8:10-11

What fell upon the freshwater rivers and springs?

What happened to one third of the waters on the planet as a result?

What happened to the people who consumed these waters?

If the people drinking these waters are in danger of dying, what must happen to the freshwater fish?

The name of the star, Wormwood, has some interesting history and significance that may give us further clues to what is going on.

First, we know that wormwood appears a number of times in the Scriptures. Throughout we see it associated with bitterness, calamity, and judgment in verses such as: (NKJV and KJV)

Deuteronomy 29:18

Lamentations 3:15

Proverbs 5:3-5 (Sin followed by deserved consequential judgment)

Jeremiah 9:13-15 (Sin followed by deserved consequential judgment)

Jeremiah 23:11-15 (Sin followed by deserved consequential judgment)

As we examine the original language we find that the Greek word for wormwood is *absinthe.* This means something that is "undrinkable without harm."

There is also a popular liqueur called absinthe. Absinthe has often been portrayed as a dangerously addictive psychoactive drug, however it has not been shown to be any more harmful than other alcoholic beverages. One imagines that at the time of the writing of Revelation that higher concentrations must have been the norm since it apparently had quite a negative reputation at the time.

Modern researchers have taken this whole subject to another interesting level. They have noticed that the word for wormwood in Russian (Ukranian) is Chernobyl. For those of us who don't remember, this is the site of the worst nuclear accident in history. Untold numbers of people in and around the area suffered from radiation sickness and died, though the government in the region has done its best to suppress this data.

The researchers who have taken this tack then posit that the star seen falling was a first century man's description of an explosive nuclear device that ended up polluting much of the world's fresh water sources. Indeed, the deleterious impact of this kind of thing can be quite insidious as we are beginning to see from the reports of the recent Fukishima nuclear accident in Japan. Scientists report that this site has been spilling out 80,000 gallons of radioactive water per day into the oceans and that reefs in its path are devoid of life.

So what is the answer?

At this point the best we can do with accuracy is to refer back to the text itself. We know what this event looks like and the impact it will have. The exact methodology is an interesting point of conjecture and will be revealed in the future when it actually takes place.

How might the events that occur as a result of the sounding of the first three trumpets alone impact the world?

Do you think there might be:

1. Food shortages?

2. Rioting?

3. Murder?

4. Rapes?

5. Anarchy?

6. Military Coups?

7. Starvation?

8. Disease?

What besides these possibilities can you envision happening as a result of the sounding of the first three trumpets?

Read: Isaiah 2:9-21

Does this sound like what is going on in Revelation? The Holy Spirit inspired the prophet Isaiah to write it about 2700 years ago.

Read:

John 1:1-3

John 8:58

Revelation 21:6

Revelation 22:13

How does it make you feel when you realize that while we have free will, Jesus Christ exists outside of the constraints of time and knows the end from the beginning?

How would you tie this concept into the passages we have read in this week's study from Revelation, Isaiah, and Exodus?

Reread: Revelation 8:12

Also read: Exodus 10:21-23

What happened at the sounding of the fourth trumpet?

How is this similar to what happened in Exodus 10:21-23?

How do you think the event Recorded in Revelation 8:12 will impact the earth on top of the first three trumpet judgments?

If unabated, how might it impact the earth to lose one third of the light and energy of the sun?

What this verse does not tell us is the length of time the sun and the celestial bodies will be darkened. We do know, however, that it will be temporary, not permanent. This is indicated by:

Revelation 16:8-9 where we see intense heat from the sun.

Matthew 24:29-30 where we see that the sun and moon are again darkened at the second coming of Jesus, indicating that they were shining between the fourth trumpet event and the time when Jesus returns.

Luke 21:25-28 which also that there will again be strange signs in the sun, moon and stars immediately prior to the return of Jesus, seeming to corroborate Matthew 24:29-30.

Taking all of this into account, do you think it might be possible that the event in Revelation 8:12 mirrors that in Exodus 10:21-23 in duration as well as impact?

As an interesting aside, when examining Luke 21:26 we see that "the powers of heaven will be shaken." The Greek words used are often the source of conjecture for scholars. They include *ouranos* which is the root word for uranium, *dunamis* which is the root word for dynamite, and *saleo* which means "to be set off balance."

Does this expansion of the Greek make you wonder about any of the things that will be happening on the earth at that time? How so?

Reread: Revelation 8:13

What does this angel say?

The Greek word *aietos* is translated by the KJV and the NKJV as angel from the context of the passage in the original language. Young's literal translation translates it to simply mean "messenger" from the context of the passage. A number of other versions translate it to mean eagle since the same word is used of an eagle in Revelation 12:14, Matthew 24:28, and Luke 17:37. This is no cause for great discussion or debate. Any way you slice it we have a message from God.

To whom in particular is this angel delivering a warning?

What should these people be thinking when they hear this message having already endured such great calamity?

We should take a moment to be clear on just who the "inhabiters of the earth" or "them that dwell upon the earth" are. We find these same words used twelve times in the book of Revelation to describe a certain "kind" of people. Take a look at the following verses to see this:

Revelation 3:10

Revelation 6:10

Revelation 8:13

Revelation 11:10 (Twice)

Revelation 12:12 (See the KJV)

Revelation 13:8

Revelation 13:12

Revelation 13:14

Revelation 14:6

Revelation 17:2

Revelation 17:8

Read 1 John 2:15-17 to see an apt description of these people.

Read Revelation 13:8 to see how God's Word makes it crystal clear that these people are not believers.

Read Philippians 3:18-21 to see that that the people just described live for the earth and the things of the earth in contrast to the believers who are "citizens of heaven."

Read 2 Corinthians 4:14-16 and discuss the attitude the believers living during the tribulation period should have.

Should we also have this attitude today? Why or why not?

Now we are about to see the Holy Spirit employing another literary device, in this case a metaphor. Merriam Webster defines a metaphor as a word or phrase for one thing that is used to refer to another thing in order to show or suggest that they are in some way or ways similar.

Read: Revelation 9:1-2

What did John see when the fifth trumpet was sounded?

How is the star described?

Read:

Isaiah 14:12-16

Luke 10:18

In Revelation 9:1-2 the star is referred to as "he." Based upon the pattern in the Scriptures, who do you think "he" is?

What was given to this star and what did he do with it?

Here we are faced with another question that bears answering; that is what is the Abyss? The Greek word for this place is *Abousso* and means "bottomless pit." We see this term used 9 times in the New Testament and 30 times in the Old Testament. Seven of the times we see the term in the New Testament are in Revelation.

Abyss in Revelation

Revelation 9:1

Revelation 9:2

Revelation 9:11

Revelation 11:7

Revelation 17:8

Revelation 20:1

Revelation 20:3

Having read these verses what further thoughts do you have about the "star" referenced in Revelation 9:1-2?

For further information on the functioning of the *Abousso* see:

Genesis 6:2 to learn about angels who stepped over their authority.

Genesis 6:4 to again see these disobedient angels.

Isaiah 24:21-22 to see the fate of these beings prophesized.

Luke 8:31 to see that the demons themselves feared the *abousso*; the bottomless pit.

Revelation 20:1 to see a mighty angel with the keys to the bottomless pit.

Revelation 20:3 to see Satan confined to bottomless pit for a thousand years.

This bottomless pit, *the abousso*, always appears as reference to a temporary place of incarceration for certain demons or for Satan himself.

The lake of fire is the final awful destiny of these demons and the enemies of God. Take a look at:

Matthew 13:40-42 to see the fiery furnace as the terrible destiny of those who do evil.

Matthew 13:49-50 to see the involvement of this place of torment in the future.

Revelation 20:10 to see the future destiny of the "star" we read about in Revelation 9:1-2

How would you feel on the way down if you fell off a cliff?

How do you imagine you would feel if falling on a continual and endless basis into a pit without a bottom?

Reread: Revelation 9:2-11

What are the first things to come out of the pit when it is opened up?

What effect does this have upon the sun and they sky?

What immediately follows the smoke out of the Abyss?

For anyone familiar with Entomology, the study of insects, it is obvious that the "locusts" in this passage are not normal locusts. They are something else. Please list the characteristics of these locusts as we find them in this passage.

1.

2.

3.

4.

5.

6.

7.

8.

9.

10.

Several things, however, are not readily apparent to those unfamiliar with locusts when reading this passage. A few of them include:

1. In Revelation 9:2-3 when we see smoke rising from the Abyss locusts are seen to come out of the cloud of smoke. When locusts travel in a large group they are often described today in exactly the same way. What appears to be a huge cloud of smoke is actually a group of locusts beyond number.

2. In Revelation 9:7 we see these locusts wearing crowns. The Greek word used to describe these crowns is *stephanos*. We would do well to remember that these are not the crowns of rulers, but of victors. These minions of Satan are victorious in torturing the non-believers. We should also remember that when the Antichrist was revealed as the rider of the white Horse in Revelation 6:1 he also wore a *stephanos*.

3. In Revelation 9:7 we see the locusts likened to horses prepared for battle. This seems strange to readers in the United States since in this country people most often think of locusts incorrectly as a different insect, the cicada, which is often colloquially referred to as a locust. This is because when cicadas emerge *en-masse* from their nymph stage they do indeed make a loud sound when they travel together in a cloud in a fashion somewhat similar to real locusts.

   Real locusts, however, have an appearance that is likened to that of horses equipped with armor. The German term applied to them is *heupferd*, which means "hay-horse" and the Italian word is *cavaletta* which means "little horse."

4. In Revelation 9:9 we see the sound of the demonic locusts described as being "like the thundering of many horses and chariots rushing into battle." This is different than the sound made by natural locusts. Natural locusts are described as making a sound like a great rainstorm. The two, while sharing some similarities, are decidedly not the same.

5. In Revelation 9:11 we see that the demonic locusts have a king. Natural locusts have none. (See Proverbs 30:27)

In his work on Revelation David Jeremiah goes further and summarizes these characteristics in other descriptive terms that include:

1. Impressive.

2. Innumerable.

3. Inhuman.

4. Indestructible.

5. Intelligent.

6. Somehow weirdly sensual and inviting.

   - (Revelation 9:8 says that their hair was like women's hair. At the time Revelation was written a woman's hair was considered the most intriguing, sensual, sexual and seductive thing about her. This knowledge also helps readers today to understand the thinking behind 2 Corinthians 11:5-16, which has often been puzzling and misleading to people without an understanding of the times.)

It is of great import that these locust-like demons had the power to sting like scorpions with their tails.

To those of us unfamiliar with scorpions we should be aware that their sting is spoken of as the most painful sting known to man. Depending upon the species of scorpion, their venom can cause swelling, skin lesions and extreme pain by essentially inflaming a portion of the nervous system. The Israeli "deathstalker" scorpion is perhaps the worst species. The deathstalker is regarded as a highly dangerous species because its venom is a powerful mixture of neurotoxins, with a low lethal dose. While a sting from this scorpion is extraordinarily painful, it normally would not kill an otherwise healthy adult human. The scorpion stings from the tails of the demonic locusts in Revelation appear to be far worse than anything known to us today. The pain of the scorpion-like sting of the locusts in Revelation is said to last for five months.

To put this in further perspective we might concentrate on the necrotic impact of the worst of the scorpion stings with which we are familiar. Necrotic pain is nerve pain and for those who have suffered from it they know that it is far worse in intensity and duration than any other pain they have experienced. Indeed, I have known a man with a rare nerve disease in which his entire nervous system was inflamed. When I visited with him he described the pain as if his whole body was constantly on fire. Nothing he or his doctors could do provided any substantive relief. All this poor man wanted to do was die, but he could not. He lived in this state of pain and torment for years on end.

In summary we see that the sting and plague of these demonic locusts is:

1. Very personal.

2. Protracted.

3. Continual.

Reread: Revelation 9:6

Can you imagine pain such that one might want to die rather than endure it?

How do you think these people will feel if they try unsuccessfully to kill themselves by:

Drowning?

Knife wounds?

Lethal injection?

Poisoning?

Jumping off a cliff?

Gunshot?

Today a person with terminal cancer pain can at least most often receive temporary pain from a shot of morphine as they move toward death. The people tormented by the demonic locusts in Revelation are unable to receive relief regardless of what they do.

Specifically what group of people is attacked by the locusts?

Read: Revelation 7:1-12

Revelation 22:1-4

2 Timothy 2:19 (God knows who are His and so do the locusts.)

What happens to the tribulation believers, including Jews and Gentiles, during this period of time?

How does this benefit them during the time of the plague of demonic locusts?

How do you think the immunity to this plague experienced by the believers with the seal of God impacts those suffering from this particular plague?

Do you think it might make non-believers even more determined to wipe out those following Jesus?

Reread: Revelation 9:10

What does John again tell us about the most important characteristic of these locusts?

For how long does this plague of demonic locusts last?

Why do you think John devotes so much time to describing this particular judgment?

Reread:

Revelation 9:1

Revelation 9:11

Who, according to our study so far in this lesson, has the keys to the Abyss?

If Satan has the keys to the Abyss and he is the king of the locusts, what must the "locusts" then be? (In case anyone has any doubt.)

Even though the people suffering for this plague deserve it, God takes no pleasure in their pain.

Read Ezekiel 33:11 to see what God wants.

In the Bible we see over 600 times when men and women are warned to turn from their evil ways and follow God. This is part of the overall pattern of blessing and curse.

If you were driving down a road and saw 600 signs in succession warning that you would die if you stayed on that road, do you think you might take a different route?

Why do so many people refuse to respond to the warnings God graciously provides to them and to then accept His offer of life through His Son?

Reread: Revelation 9:13-21

What happened when the four angels were released?

Note: These are not good angels. Scripture has no record of the angels serving God being bound by Him. These particular followers of Satan have been bound until just this time in history.

How many people were killed by this onslaught?

Read: Revelation 6:8

Mathematical Question: If one fourth of the population of the world died in this passage and one third of those remaining die at the time of Revelation 9:15, what percentage of the world's people will have been killed? (A close approximation will suffice.)

The Euphrates River

For those of us unfamiliar with this part of the world we should realize that the Euphrates River:

1. Is the longest river in Western Asia. (It is approximately 1,740 miles long.)

2. Flows from Turkey in the north through Syria and Iraq to the Persian Gulf.

3. Is unnavigable except for very shallow-draft vessels.

4. Is the Eastern boundary of the land given to Israel. (See Joshua 1:1-4)

5. Is the traditional boundary between the East and the West.

6. Was the boundary or division that separated the Romans from the Parthian Empire. (The Romans greatly feared these fierce peoples.)

7. Served as the impassable obstacle that trapped the elite Iraqi Republican Guards when pursued by the United States 101st Airborne Division and the Army's 24th Mechanized Division during the 1991 Gulf War.

What does Revelation 9:16-19 passage tell us about the army that is released?

Note: There remain some unanswered questions about this 200 million being army. Some researchers attempt to fit this army into the mold of the massive Chinese military establishment. Other scholars believe that the army in this passage appears to simply be demonic in origin, much like the locusts we just studied.

In thinking about this one might look at Revelation 16:12 where we see a direct reference to the Kings of the East. We have generally been treating the various judgments in Revelation as events that unfold consecutively. However, some scholars believe that there is so much going on here that they think some of the things happening during the time of the trumpet judgments are occurring concurrently with what we see happening in the time of the bowl judgments.

Putting Revelation 16:12 together with Revelation 9:13-19 certainly has some interesting implications if the events are occurring at the same time. We would note:

1. The Euphrates River would have to be dried up or at least somehow crossed for a great army to advance from the East. (The Ataturk dam in Turkey, constructed in 1990, reportedly has the ability to reduce the great river to a trickle.)

2. China and India are two great superpowers who have the ability to put huge armies into the field.

3. China has built a road system capable of transporting an immense army to the Middle East.

4. From the point of view of history and prophecy the statement about the size of this force is quite incredible given the time at which the book of Revelation was written. At that point in history the entire population of the planet is thought to have been between 170 Million and 400 Million persons. Thus, the prophecy seems to indicate a potential army that might have been so large as to be hard to comprehend in the first years of the first century A.D.

5. Some scholars posit that the destructive characteristics imputed to the horses and riders in Revelation 9:17-19 might be a first century man's

way of describing modern mechanized warfare. They would go somewhat further in suggesting that the fire, brimstone, smoke and burning described are suggestive of tactical nuclear weapons.

6. We cannot, however, at this point make a definitive statement about the nature of the army in Revelation 9:17-19.

7. Different serious and committed believers view this passage in various ways. This is not a point at which anyone should separate from fellowship with a believer with a divergent view of this subject. We will review the topic of the Kings of the East in more depth in Chapter 19.

8. If one is a believer who feels certain that the Rapture occurs prior to the Tribulation or mid-way through (that is before the Great Tribulation) they will be watching this from the mezzanine anyways. Anyone believing in a post-Tribulation rapture will view it with much greater concern.

9. Anyone reading this passage who is not a believer should by now be viewing all of history to come with great alarm.

Reread: Revelation 9:20-21

What do we learn about the people (the non-believers) who are still living at this point?

Question: How can these people possibly not see and respond to:

The error of their ways?

The power of God?

The coming doom of Satan?

The life offered through Jesus Christ?

How can you explain the fact that the surviving non-believers are actually choosing to worship demons and idols at this point in history?

Dr. David Jeremiah, in his commentary on this subject. makes an excellent point. He says we need to remember that "A man is not changed because of punishment. He may desist from doing evil because he is afraid of punishment (actually quite effective), but his acts of will are based on what is going on inside him." (See Mark 7:20-22)

How do you feel about what Dr. Jeremiah has said?

Read:

Hebrews 3:12

Hebrews 3:15

Hebrews 10:16

Ephesians 4:18

Luke 21:34

Acts 28:27

Zechariah 7:12

Why do people sometimes harden their hearts?

What happens to people when their hearts become hardened?

Conversely, please read the following verses and list what we learn about our hearts when they are as God intended and wants them to be?

1 Thessalonians 3:12-13

2 Thessalonians 3:5

1 Timothy 1:5

James 1:21

Ephesians 3:17

Galatians 4:6

2 Corinthians 1:21-22

Luke 6:45

Philippians 4:6-7

Read: Ezekiel 36:26

Psalm 51:10

So where can one get the kind of a heart that pleases God?

Read:

John 16:33

Romans 10:10

How does one go about obtaining the kind of peace offered by God and a heart that pleases Him?

Read: 2 Corinthians 6:2

If one is not a believer, how soon should they take this step?

Why do you think the plagues described in Revelation are progressive? Why doesn't God just wipe out the evil-doers, condemn them, reward His followers, and go on to the new heaven and new earth?

Read: 2 Peter 3:3-9

Question: How might this passage from Peter tie into the previous question which we are now considering?

Application Questions

What changes might you make in your prayer life this week as a result of what you have studied in this passage?

As a result of this study, are there any changes you should make in your life to be sure that your actions and attitudes are consistent with what God desires to produce in us? (See Galatians 5:22-23)

Close in Prayer

THE MESSENGER AND THE LITTLE SCROLL
REVELATION 10:1-11

Opening Prayer

Group Warm up Question

On a scale of one to ten (with ten being great and one being terrible), how good are you at keeping secrets? How good should you be?

We now enter an interlude between the sixth and seventh trumpets in Revelation.

Read: Revelation 10:1-10

I suggest that this passage be read in Young's Literal Translation in addition to any other versions of the Bible one might be using. Since everyone might not have this version at their disposal I am including it here.

Revelation 10:1–11

1 And I saw another strong messenger coming down out of the heaven, arrayed with a cloud, and a rainbow upon the head, and his face as the sun, and his feet as pillars of fire, 2 and he had in his hand a little scroll opened, and he did place his right foot upon the sea, and the left upon the land, 3 and he cried with a great voice, as a lion doth roar, and when he cried, speak out did the seven thunders their voices; 4 and when the seven thunders spake their voices, I was about to write, and I heard a voice out of the heaven saying to me, 'Seal the things that the seven thunders spake,' and, 'Thou mayest not write these things.' 5 And the messenger whom I saw standing upon the sea, and upon the land, did lift up his hand to the heaven, 6 and did swear in Him who doth live to the ages of the ages, who did create the heaven and the things in it, and the land and the things in it, and the sea and the things in it—that time shall not be yet, 7 but in the days of the voice of the seventh messenger, when he may be about to sound, and the secret of God may be finished, as He did declare to His own servants, to the prophets. 8 And the voice that I heard out of the heaven is again speaking with me, and saying, 'Go, take the little scroll that is open in the hand of the messenger who hath been standing upon the sea, and upon the land:' 9 and I went away unto the messenger, saying to him, 'Give me the little scroll;' and he saith to me, 'Take, and eat it up, and it shall make thy belly bitter, but in thy mouth it shall be sweet—as honey.' 10 And I took the little scroll out of the hand of the messenger, and did eat it up, and it was in my mouth as honey—sweet, and when I did eat it—my belly was made bitter; 11 and he saith to me, 'It behoveth thee again to prophesy about peoples, and nations, and tongues, and kings—many.' (YLT)

As we work through this passage there are two primary questions that seem to keep popping up for students of the Bible.

1. Who exactly is the messenger from God mentioned?

2. What is the mystery that will be revealed?

   To the end of investigating the question of the identity of the messenger in this passage we will progressively look at some of the clues we find in the text as we work our way through these verses. (While this investigation is interesting and instructive, it is not one that should be a point of division among believers.)

Clue One to the identity of the messenger: In the very literal translation of this passage the one delivering the message from God is referred to as a messenger. Other translations refer to this messenger as an angel.

Reread: Revelation 10:1

After the first six trumpets of judgment, what did John see?

What did this messenger look like?

Clue Two

Read the following verses for the second clue to the identity of the messenger:

Exodus 16:10

Exodus 19:9

Exodus 24:15

Exodus 34:5

Psalm 104:3

Matthew 17:5

Luke 21:27

Acts 1:9

Revelation 1:7

Who do we see coming in the clouds?

Clue Three

Read the following verse for the third clue of the identity of the messenger:

Revelation 4:3

Where else did we see a rainbow in the book of Revelation? Hint: Review today's main passage.

Clue Four

Read the following verse for the fourth clue to the identity of the messenger:

Habakkuk 3:2

Who in Scripture remembers His mercy even in the midst of His wrath?

Clue Five

Read the following verses for the fifth clue to the identity of the messenger:

Revelation 1:16

Matthew 17:1-2

Who else had a face that shone like the sun?

Clue Six

Read the following verse for the sixth clue to the identity of the messenger:

Revelation 1:15

Who else in Revelation had feet that shone like fire or polished bronze?

Reread: Revelation 10:2

What did this messenger have in his hand?

How was this messenger standing?

Reread: Revelation 10:2-3

What two things did this messenger do at this point in the passage?

Clue Seven

Read the following verses for the seventh clue to the identity of the messenger:

Isaiah 31 4-5

Hosea 5:14

Hosea 11:10

Amos 3:8

Revelation 5:5

Who else in Scripture is pictured as a mighty lion?

Clue Eight

Read the following verses for the eighth clue as we try to determine the identity of the messenger in this passage:

Joel 3:16

John 12:28-29

Revelation 10:3

Who else do we see described as making a loud roaring?

(This is quite different from the imagery used to depict Satan as a predatory lion in I Peter 5:8. Satan roars to frighten his prey. The Lion of Judah roars to announce His victory.)

Clue Nine

Read the following verses for the ninth clue as we investigate the identity of the messenger in Revelation 10:

Exodus 3:2

Judges 2:4

Judges 6:11-12

2 Samuel 24:16

Jesus Christ makes a temporary appearance as the Angel of the Lord a number of times in the Old Testament. How might this be similar to the messenger in Revelation 10?

Clue 10

The tenth clue to the identity of the messenger in this passage comes from an examination of the original language.

Revelation 10:1 refers to this messenger as "another messenger (YLT)" or "another angel." In the English this can be somewhat confusing. In the Greek it is pretty clear. If the Greek word used had been *heteros* it would have indicated "another of a different kind." However, the work used is *allos*, which means "another of the same kind."

Since the word used is allos, we must ask what comparison is being made. When we do this we find that this is the third instance where we have seen the appearance of a distinctive messenger.

In Revelation 7:2 we see a powerful angel holding back judgments until the 144,000 Jewish believers have been marked with the seal of God.

In Revelation 8:3-5 we see a powerful angel acting as messenger of the covenant and pouring out judgment.

Other places in Scripture we see the archangel Michael, which means "who is like God" mentioned in:

Daniel 10:13

Daniel 12:1

Jude 1:9

Revelation 12:7

We see the archangel Gabriel, which means "strength of God" mentioned in:

Daniel 8:16-18

Daniel 9:21

Luke 1:19

Luke 1:26

Luke 1:28

These references about powerful angels, especially in relationship to the use of the word *allos*, have led many Bible scholars to believe that while there are similarities between this messenger and Jesus Christ, it must in actuality be a special angel.

Reread: Revelation 10:4

Before we proceed, let's try to identify the seven thunders. To aid us in our inquiry please read Revelation 1:4.

How is God described in this verse?

How is the Holy Spirit referred to?

This appears to be an allusion to Isaiah 11:2. The Holy Spirit is spoken of as the Seven Fold Spirit; part of the trinity. How do you identify the seven characteristics of the Holy Spirit when you put Isaiah 11:2 together with Revelation 1:4?

1.

2.

3.

4.

5.

6.

7.

What did John try and do after he heard what the seven thunders said?

What did the voice from heaven say to John about what he wanted to do?

Note: About 2,600 years ago Daniel was given information that was to be sealed until the time of the end.

In Revelation 22:10 John is instructed to not seal up the prophetic words of the book of Revelation.

Whatever the seven thunders said is the only "sealed" thing in this book. Why do you think God did this?

What do you think the thunders said?

Theologians, Bible students, and others have spent thousands of hours speculating what the seven thunders said. We know only two things about these utterances:

1. As part of Scripture they must be consistent with the rest of God's Word.

2. The specific utterances are, at this point, unknown to us.

Is there any real profit to believers in everyday life in speculating upon the content of these utterances?

Read:

John 13:34-35

Galatians 6:15

What is it that really matters in the life of believers?

Reread: Revelation 10:5-6

What did this messenger do next?

Does it seem strange to you that this messenger took an oath in the name of God?

Clue Eleven

Please read the following:

Hebrews 6:13-20

Hebrews 7:20-22

If the Angel or messenger in Revelation 10 is Jesus Christ, why might He be taking an oath?

Reread: Revelation 10:6

In Revelation 10:6 we also see that there will be no more delay. We also see the subject of God's delay up until this point in:

2 Peter 3:1-9

Revelation 6:10-11

How have some of the people of the world incorrectly interpreted God's delay?

What has been the real purpose of God's delay?

Reread: Revelation 10:7

What announcement did the messenger make?

What mystery of God do you think is being referred to in this verse?

This question has been confusing to many. Certainly, many "mysteries" have been mentioned in Scripture and have then also been explained in the text itself. See several examples below:

Matthew 13:11

He replied, "You are permitted to understand the secrets of the Kingdom of Heaven, but others are not.

Mark 4:11

He replied, "You are permitted to understand the secret of the Kingdom of God. But I use parables for everything I say to outsiders,

Romans 11:25

I want you to understand this mystery, dear brothers and sisters, so that you will not feel proud about yourselves. Some of the people of Israel have hard hearts, but this will last only until the full number of Gentiles comes to Christ.

1 Corinthians 15:51

But let me reveal to you a wonderful secret. We will not all die, but we will all be transformed!

Ephesians 1:19

I also pray that you will understand the incredible greatness of God's power for us who believe him. This is the same mighty power

Ephesians 5:32

This is a great mystery, but it is an illustration of the way Christ and the church are one.

Ephesians 3:4

As you read what I have written, you will understand my insight into this plan regarding Christ.

Colossians 1:26–27

26 This message was kept secret for centuries and generations past, but now it has been revealed to God's people. 27 For God wanted them to know that the riches and glory of Christ are for you Gentiles, too. And this is the secret: Christ lives in you. This gives you assurance of sharing his glory.

Colossians 4:3

Pray for us, too, that God will give us many opportunities to speak about his mysterious plan concerning Christ. That is why I am here in chains.

Colossians 2:2

I want them to be encouraged and knit together by strong ties of love. I want them to have complete confidence that they understand God's mysterious plan, which is Christ himself.

1 Timothy 3:9

They must be committed to the mystery of the faith now revealed and must live with a clear conscience.

1 Timothy 3:16

Without question, this is the great mystery of our faith: Christ was revealed in a human body and vindicated by the Spirit. He was seen by angels and announced to the nations. He was believed in throughout the world and taken to heaven in glory.

Revelation 1:20

This is the meaning of the mystery of the seven stars you saw in my right hand and the seven gold lampstands: The seven stars are the angels of the seven churches, and the seven lampstands are the seven churches.

Revelation 17:5

A mysterious name was written on her forehead: "Babylon the Great, Mother of All Prostitutes and Obscenities in the World."

Revelation 17:7

"Why are you so amazed?" the angel asked. "I will tell you the mystery of this woman and of the beast with seven heads and ten horns on which she sits.

Many great Bible scholars believe the mystery mentioned in Revelation 10:7 to be that of the problem of evil in the world. We see that:

1. Evil has been permitted to increase until the world is ripe for judgment. (2 Thessalonians 2:7 and Revelation 14:14-20)

2. The price for sin has been paid.

3. As Dr. Charles Missler says "It may come as a surprise to learn that God has never reigned on the earth. Surely He is, indeed, the sovereign King over all of the universe---over both heaven and earth. He has ruled, overruled, and intervened upon the earth. He governs in a manner that seems remote and incomplete. *He has never used His absolute power to bring about an end to demonic evil, human rebellion, and global injustice and suffering. (Italics from Chuck Missler.)* And He does not receive the worship and honor that is His due. This is all about to change. That is what we pray for when we pray, "Thy kingdom come, thy will be done on earth as it is in heaven." *This reign will be inaugurated in Revelation 11:17.*"

How do you tie this concept into what we learned in 2 Peter 3:1-9?

Reread: Revelation 10:8

What did the voice from heaven tell John to do?

Clue Twelve

Clue twelve to the identity of the messenger in Chapter 10

Throughout the tenth chapter of Revelation we see the messenger referred to in a specific fashion relating to the whole of the earth and seas. Please read the following verses to see this:

Revelation 10:2

Revelation 10:6

Revelation 10:8

These verses seem to echo the following references from the Old Testament:

Psalm 95:3-5

Isaiah 40:12

Psalm 2:6-8

Putting these New and Old Testament references together, what do you think about the identity of the messenger in Revelation 10?

Thirteenth Clue

The thirteenth clue we will examine in terms of the identity of the messenger in Revelation 10 takes us to the role this personage seems to be filling. He seems to be acting as a prophet (speaking forth the message of God), a priest (interceding between men and God), and king (with dominion over all of the earth.) In the Scriptures we see these characteristics incorporated into Melchizedek, a type of Christ, and Christ Himself.

One can see this in:

Genesis 14:20

Psalm 110:4

Hebrews 5:6

Hebrews 7:2

Final and Most Important Clue

Reread: Revelation 10:6

Also read: John 1:1-3

If the messenger in Revelation 10 is swearing by the Creator Himself, who must the messenger then be?

Most Bible scholars, after considering all of the evidence, feel that this messenger is a special and powerful angel.

In the final analysis, who do you believe the messenger in this chapter to be?

If you are wrong in your conclusion, does this have any bearing upon your life or eternal destiny?

What profit is there in searching the scriptures to try and understand a tricky subject like this? (Read Isaiah 55:11 as you construct your answer.)

Reread: Revelation 10:9

What did the messenger tell John to do with the little scroll?

What warning did the messenger give John about what he told John to do?

Reread: Revelation 10:9-10

Read: Ezekiel 2:9-3:4

What actually happened when John followed the instructions given him by the messenger about the little scroll?

What do you think might be symbolized by John's eating of the scroll of God's words and finding it sweet in his mouth but sour in his stomach?

Read:

Acts 20:27

2 Timothy 4:1-5

How do these verses and the concepts therein tie in with Revelation 10:9-10?

The imagery of consuming the Word of God and assimilating it into every area of our lives is a thread that is woven throughout Scripture. Read the following verses and note what you learn about this process and practice:

Matthew 4:4

1 Peter 2:2

1 Corinthians 3:1-2

Psalm 119:103

Psalm 19:7-11

Jeremiah 15:16

Reread: Revelation 10:11

What was the last thing the messenger told John to do?

Application Questions

What steps can you take this week to help you internalize God's Word?

To whom in your life has God called you to speak the truth of His Word this week?

Close in Prayer

WEEK 20

THE TWO WITNESSES
REVELATION 11:1-14

Opening Prayer

Group Warm-up Questions

Why do you think people today are so often turned off by fire and brimstone preachers?

Why do you think so many people in the world are gleeful when someone claiming to be a believer is publicly found to be in moral failure?

Read: Revelation 11:1-14

Here we find some important augmentative data regarding the Tribulation. The Temple in Jerusalem has been rebuilt during the first half of the Tribulation. We see the two witnesses beginning their work during the first part of the Tribulation with it culminating in the events of this chapter. Many scholars believe that the two witnesses were in part responsible for the conversion of 144,000 Jewish believers who have been proclaiming God's message throughout the world at this point in history.

Chapter 11 in Revelation flows directly from Chapter 10 in a continuum. It is part of the interlude between the sounding of the sixth and seventh trumpets. Interpreting this chapter has been a point of difficulty for many people over the years, especially for those who prefer to allegorize or symbolize Scripture. Imputing one's fanciful notions into the text results in no end to the ridiculous interpretations one can find in less scholarly literature about this book and particularly this chapter of Revelation.

(This is the same problem encountered by people when they adhere to "replacement theology." Replacement theology had its genesis, at least in part, when well-meaning people lacking in confidence in the prophetic Scriptures read the Old Testament passages about Israel being reestablished as a Nation. When they looked and saw that there was no longer a nation of Israel (prior to 1948), they thought they would help God along by declaring that what He meant to say in His Word was that the church would become and replace Israel in the plan of God. This, of course, went out the window for any thinking person when the prophecies about the literal return of the Jews to their ancient homeland were fulfilled.)

The difficulties encountered when one unnecessarily and capriciously allegorizes and symbolizes this passage disappear when one adopts a high view of the Word of God and realizes that:

1. This chapter is essentially Jewish in nature. (Emanating from the Hebraic roots of Christianity.)

2. This chapter is prophetic and not historic.

3. It is presented and to be understood in a literal fashion. This means that:

- The two witnesses are real people.

- The temple is a real temple.

- The time periods mentioned are real and accurate time periods.

- The powers granted to the two witnesses are actual.

- The death of the two witnesses is factual.

- The claim that the two witnesses can be seen around the globe by all peoples, tribes, nations and languages actually occurs.

- The city mentioned is Jerusalem as stated in the text.

- The two witnesses are really resurrected.

- There is a real earthquake.

- The number of people who die in the earthquake is accurately recorded.

- The type of people who die in the earthquake is likewise accurately stated.

- People will actually celebrate the death of these two godly witnesses.

- The "earth dwellers" will watch in terror and amazement as the two witnesses rise from the dead and are taken up to heaven in a cloud.

- The people not killed in the earthquake will actually give glory to God.

Reread: Revelation 11:1-2

What was John given?

What was John told to measure?

What was John told to leave out of his calculations?

Do you think God wanted John to take these measurements because He didn't know how big the temple was?

In order to simplify things permit me to first do my best to summarize what Scripture seems to tell us about the timing in these verses as they relate to the Tribulation period. After my attempt at a summary we can view the specific references that help one understand it with more in-depth study.

1. The two witnesses boldly proclaim the message of God and repentance for three and one half years.

2. The witnesses are killed.

3. The whole non-believing world celebrates their death.

4. The witnesses are resurrected.

5. The anti-Christ begins to continue his program more viciously than ever.

Interpreting the opening verses of Revelation 11 requires knowledge of not only the Old Testament, but of history. To aid us in this study we should understand the following:

1. The use of a rod in scripture is itself quite symbolic. We see it specifically used in relationship to an instrument of chastisement and ruling authority. See:

   • Revelation 2:27

   • Revelation 12:5

   • Revelation 19:15

2. The part of the temple to be left out of John's measurements was the outer Court of the Gentiles containing the brazen altar. This marked the boundary beyond which Gentiles were not permitted to go. (See Acts 21:28-29) During what one might call the New Testament times the Romans gave the Jews the right to execute any Gentile who went beyond the Court of the Gentiles.

John was told to not measure this court as we see in Revelation 11:2.

Revelation 11:2

"But exclude the outer court; do not measure it, because it has been given to the Gentiles. They will trample on the holy city for 42 months."

This corresponds to the final years of the career of the Antichrist as well as to the end of the Times of the Gentiles referenced by Jesus Christ himself in Luke 21:24. This period of time began in 606 B.C. when Babylon began to devastate Judah and Jerusalem and will continue until Jesus Christ returns to deliver the Holy City of Jerusalem and Israel.

3. We see the act of taking measurements as a prelude to judgment and/or destruction in:

   • Jeremiah 31:38-39

   • Lamentations 2:8

   • 2 Kings 21:13

   • Amos 7:8-9

   • Isaiah 34:11

4. We see measurement in preparation for judgment beginning at the temple in Ezekiel 40:2-6.

5. We see measurement in preparation for the Lord's coming to dwell upon the earth (the Second Coming) in Zechariah 2.

6. The Holy City referenced is none-other than Jerusalem. We see no other city labeled such in all of Scripture. This is corroborated in:

   • Nehemiah 11:1

- Nehemiah 11:18

- Isaiah 52:1

- Daniel 9:24

- Matthew 4:5

- Matthew 27:53

7. The temple referenced did not exist at the time John penned the book of Revelation. The temple of John's time was destroyed by the Romans in 70 A.D. as predicted by Jesus himself. (See: Luke 21:5-6) The temple referenced in Revelation 11 is the one that will be rebuilt during the first half of the Tribulation when the Antichrist lures Israel into a false sense of security and peace with a disingenuous treaty. This temple will ultimately be desecrated when the Antichrist breaks his treaty with Israel.

   We see this foretold by:

   - Daniel in Daniel 9:27, Daniel 11:31, and Daniel 12:11.

   - Jesus in Matthew 24:15 and Mark 13:14.

   - Paul in 2 Thessalonians 2:3-4.

   - John in Revelation 11:2

8. The Temple Institute in Israel is preparing for the rebuilding of the temple, the very temple mentioned in Revelation 11, as we speak. To that end:

   - There are today several hundred young men in training in Israel to serve in this temple.

   - They have manufactured the temple implements and vessels to be used in the temple according to the instructions in the Old Testament.

- They have prepared the vestments to be used in the temple according to the instructions in the Old Testament.

- They are breeding red heifers to be used in sacrifices at the temple as seen in the Old Testament.

- They have actually rehearsed the sacrifice of the Passover lamb (with protestations from animal rights groups.)

- For more information on this fascinating organization I suggest one view their website at www.templeinstitute.org.

9. The temple in Revelation 11 is generally regarded as the third temple. It is not to be confused with the Millennial Temple or the Heavenly Temple which we will see later on in our study.

Reread: Revelation 11:2-3

In the Bible we oftentimes see this period of time referenced in a way that is strange to our ears.

Seven years is sometimes referred to as "seven times" as we see in the following verses:

Daniel 4:16

Daniel 4:23

Daniel 4:24-25

Half of this time period is sometimes referred to as either a number of days, months, or "a time, times, and half a time." We can see this in the following verses.

Revelation 11:3

Revelation 12:14 (More on this later)

Revelation 13:5

Daniel 7:25

Daniel 12:7

As we read Revelation 11 it appears that the duration of the ministry of the two witnesses during the first half of the Tribulation lasts 1,260 days. (Revelation 11:3) Jerusalem is then overrun by the Gentiles for 42 months. (Revelation 11:2)

In Daniel 9:25 we see a reference to 69 weeks of years. This then culminates in the final seventh week of years (Daniel 9:27—often referred to as the 70th week of Daniel) that directly precedes the Second coming of Jesus Christ and the thousand year reign of Christ on earth. (The Millennium)

Reread: Revelation 11:3-6

How are the two witnesses dressed?

Dressing in sackcloth speaks of repentance and is a motif we see frequently in the Old Testament.

What is the mission of these two witnesses?

What special powers are granted to these prophets?

Who do you think these witnesses might be?

The identities of these witnesses have been debated by Bible scholars many times over. This is not completely clear and agreeing on who they are is not a point of faith. That being said many people take the following characteristics of these two men to indicate that they are Moses and Elijah.

Like Moses they have:

The ability to turn water into blood.

- See Exodus 7:19-20

The ability to strike the earth with plagues.

- See Exodus 8-12

Like Elijah they have:

The ability to call fire down from heaven.

- 1 Kings 18:37-38

- 2 Kings 1:10

- 2 Kings 1:12

The ability to stop and start the rain.

- 1 Kings 17:1

- Luke 4:25 (Note the period of time.)

- James 5:17

- James 5:8

And, we do see Moses and Elijah having a "staff meeting" with the Lord in Matthew 17:1-5

While there are a number of other references we might access to try and ascertain whether or not these two witnesses are Moses and Elijah, knowing their identity at this point in time is not crucial to one's faith or their understanding of the book of Revelation.

The text itself, in Revelation 11:4 specifically identifies these witnesses in the same terminology as Zechariah 4:10-14.

Zechariah 4:12, by the way, is taken to mean that these two personages are continuously filled with the Holy Spirit.

Having said all of this, the identity of the two witnesses is not sure. Some people even think they may relate to other personages in the Scripture including Enoch, Lazarus, John the Apostle, or John the Baptist. While this is interesting, one should not get too caught up on it. The important thing is to understand their mission in the plan of God as we see it in the book of Revelation at this point in time.

Question: These two witnesses had a difficult job in proclaiming the Word of God during the Tribulation. However, God granted them the ability to perform the work He had set out for them to do in this difficult situation. Does God do the same for believers today? How so?

Reread: Revelation 11:7

What will happen after the two witnesses complete their God-ordained purpose and ministry?

Why do you think the enemy was unable to stop these witnesses until after their mission was complete?

Are believers today likewise protected until they complete the plans God has for them?

What examples have you seen of this in your experience?

What does this mean for you, your life and carrying out the will of God in your life?

Are you, in some sense, invulnerable until your testimony is complete?

Illustration

One of my best friends over the years was a man named Phil Evans. He and I became believers at about the same time in life when we were in high school. We played football together, vacationed together, led Bible studies together, hunted together, and enjoyed each other's company. He was my brother as a believer and like my brother in every other sense of the word. As we grew older we lived in different places, but whenever we spoke on the phone or met it was if no time had passed since our last contact. We shared each other's triumphs and tragedies through the years, sometimes from afar.

Over the years we each continued to grow in our faith and in our knowledge and sharing of God's Word. Phil was doing a great deal of work not only with the adults at his church, but was also spearheading a large and effective program with high school students. He was likely the single most effective believer in the large church in which he was involved.

Early one morning, when Phil was about 55 years old, his wife Chris was reading her Bible in the kitchen when she heard a noise in the bedroom where Phil was "sleeping in." He had gotten up from bed, fallen over, and died on the bedroom floor. His crying grief-stricken mother called me as I was driving home from work that day to tell me about it.

Phil's memorial service filled the sanctuary at Graystone church. My wife Sally and I saw the old football coach and his wife with whom Phil and I had worked when involved with the Fellowship of Christian Athletes. We saw old friends, people of all ages from the church and community, and most notably a huge number of high school students who Phil was leading in Bible study groups.

I believe Phil died at the point of maximum effectiveness both in terms of what God had set out for him to do and in terms of the impact of his memorial service and legacy.

Reread: Revelation 11:7-10

How are the two witnesses killed?

What happens to their bodies after they are killed?

How will people from around the world react to the deaths of these two great men?

The book of Revelation was written about two thousand years ago. It says that people from around the world will stare at their bodies and gloat over them? How is this possible?

Could this end up being a major news event on the television networks?

Note: The Antichrist (the beast) is now in power and wants to take over the temple. He has not been able to succeed up until this point because the two witnesses are in the way. The road is now opened for the foretold desecration he will bring to the temple.

Reread: Revelation 11:11-12

What happens to the two witnesses after three and a half days?

How will the people observing this event respond?

How do you think you would respond if you saw two men dead for half a week come back to life?

Do you think this event, like the gloating over the murder of these two witnesses, will be viewed around the world?

Reread: Revelation 11:13-14

What else will happen at the same time these witnesses are resurrected?

The original language suggests that the 7,000 men who died were men of prominence. What might be the significance of this fact?

How will the people who observe the death and resurrection of these two witness, the great earthquake, and the death of 7,000 prominent men respond to these events?

Note: An even greater earthquake will occur when the seventh bowl is poured out in Revelation 16:18-20. (Interestingly, the greatest fault line in the world runs east of Jerusalem down the Jordan called the Great Rift Valley, running underneath the Dead Sea into Africa.)

How do you see God using these two witnesses, even unto the point of their death?

Application Question

What can you do to be sure that your work for God continues to have a profound and positive impact up until and including the time of your death?

Close in Prayer

THE SEVENTH TRUMPET
REVELATION 11:15-19

Opening Prayer

Group Warm-up Questions

Who is one famous believer who you think will receive great reward in heaven?

Who is one not-so-famous believer who you think will also receive great reward in heaven?

Read: Revelation 11:15-19

Reread: Revelation 11:15

What did John see and hear in Revelation 11:15?

What did the voices say about the world?

What did the voices say about the reign of Jesus Christ?

How is the promise that Jesus Christ will reign over the earth significant to you?

The Greek word used for kingdom in this verse, *basileia*, is singular. Satan has had the world under his control. We see this in:

Matthew 4:8-9

Matthew 12:25-27

John 12:31

John 14:30-31

John 16:11

The sounding of the seventh trumpet announces the coronation of Jesus Christ, the beginning of His reign on the earth. One can see trumpets sounded at the coronation of a new king in:

2 Samuel 15:10

1 Kings 1:39

2 Kings 9:13

2 Kings 11:12-14

Reread: Revelation 11:16-17

What group of people, in addition to John, heard the voices from heaven?

How was the group of twenty-four elders seated?

How did the elders respond to the sounding of the seventh trumpet and the voices from heaven?

What did the twenty-four elders say at this point in time?

The twenty-four elders are seen praising God for:

1. His eternal nature.

2. His irresistible and omnipotent power.

3. His sovereignty and beginning His reign. (The rendering "has begun to reign" is the most accurate translation of the verbs used in this passage.)

It is of great import that the power of God is emphasized not only in these verses, but throughout the book of Revelation. We see God's "almighty or omnipotent" power described in just those terms 10 places in the New Testament with nine of them in this book. We see this in:

Revelation 1:8

Revelation 4:8

Revelation 11:17

Revelation 15:3

Revelation 16:7

Revelation 16:14

Revelation 19:6

Revelation 19:15

Revelation 21:22

Why do you think the Holy Spirit is emphasizing this attribute of God in the book of the Bible in which all of human history culminates?

Reread: Revelation 11:16-18

What three acclamations of praise do we see coming from the twenty-four elders in these verses?

   1.

   2.

   3.

After constructing your list it should include that God is being praised because:

1. Christ reigns supremely. (Revelation 11:17)

2. He judges righteously. (Revelation 11:18)

3. He rewards graciously. (Revelation 11:18)

Reread: Revelation 11:18

How will the nations of the earth respond when Jesus Christ begins His reign?

Read Psalm 2:1-3 to see this spoken of thousands of years before it happens.

Why are the nations angry?

Later in the book of Revelation we will see that the nations become so angry that they actually go to war against God? What are your thoughts about this?

Read Revelation 11:18 again.

What time has now come?

Note: This passage looks forward to coming judgment and rewards without differentiating future judgments from each other. We will see more detail on this as we continue our study in Revelation.

What does the promise of both reward and judgment mean to you personally?

Who did the elders describe as deserving a reward?

The promised rewards will involve all believers. In thinking about this it is helpful to review some of the truths about rewards in the following Scripture references. Please note what you discover in each passage.

Revelation 22:12

1 Corinthians 3:8

Matthew 25:34-40

Mark 10:29-31

Revelation 21:7

2 Timothy 4:8

James 1:12

Revelation 2:10

1 Peter 5:4

In thinking about rewards we also see special mention given to prophets. (That is those who speak forth the word of God, not necessarily only those who have spoken of the future in advance in the Scriptures.) Take a look at the following verses:

Matthew 10:41

2 Kings 9:7

Ezra 9:11

Jeremiah 7:25

Ezekiel 38:17

We should also note that all believers (all of the redeemed), whether living in Old or New Testament times, whether small or great, will be included in this. Take a look at the following verses and see what we learn:

Psalm 34:9

Luke 1:50

Revelation 8:3-4

Psalm 16:3

Daniel 7:18

Matthew 27:52

Romans 1:17

Romans 8:27

What do you think determines whether a believer receives either a large or small reward?

What is communicated to us when we realize that even the mighty angels and the twenty-four elders worship and serve God in total humility? What do we learn from this?

Who did the elders say deserves destruction?

Note: Those who "destroy" the earth is not a reference to those who cause water or air pollution. It is a reference to those who pollute and corrupt the earth with sin.

Reread: Revelation 11:19

What happened next in heaven?

What things happened upon the earth when the temple in heaven was opened? Please list them.

1.

2.

3.

4.

Based upon what we have read and studied today, why do you think these things happen at this point in time?

Note: Some people are fascinated with the location of The Ark of the Covenant here on earth. While this is interesting and has been the topic of a number of books and movies, we should realize that what we have seen on earth is a copy of the real thing in heaven. (See Hebrews 9:23)

Application Question

What is one specific thing you can do this week to advance the kingdom of God in your neighborhood, school, place of work, or home?

Close in Prayer

THE WOMAN, THE SON AND THE DRAGON
REVELATION 12:1-13:1

Opening Prayer

Group Warm-up Question

What are the clearest examples of the existence and activity of Satan in the world today of which you are aware?

Read: Revelation 11:19

The last sentence in this verse actually introduces the important events in Revelation 12.

Read: Revelation 12:1-Revelation 13:1

Reread: Revelation 12:1-6

What did John witness in heaven in the first six verses of Revelation 12?

The appearance of this woman begs the question, "Who is she?"

Fortunately the answer to this question is clear as we relate what we read in Revelation 12:1-6 to the rest of Scripture. In order to ferret out the identity of this woman we must first dissect what we learn of her in these two verses. Please list her observable characteristics below:

1.

2.

3.

4.

5.

6.

7.

Some writers have initially identified this woman as the church. While the church, the community of believers, is described in Scripture as a woman, the descriptors indicate that she is a different woman than the one we see in the first six verses of Revelation 12. The church, as the bride of Christ, is described in the following verses:

Revelation 19:7

Revelation 21:9

2 Corinthians 11:2

In addition we would note that in Revelation we see the woman giving birth to Jesus Christ. Jesus Christ gave birth to the church, not the other way around.

The woman in Revelation 12 is clearly Israel as we see when her characteristics are related to the whole of Scripture. Read the following verses and list what we learn about the past, present, and future role of Israel in the plan of God.

1. A woman in travail (a difficult experience or situation).

    Jeremiah 3:6

    Micah 4:9-10

    Micah 5:2-3

    Isaiah 66:7

    Isaiah 54:1-5

2. An unfaithful wife.

    Jeremiah 3:20-22

3. The Source of the Messiah who will bless and reign.

    Revelation 12:5

    Genesis 12:3

Romans 1:1-3

Romans 9:4-5

Isaiah 9:6 (Written by an Israelite to Israelites.)

Psalm 2:9

Revelation 12:5

Revelation 2:27

Revelation 19:15

Jeremiah 31:31

Genesis 37:9-10 (KJV) and Revelation 12:1 help to complete this imagery.

What do you make of the twelve stars on the head of this woman?

Could the twelve stars have anything to do with the twelve tribes of Israel? (Most scholars say this is one of the ways we identify the woman as being representative of Israel.)

Reread: Revelation 12:3-4

How is the dragon described?

We might note that the word "devil" means slanderer in Greek and that the word "Satan" means adversary in Hebrew.

What insights do you gain from understanding the meaning of the original language when the dragon is described?

Read: Isaiah 14:12-17 and Daniel 8:10 to get a picture of the revolt in heaven that has already occurred. Here we see Satan and his angels (symbolically referenced as stars) falling from heaven.

Note: The crowns and horns on the dragon are significant. While we will hear more about them later we will here note several points of interest.

1. The crowns are diadems and indicate ruling authority.

2. John MacArthur and many other scholars interpret the seven heads of the monster to be seven consecutive world empires running their course under the dominion of Satan. These would be:

   - Egypt

   - Assyria

   - Babylon

   - Medo-Persia

   - Greece

   - Rome

   - The Antichrist's future empire.

3. The future and final worldly kingdom ruled by the antichrist is expected to be a ten nation confederacy with the ten horns representing the kings or tyrants that will rule under him. (Revelation 17:12)

4. The shifting from the diadems on the dragon's heads to the horns of the beast is said to show the shift of power from the six consecutive world powers to the ten kings ruling under the authority of the Antichrist.

Reread: Revelation 12:5

We have already seen the way in which the Messiah will "Rule with a Rod of Iron" is mentioned elsewhere in Scripture.

Here we also see the Messiah being "caught up" to God and His throne. What do you think this means?

Note: This verse has generally been seen to relate to the ascension. That being said, G. H. Pember and others have noted that the Greek word translated "caught up" is *harpazo,* which is also used in relationship to the Rapture. These people suggest that this sentence refers to the body of Christ being caught up rather than the ascension. (This is not a point of faith. It will someday become clear to everyone as history progresses.)

Reread: Revelation 12:6

Also Read: Revelation 12:14

Note: The terms time, times and half a time represent three and a half years as follows:

Time = 1 year.

Times = 2 years.

Half a time = one half year.

These verses refer to the same three and a half year period of time when Israel will be preserved when the subject of Satanic attack.

Reread: Revelation 12:7-9

Read: Daniel 12:1 to see this same event spoken of about 2600 years before 2014.

What did John see taking place in heaven?

What happened to the dragon, Satan, and his angels?

Read Daniel 10:12-20 and Jude 1:9 to see that the event in Revelation 12:7-9 is not the first time the archangel Michael has fought against Satan and his minions.

Read 1 Thessalonians 4:16 for a reminder of the prominence of the archangel in the army and plan of God.

Read 2 Kings 6:15-17 to gain an understanding of the spiritual warfare that goes on around us even if we don't realize it.

Activity of Our Adversary

This is a good juncture for us to take a brief look at the history of Satan.

Read Job 1:1-2:10 and Zechariah 3:1-2 to see Satan's access to heaven even after his fall as recorded in Isaiah, and his practice of accusing those who follow God.

Read the following verses to see examples of Satan's ongoing activity on the earth.

1. 1 Peter 5:8

2. 2 Corinthians 4:3-4

3. John 8:44

4. 2 Corinthians 2:10-11

We would be remiss if we did not review the powerful weapons at the disposal of all believers that enable them to resist and defeat the evil one. Read Ephesians 6:10-18 and enumerate the weapons and stratagems God has provided us in this conflict:

1.

2.

3.

4.

5.

6.

7.

8.

9.

10.

11.

12.

Is this passage from Ephesians a list of suggestions or is it a battle plan that we have been directed to follow from the Lord Himself?

Looking at the text of this passage from Ephesians, what promises do we have if we are obedient and follow the battle plan of God? Please list them.

Reread: Revelation 12:10-11

What did the loud voice declare?

How is Satan referred to in these verses?

Question: In what three ways were the believers herein referenced able to defeat Satan?

1.

2.

3.

We can see these same principles incorporated into the following references. Please explain in your own words what each of these means.

Hebrews 9:12 regarding the blood of Jesus.

Explanation:

Matthew 4:4, 7, 10 directly from Jesus Himself.

Explanation:

Ephesians 6:10-18 as we already investigated earlier.

Explanation:

Romans 6:11-13 and Acts 20:24 regarding our lives and bodies.

Explanation:

Read: 2 Timothy 1:12

What confidence do we have in the promises of God and our ultimate victory?

Read: Revelation 12:12

How will the heavens and those who live in them react when Satan is expelled from heaven?

How will Satan react to his expulsion from heaven and the realization that his time is running out?

Reread: Revelation 12:13-14

What, in particular, will the dragon do when he is hurled down to the earth?

What will happen to the woman (Israel) in response to the efforts of Satan?

Here we see Israel being preserved and protected for a period of three and a half years. Some researchers believe that the eagle's wings herein mentioned refer to a future airlift to the safety of Petra at this point in time. While the specifics of the prophecy are not completely clear, it is completely apparent that Israel will be supernaturally preserved. These two verses are taken by most scholars with a high view of God's Word to refer to Satan's general plan against Israel and all Jews.

We do, of course, see other figurative references in the Old Testament to God rescuing His people Israel on His wings or wings of eagles.

See: Exodus 19:4, Deuteronomy 32:11-12, and Isaiah 40:31

Read:

Jeremiah 30:4-7

Matthew 24:16-22

Here we see this period of time in Revelation referred to in advance by:

1. The prophet Jeremiah about 2600 years prior to the preparation of this study.

2. Jesus Christ about 2000 years from this writing (in 2014).

Read: Revelation 12:15-16

What did the dragon do next in his attack on the woman? (Israel)

This reference to a flood is interesting. Some take it to refer to a literal flood. The geography of the middle-east makes this somewhat hard to imagine. However, most take it to indicate the tremendous effort Satan will direct to his attack upon Israel and the Jews. We can see a number of symbolic flood references in Scripture that seem to give weight to this interpretation. This includes:

Jeremiah 46:8

Psalm 69:2

Isaiah 28:2

Isaiah 59:19

Nahum 1:8

Amos 5:24

Psalm 18:4

1 Peter 4:4

2 Samuel 5:20

Genesis 49:4

Going one step further we also see God swallowing up His enemies by opening the earth in Numbers 16:31-33.

And, we also see God delivering His people symbolically in these same terms in Psalm 124.

Reread: Revelation 12:17

Note: Most scholars tend to relate these verses to Satan's specific anger against the 144,000 believing Jewish evangelists we read about earlier in Revelation. On an historical note we should realize that Satan's effort to exterminate the Jewish people has been one of his prime modes of operation. We can see this:

1. Repeatedly throughout the Old Testament.

2. In the effort to kill Jesus when he was an infant.

3. In the Secular histories of the world.

4. In the various pogroms that have taken place. (The Merriam Webster dictionary defines a pogrom as the organized killing of many helpless people usually because of their race or religion, particularly one aimed at Jews.)

5. In the holocaust in the Second World War.

6. In the efforts of many Islamic countries in the middle-east to wipe Israel from the face of the earth since 1948.

It would seem that somehow:

1. Satan hoped to prevent his defeat by preventing the Messiah from being born by trying to exterminate the Jews prior to the birth of Christ.

2. This having failed he tried to kill Jesus as an infant.

3. This having failed he inspired the plot to kill Jesus when He walked the earth.

4. This having been thwarted by the resurrection he tried to prevent Jesus' triumphant return to rule by destroying the Jews.

Satan knows scripture.

He knows that there is a precondition for the second coming of Jesus Christ.

He knows that in the Old Testament we see that the Messiah will return only when Israel admits her guilt and turns to him crying out for his help.

See Hosea 5.

Jesus also echoed this in Matthew 23:29.

It would seem that our adversary believes that Israel and the Jews cannot cry out for Jesus to return if he can annihilate them.

It is interesting to realize that some radical Islamist groups have similarly thought that they could prevent Christ from returning to rule in Jerusalem by either occupying or destroying the city. These same groups, when aware of the prophecy about the Jews crying out to the Messiah, also calculate that they cannot cry out if they are all dead.

Reread: Revelation 12:17-13:1

Here we see a prelude to our next lesson. Satan is standing on the shore of the sea. Warren Wiersbe understands the sea to symbolize the Gentile nations. He feels that the emergence of the Antichrist, the beast, from the sea shows his coming from one of them. This is not conclusive so we cannot hang our hat on it. We can, however, be sure that we will learn more of this evil man in the coming sessions.

Application Questions

What specific steps can you take this week to be sure that you are able to stand up to the attacks of our adversary, Satan?

What steps can you take to be sure that your friends, family, and fellow believers are able to also stand?

Close in Prayer

THE BEAST OUT OF THE SEA
REVELATION 13:1-10

Opening Prayer

Group Warm-up Question

What names of living or dead persons have your read or heard mentioned as the "Antichrist?"

Read: Revelation 13:1-10

Reread: Revelation 13:1

There is likely more symbolism here than might be apparent on the surface. A literal reading of the original text indicates that he, the dragon, stood on the sand of the seashore. (Some translations read "I saw a beast rising up out of the sea." However, the most accurate ones read that "the dragon stood" there.) The imagery of the sand seems to depict the nations of the world as seen in Revelation 20:8.

The dragon, Satan, seems to be taking his place among the nations which he is attempting to claim as his possession.

From where did the beast arise?

How might this be symbolic?

Read: Revelation 17:15

Most students of prophecy tie this verse in with Revelation 13:1 and conclude that the Antichrist must be a Gentile. From time to time one also hears people claim that he is a Jew because he is able to broker peace in the middle east for 3 and a half years. (This is, of course, conjecture since there is no definitive scriptural basis for it.)

This is also a good time for a quick overview of the career and character of the Antichrist.

We might recall that:

1. He will begin his career as peacemaker as we saw in our study of Revelation 6. (See Revelation 6:2)

2. He settles the Arab-Israeli conflict with a temporary peace agreement that is to last for seven years. (See Daniel 9:27)

3. This peace accord will enable the temple to be rebuilt.(See Daniel 9:27 and Revelation 11:1)

4. He violates the peace accord half way through. (See Daniel 9:27)

5. He ultimately stops the temple ceremonies and sets himself up to be worshipped in the temple and proclaims himself to be God. (See Daniel 9:27 and I Thessalonians 2:1-12)

6. He will essentially be like Satan acting in a human body in a fashion similar to the time when Satan inspired Judas. (See John 13:2 and John 13:27)

How many heads did the beast have?

What was written on each head?

These seven heads are thought to represent seven successive world empires:

1. Egypt.
2. Assyria.
3. Babylon.
4. Medo-Persia.
5. Greece.
6. Rome.
7. The Antichrist's final world kingdom.

Dr. Charles Missler and others attempt to clarify this by relating the seven heads to the Seven Hills of Rome. Rome is represented in two phases. The first encompasses the first six kingdoms. The last encompasses the first six at the time of the Antichrist. (This allusion would have been clearer to the people of the Roman Empire at the time John wrote the book.)

A reading of Revelation 17:9-13 may also help to shed more light on this for the student of the scriptures and Revelation in particular.

How many horns did the beast have?

In scripture we find that these horns:

1. Represent 10 kings. (See Daniel 7:24 and Revelation 17:12)

2. Embody the world's political and military power. (Daniel 7:23-24)

The Apostle John also tells us that on the beasts heads were written blasphemous names. John MacArthur says it this way; "like many of the Roman emperors and other monarchs before them, these rulers will choose divine names and titles that dishonor the living God."

Reread: Revelation 13:2

What did the beast look like? What animals did it resemble?

John listed the characteristics of this beast in resemblance to other animals in a certain order. Please list these animals in the order they are mentioned:

1.

2.

3.

It is interesting to note that Daniel also mentioned these 3 animals in a different order in Daniel 7:3-8. Please list the order in which Daniel lists them.

1.

2.

3.

Why do you think these beasts are listed in reverse order in these two passages?

Warren Wiersbe and others feel this is because in the book of Daniel the scene is being viewed ahead while in Revelation it is viewed looking backward. What do you think?

Dr. Charles Missler adds to our understanding of what is being communicated by the symbolism of these three animals. This is particularly helpful to any of us unfamiliar with the characteristics of such creatures.

Dr. Missler says:

1. The lion communicates arrogantly.

2. The bear controls extensively.

3. The leopard conquers quickly.

What power did Satan give to this beast?

What does this tell you about the nature and capabilities of the beast?

Reread: Revelation 13:3

What happened to one of the heads of the beast?

How will the people of the world respond to this event?

We also see this spoken of prophetically in Zechariah 11:17.

This wound must be important because John mentions it three times and is sure to remind us that it is inflicted by a sword.

See:

Revelation 13:3

Revelation 13:12

Note: The original language in these first two verses indicates that this wound was inflicted by a deadly stroke, as of a sword. (See Young's literal translation.)

Revelation 13:14

Reread: Revelation 13:4

What step did the people of the world take next?

What do you imagine it would feel like living in the world with so many people openly worshipping Satan and the Antichrist?

How does the character of the personage being worshipped impact the worshipper?

Read: Ephesians 2:2

What insight does this verse give you into what we see happening in Revelation?

Reread: Revelation 13:5-6

Please also read the following verses which speak of this same period of time prophetically.

Daniel 7:8

Daniel 7:25

Daniel 11:36-38

2 Thessalonians 2:4

Against whom did the beast speak?

What does the Antichrist say? Please make a list.

1.

2.

3.

4.

5.

6.

For how long will the beast be in power? (Note: This is the second half of the Tribulation period known as "The Great Tribulation.")

What does the Antichrist do during this period of time?

Please make a list from what we have studied so far today.

1.

2.

3.

4.

5.

6.

Reread: Revelation 13:7

What will the beast do in relationship to God's holy people?

Over whom will the Antichrist rule at this time?

If you are someday facing death because of your trust in Jesus Christ, how will you respond? (As we saw in our review of the second and third chapters of Revelation, the time to come to terms with this question is now.)

Reread: Revelation 13:8

Who worshipped the beast?

Earlier in our study of Revelation we discussed the concept of the "earth dwellers" or "those who belong to this world." Please read the following verses and discuss what we learn about those who belong to this world in contrast to those who are traveling through this world and belong to the Father. Please make separate lists of the characteristics of those belonging to each group.

Revelation 13:8

Matthew 4:8-9

John 12:31

John 14:30

John 18:36

Ephesians 2:2

Ephesians 6:12

1 John 2:15-17

1 Peter 2:11-12

The Earth Dwellers or Those Who Belong to This World

    1.

2.

3.

4.

5.

6.

Those Who Are Traveling Through and Belong to The Father

1.

2.

3.

4.

5.

6.

What will happen to those who would not worship the beast; whose names are written in the book of life?

The Book of Life is seen throughout the New and Old Testament. A few of the references that mention it are:

Exodus 32:32

Daniel 12:1

Isiah 4:3

Luke 10:17-20

Revelation 20:11-15

What will happen to those whose names are not written in the book of life?

This is obviously an important book in which to be included and we will learn more about it as we proceed through Revelation. For now, however, the most pressing issue is that those participating in this study be sure that their names are, in fact, included in the book. While there is more to understand, Scripture does tell us in the most succinct terms the basics of what one must do to find themselves in this book.

1. What they must do: Romans 10:10-13

2. What they are offered in addition to eternal life: John 16:33

3. When this decision should be made: 2 Corinthians 6:2

Reread: Revelation 13:9-10

What warning did John give to all who would listen?

What will believers who experience this event need to do at this point in time?

What lessons do we need to draw from what is described in Revelation 13:9-10?

Application Questions

What situations are you facing right now that call for patience, endurance, and faithfulness?

How can you prepare for future times when you will be required to be faithful and to patiently endure?

How can you prepare for a time when you must endure to the end?

Close in Prayer

THE MARK OF THE BEAST
REVELATION 13:11-18

Opening Prayer

Group Warm-up Question

What is the most amazing trick you have ever seen a magician or illusionist perform?

Read: Revelation 13:11-18

Reread: Revelation 13:11

How did John describe the beast he saw coming up out of the earth?

From our earlier studies you may recall that horns as we see them here are symbols of authority or dominion.

Note: We also see this beast described as the false prophet in Revelation 16:13, Revelation 19:20 and Revelation 20:10.

Read Matthew 24:11 and Matthew 24:24 to review Jesus' warning against false prophets and false messiahs.

Do you think these warnings apply to the beast out of the earth? How so?

Reread: Revelation 13:12

Who did this beast represent?

What did this second beast require all of the people on the earth to do?

Reread: Revelation 13:13

What powerful signs did the second beast do on behalf of the Antichrist?

Reread: Revelation 13:14-15

What other amazing miracles did the false prophet appear to perform?

How would you respond if you saw someone rise from the dead?

How would you respond if you saw a statue come to life and speak?

Note: Dr. David Jeremiah says that in the original language it appears that the false prophet was able to give the impression that the statue was alive as differentiated from actually giving it life.

What was the result of the signs and wonders performed by the second beast? How did it impact the people of the world?

Here we should also note that those who belong to Jesus Christ will not and cannot be deceived by the Antichrist.

Read Mark 13:22 to be reminded that our adversary will try to deceive believers.

Read the following verses to reinforce the fact that believers will recognize the teaching of the false prophet and the Antichrist as lies:

John 10:3-5

John 10:14

John 10:27-30

Read: 2 Thessalonians 2:9-10 to see how these false signs and counterfeit miracles impact those who choose to follow Satan.

What purposeful behavior will prevent these people from choosing life?

What two things did the false prophet order the people of the world to do in Revelation 13:14-15?

1.

2.

This is a crucial and pivotal point in prophecy and history.

To students of the Bible this is not news. They know that this has all been foretold. As amazing as it seems, this all appears to occur in God's holy temple in Jerusalem. Read the following verses to see this clearly.

Daniel 9:27

Daniel 11:36

Daniel 12:11

Matthew 24:15

Matthew 24:15-17

2 Thessalonians 2:4

Some students of prophecy will also realize that some of the prophecies in Daniel regarding the abomination of desolation have a double meaning. In addition to pointing us to events in Revelation they also point forward to a personage prior to the birth of Christ by name of Antiochus Epiphanes, who was a type of the Antichrist. Larry W. Cockerham has written an interesting and very scholarly article on this subject entitled *Antiochus IV Epiphanes: The Antichrist of the Old Testament.*

Here I quote from the text of his writing. "The prophecies of Antiochus Epiphanes in Daniel (Dan. 8:9-14; 23-25; 11:21-35) have both a historical as well as future fulfillment. Because these prophecies point both to Antiochus Epiphanes as well as the future Antichrist of the New Testament Bible students call them a *double reference prophecy*".

To view this interesting and informative piece of scholarship in full I commend you to http://www.prophecyforum.com/antiochus.html.

Depending upon the time available it might be of interest to consider having a member of the group report on this material during the next session together.

What happened to anyone who refused to worship the image of the beast?

In what way are people deceived or blinded by Satan today?

How might you respond to someone who insists that every miracle comes from God?

How can you tell if some miracle or other great work comes from God or Satan? (It might help to recall some of our favorite memory verses as we consider this question including 2 Timothy 3:16-17 and Acts 17:11)

Reread: Revelation 13:16

Who did the false prophet require to receive a special mark?

Where upon their body did the false prophet require that these people receive the mark of the beast?

Note: Some researchers link the placement of this mark to Revelation 13:3 where we learn about the wounds received by the Antichrist. They feel that the mark will be taken on these sites partially in sympathy for and solidarity with the beast.

Warning: At this point in our study alarm bells should be going off for any student of the Old Testament Scriptures. Here we find verses indicating that we should bind the Word of God upon our foreheads and hands.

In Revelation the Beast or the Antichrist is introducing a counterfeit to this practice. This should not surprise students of the Judeo-Christian Scriptures as throughout history we see Satan introducing counterfeits of the good things of God. In fact, whether one realizes it or not, the term "Antichrist" does not indicate one who is against Christ or counter to Christ. The term "Antichrist" indicates one who is in place of Christ; in other words, a counterfeit.

Orthodox and conservative Jewish men throughout the centuries have taken the passages in the Tanakh, the Old Testament, literally in regard to binding the Word of God on their forehead and hand. They take small boxes called Tefillin containing pertinent passages of Scripture and bind them to their foreheads and weak hand during weekday morning prayers. The small box on the hand is held in place with straps attached to the Hand Tefillin which are wrapped around the arm seven times. Nowadays, orthodox Jewish women sometimes also engage in this practice. (The English word for the Hebrew word Tefillin is Phylacteries and readers may be more familiar with this term.)

The four full passages of Scripture written on four separate scrolls inside the Tefillin boxes are:

Deuteronomy 6:4-9

Exodus 13:1-10

Exodus 13:11-16

Deuteronomy 11:13-21

During the morning prayers when the Tefillin or Phylacteries are bound to one's forehead and hand the famous Sh'ma is usually recited. It is:

Deuteronomy 6:4

Hear, O Israel: The LORD our God, the LORD is one.

Extracting the Key portions of the four passages in the Tefillin we find:

Deuteronomy 6:6–8

6 These commandments that I give you today are to be upon your hearts. 7 Impress them on your children. Talk about them when you sit at home and when you walk along the road, when you lie down and when you get up. 8 Tie them as symbols on your hands and bind them on your foreheads.

Exodus 13:9

This observance will be for you like a sign on your hand and a reminder on your forehead that the law of the LORD is to be on your lips. For the LORD brought you out of Egypt with his mighty hand.

Exodus 13:16

And it will be like a sign on your hand and a symbol on your forehead that the LORD brought us out of Egypt with his mighty hand."

Deuteronomy 11:13

So if you faithfully obey the commands I am giving you today—to love the LORD your God and to serve him with all your heart and with all your soul—

Deuteronomy 11:18

Fix these words of mine in your hearts and minds; tie them as symbols on your hands and bind them on your foreheads.

How do these Old Testament verses apply to believers today?

Reread: Revelation 13:17

What did receiving the mark of the beast enable people to do?

Thinking of the technology in the world today, how do you think this monetary control might be implemented and enforced (Credit Cards, virtual currencies, electronic transfer.)?

How might people obtain food, clothing, water and pay for their housing if they do not have the mark?

Given the ease with which electronic media and currency can be manipulated, how much power could the Antichrist exercise over the world?

What economic impact do you think this will have upon the world?

Does the fact that the false prophet "required" people to take the mark of the beast and that many of them had to be forced to do so imply that it was in some way voluntary?

What does the mark represent?

Reread: Revelation 13:18

What is the numerical value of the mark of the beast?

What do you think it will mean for someone to take the mark of the beast voluntarily besides obtaining material goods and comfort?

Note: The word used for mark in Greek is *charagma*, which means a brand or a seal. It is like a mark of ownership and allegiance.

On an historic basis the *charagma* was the term for the imperial stamp of the Roman emperor at the time that John was writing. It included the name of the emperor and the date of his reign. It was used as a seal on commercial documents and also stood for the likeness of the emperor that was on coins.

However, the use of *charagma* that seems to most closely fit the way in which it was used at this point in Revelation adds more information as we alluded to above. Paul Kroll writing for Grace Communion International at www.gci.org says it well. He states that at the time of John's writing "The *charagma* was also a type of brand. In Roman times, disobedient slaves were often branded with marks of ownership, much like cattle are today. Religious tattooing was also widespread. Soldiers had a custom of branding themselves with the name of a favorite general. Devotees of a god labeled themselves with tattoos to designate their loyal devotion."

People have speculated for years about the form this mark might take in the future. Some people believe it will be in the form of implantable computer chips smaller than a grain of rice powered by the miniscule electric currents naturally occurring within the human body. This would be recognized by some sort of a scan when buying or selling.

Others believe it will simply be some sort of invisible or perhaps visible tattoo.

What form do you think the mark of the beast will take?

What does understanding the meaning of the Greek imply about someone who takes the mark of the beast?

Believers also have a mark upon them.

We see this in Ephesians 4:30 which says "And do not make God's Holy Spirit sad; for the Spirit is a mark of ownership on you, a guarantee that the Day will come when God will set you free." GNT

How would you compare and contrast the import of taking the mark of the beast with receiving God's mark of ownership?

In addition, we might also remember that the 144,000 Jewish Evangelists so prominent in Revelation are marked by God in a special way. We see this in Revelation 7:3 and Revelation 14:1.

Some people have thought that perhaps it might be ok for someone to take the mark of the beast so that they could survive during the Great Tribulation. They feel that it might be possible to take this mark as a utilitarian measure, but without a real commitment to the Antichrist and Satan. They could, so to speak, have their cake and eat it too. However, Scripture tells us that this is just not so. Purposefully taking the mark or not taking the mark is an irreversible act of the will with eternal consequences. Read the following verses to see this:

Revelation 14:9

Revelation 14:11

Revelation 16:2

Revelation 20:4

In the best-selling *Left Behind* series of books the author raises the question of what might happen to a believer if somehow he or she were involuntarily forced to take the mark of the beast. What do you think?

In this particular study we have given little time to trying to "decode" 666. There are many interesting books on this subject that students of prophecy may enjoy.

Some people have tried to use various number codes to see if somehow 666 has an alpha numeric equivalent that reveals the name of the Antichrist. Indeed employing such contrived codes can result in anyone from your mother to the pope being incorrectly identified as the beast. In fact, by manipulating such a code one can imply that any one they wish to designate is the Antichrist. Going in that direction results in pointless misdirection and distraction from experiencing a full life in Jesus Christ here and now. (This is not to diminish the study of numbers in Scripture, sometimes called Gematria. The intention here is for us to maintain our focus.)

If we are correct that the rapture of believers occurs prior to this point in time, must those to be raptured be concerned with this mark?

Of what value then is it to study this mark?

If the book of Revelation is read by people after the rapture and at the time of the Great Tribulation, how might reading about the mark of the beast as well as the rest of the Bible help them? (Believers will be raptured, Bibles and books will not.)

Note: Dr. David Jeremiah and Dr. Charles Missler warn us to not become so entranced by the signs and wonders in the book of Revelation that we miss the point of the book.

Why do you think they found it important to put forth such a warning?

Application Questions

What should we do today to be wise about the schemes of Satan?

What can you do today to help guide or instruct a newer believer so that they can avoid deception and develop a victorious and meaningful life?

Close in Prayer

SONG OF THE
UNSCATHED 144,000
REVELATION 14:1-5

Opening Prayer

Group Warm-up Question

Have you ever felt invulnerable? How so?

Read: Revelation 14:1-5

Reread: Revelation 14:1

What Singular Central Personage does John see before him?

Who, exactly, is the Lamb?

Read: Revelation 7:3-4

Who is with the Lamb?

Where in this vision are the Lamb as well as the 144,000 standing?

Note: Most biblical scholars feel that at this point we are looking at the heavenly Mount Zion. They say that the scene anticipates the coronation of Jesus Christ and the establishment of His Kingdom when He returns to the earth.

For information on the heavenly Zion see:

Hebrews 12:22-24

Ephesians 2:6

Psalm 2 6-9

For a description of what is going on with Jerusalem now and will continue until the second coming of Jesus Christ see:

Zechariah 12:2-3

For a description of Jerusalem during Jesus' coming Millennial Kingdom on earth see:

Isaiah 2:2-4

Micah 4:1-4

Isaiah 60:1-5

How many of the original 144,000 Jewish evangelists made it through the tribulation?

This band of believers has come through the worst holocaust in human history. Do you think there has there ever been a more triumphant group?

It appears that the 144,000 Jewish evangelists will enter the Millennial kingdom as men. It further appears that these people may still be among the Jews being used by God in that kingdom. (See Zechariah 8:23)

This group of servants was apparently invulnerable as they went about the special task God gave them. Some people say that a believer is "invulnerable" until they have finished the task God has given them on this earth.

How do you feel and think about this statement in relationship to your life today?

Reread: Revelation 14:2

What did the sound John heard from heaven remind him of?

This sound from heaven had three primary attributes:

1. It was loud and continuous. We see also see such a sound coming from heaven in:

   • Ezekiel 43:2

   • Revelation 1:15

   • Revelation 19:6

2. It was associated with the music of the harp. We should realize that such music is associated with great joy in Scripture. See:

   • 2 Samuel 6:5

   • 2 Chronicles 13:8

   • 1 Chronicles 15:16

   • 1 Chronicles 15:28

   • 2 Chronicles 5:12-13

   • Nehemiah 12:27

   • Psalm 33:2

   • Psalm 71:22

   • Psalm 144:9

   • Psalm 150:3

3. It was in the form of a new song. A new song sung before the Lord is different from any other song.

   • A new song sung before the Lord involves joyful praise and worship. See:

     ◆ Psalm 33:3

- ◆ Psalm 40:3

- ◆ Psalm 96:1

- ◆ Psalm 98:1

- ◆ Psalm 144:9

- ◆ Psalm 149:1

- This new song could only be learned by these 144,000 Jews redeemed from the earth. It appears to be clear that the song has to do with the redemptive work of Jesus Christ. See:

  - ◆ Revelation: 14:3

- This particular new song is sung in the presence of the elders and angels before the throne of God in heaven. Again see:

  - ◆ Revelation 14:3.

Why do you think only these particular 144,000 Jews are able to learn this new song of praise?

Reread: Revelation 14:4-5

How does John further describe these 144,000 men? There are several characteristics listed.

  1.

  2.

  3.

4.

5.

In constructing your list I suggest that it should include:

1. They were literal virgins.

   - This seems to be indicated by the original language.

     - In Jeremiah 16:1-4 we see that he was forbidden to marry for a period of time.

     - In Matthew 24:19 we see the difficultly that would have ensued if these men had started families during the tribulation period.

2. They were spiritual virgins.

   - We see this same concept in II Corinthians 11:2.

3. They follow the Lamb wherever He leads.

4. They were purchased by the blood of Christ.

5. They are offered as first fruits to God and the Lamb.

6. There is no lie in them.

7. They are blameless.

It seems strange to hear that these men were rendered blameless. After all, even though they were greatly used by God, they were also human beings.

Read:

Ephesians 5:25-27

Galatians 5:22-23

1 Thessalonians 5:16-23

Now please enumerate how these men became blameless. (You should be able to come up with at least four if not more ways.)

    1.

    2.

    3.

    4.

    5.

Should we also "follow hard after Christ" and seriously and earnestly strive to live blameless lives?

What does it mean to follow the Lamb wherever He goes?

Are we also called to follow the Lamb wherever He may lead?

Note: "Following hard after Christ" is something every believer ought to be doing. However, in doing so one must be sure that they are in fact following God and not some personal desire or whim. God has given us a number of tools to enable us to be sure that we are on the right path. They include:

1. His Word. See 2 Timothy 3:16-17 and Acts 17:11.

2. His Spirit. See Galatians 5:22-23.

3. Prayer. See 1 Thessalonians 5:17.

4. The counsel of other mature believers. See Hebrews 10:25.

5. All of the above in relationship to the circumstance at hand.

Application Question

What is one thing you can do today to make sure you are open and willing to following God wherever He leads you?

Close in Prayer

THE THREE ANGELS
REVELATION 14:6-13

Opening Prayer

Group Warm-up Question

If you could go on the internet, television, and radio and deliver a message that you were guaranteed everyone in the world would see and hear in their own language, what would you say? (Assume that you have 10 seconds to speak and that during those 10 seconds everyone accessing your message would listen with intensity.)

Read: Revelation 14:6-13

Reread: Revelation 14:6

What did John see?

What was the specific task given to this angel?

Why do you think God is making this great effort when so many people are overtly opposing Him?

Read: Matthew 24:14 to see Jesus Himself speaking about this period of time.

Reread: Revelation 14:7

This angel tells people to do three important things. Please list them.

1.

2.

3.

Why do you think the angel tells people to fear God?

What does it mean to you to fear God?

A discussion of the fear of God might encompass many books. The fear of God is mentioned in over 300 places in the New and Old Testament Scriptures. It means far more than fear as we commonly understand it today and goes far beyond respect. Read the following verses that speak of this and list the important aspects of fearing God as you understand them. In each case we should ask ourselves what the fear of God means in the context of the situation.

Genesis 42:18

Exodus 1:17

Exodus 9:29-31

Exodus 18:21

Exodus 20:20

Leviticus 19:14

Leviticus 19:32

Matthew 10:28

2 Corinthians 7:1

1 John 4:18

John 15:13 (Yes, this verse helps us understand the concept when we realize Who had done what for us.)

Aspects of Fearing God

1.

2.

3.

4.

5.

6.

7.

8.

9.

10.

Why do you think the angels' admonition to give glory to God is tied into the coming judgment?

Why do you think the angels' directive to worship God is tied into recognizing Him as the creator?

Why is it important that people realize that God is the creator instead of giving credit to the pseudo-science of Darwinism or other misleading humanistic theories?

In the not too distant past science in North America was thought of as the search for truth. Now, it has become co-opted and often involves an attempt to make initially objective findings fit into an entirely subjective worldview dominated by secular humanism, evolution, or other man-made philosophies.

Students of the Bible understand that this is not the first time in history that such a state has existed.

Read: Colossians 2:8 to see the apostle Paul writing about this 2000 years ago.

When else in history have you read about this type of problem occurring?

Might this type of problem have been evident in the eugenics movement in Nazi Germany?

Might this type of thinking have also been evident during the period of the Spanish Inquisition?

Might thinking of this nature even been evident during the crusades?

Don't be misled by anyone putting forth the notion that scientists do not believe in creation or God. Many of the greatest scientists who ever lived have been followers of Jesus Christ.

Sir Isaac Newton, the "Father of Physics," said "This most beautiful system of the Sun, planet and comets could only proceed from the counsel and dominion of the intelligent and powerful Being." Newton wrote about and studied the New and Old Testament extensively. He penned commentaries of over 1,000,000,000 words on Revelation and Daniel. Sir Isaac took his Bible study literally and seriously.

Johannes Kepler, the "Father of Astronomy," spoke of the "Divine Mathematician whose mind could be discovered in the precise mechanics of the universe."

Blaise Pascal, famous French mathematician, logician, and theologian said:

"If you gain, you gain all. If you lose, you lose nothing. Wager then, without hesitation, that He exists."

and

"There is a God shaped vacuum in the heart of every man which cannot be filled by any created thing, but only by God, the Creator, made known through Jesus."

The tradition of top scientists who understand and fear God and have trusted Jesus Christ continues today.

Creation International works with many leading international scientists and provides erudite programs to other scientists, educators and the public showing the irrefutable reality of God's direct hand in creation.

The Institute for Creation Research provides literature and speakers showing the truth of God's creative and redemptive work in Jesus Christ.

There are also many other fine organizations dedicated to spreading the truth of the Scriptures and the Creator as evidenced in all of creation and science.

We should realize that those opposing the truth of Creation:

1. Have often simply been misled.

2. Have often swallowed what they were taught without investigation.

3. Have adhered to alternative views that are at the most simple theories because of their own personal and/or spiritual presuppositions and desires.

Opposing the truth of God as creator also has many negative implications and results for individuals as well as society as a whole. Read: Romans 1:19-32 and list the many things that result from this distorted view of reality.

1.

2.

3.

4.

5.

6.

7.

8.

9.

10.

11.

12.

13.

14.

15.

16.

17.

18.

19.

20.

Reread: Revelation 14:8

What announcement did the second angel make?

Note: This pronouncement anticipates the events that we will see in more detail in Revelation 16:18-19. We will investigate it in more detail at that time.

Why did the second angel say that Babylon has fallen twice and what do you think this means?

Note: Linguistically in the Greek repeating a phrase like this indicates the near-term and impending timing of an event yet to come.

Who or what do you think is meant by "Babylon?"

Many scholars, including Warren Wiersbe say that "Babylon is God's name for the world system of the beast, the entire economic and political organization by which he rules." This system is also associated with a city. We will consider the topic of Babylon and what it appears to mean later in our study of Revelation. For now you may wish to read the following verses to help prepare your mind for this inquiry.

Jeremiah 51:6-9

Isaiah 13:11

Isaiah 13:19

Jeremiah 25:15-26

Reread: Revelation 14:9-11

Who will drink the wrath of God's anger?

What exactly are the characteristics or components parts of suffering this punishment? Please list them below:

1.

2.

3.

4.

5.

6.

People are sometimes heard to ask how a loving God can subject His creatures to suffer eternal torment. How might you answer them?

God's character includes not only love, but justice and holiness. In what way does His character demand:

1. A consequence for disobedience?

2. A sacrifice for sin? (Satisfied in Jesus Christ.)

Understanding God's character, why must hell and heaven both exist?

Let's talk further about hell. This is a very unpopular topic in the world today. The very idea of a literal place where one suffers forever not just for their bad behavior, but for rejecting Jesus Christ (the means provided by God for them to experience never ending life, fulfillment, and peace) is offensive to many people.

Why do you think many people find the idea of a literal hell offensive?

It is a sad fact that many members of the clergy also find the idea of a literal hell disturbing.

In his lecture series entitled *Escape the Coming Night* Dr. David Jeremiah reports that a recent survey conducted by George H. Betts at Northwestern University about the reality of a literal hell found:

96% of Congregational Pastors do not believe in a literal hell.

92% of Methodist Pastors do not believe in a literal hell.

85% of Presbyterian ministers do not believe in a literal hell.

50% of Baptist pastors do not believe in a literal hell.

30% of Lutheran pastors do not believe in a literal hell.

Why do you think many members of the clergy seem to find the idea of hell disturbing?

Dr. Jeremiah also reports that a Pew survey from 2001 showed that 71% of respondents believed in a literal hell.

On August 8, 2009 USA Today reported that according to a subsequent and recent Pew Survey only 59% of Americans believed in hell, but 74% believed in heaven.

The disparity between those who believe in heaven and hell has apparently widened over time. On June 4, 2013 The Catholic Prewire reported on a survey commissioned by the True Life in God Foundation, established by international author and humanitarian Vassula Ryden (author of the bestseller *Heaven is Real But So Is Hell*; released in March, 2013). This survey found:

1. 56% of Americans interviewed believed in the devil.

2. 53% of Americans queried believed in hell.

3. 43% believed in a literal hell where some people go when they die.

4. 38% believed that those who go to hell have committed violent criminal acts as well as those who do not ask God's forgiveness of sin before they die.

The most interesting statistic from this survey is likely that:

1. 61.5% of those interviewed believe they are going to heaven when they die.

2. Only 1.5% of those surveyed believe they are going to hell.

Why do you think that many of the people who believe in heaven do not want to believe in hell, and certainly do not believe that they will ever go there?

This situation is not new. Indeed, on July 8, 1912 the International Bible Students Association passed a resolution at their Mid-Summer Convention in Washington, D.C. generally repudiating the idea of a literal hell. They felt uncomfortable with this concept and said that it was not biblical.

Apparently these people neglected to actually study the New and Old Testament documents from which they claimed to derive their conclusions.

Jesus Christ himself would have been surprised to hear that hell could not be found in Scripture.

In point of fact:

1. Jesus Christ and His disciples said more about the doctrine and reality of hell than all of the other contributors to the New Testament combined.

2. Hell or Gehenna is mentioned twelve times in the New Testament. Eleven of these twelve times the mention is made by Jesus Christ Himself.

3. There are also 19 references to hell fire in the New Testament. Twelve of these references were made by Jesus.

4. Jesus Christ made more references to hell than any other person in the New Testament.

5. Those "biblical scholars" who say that hell is not real either do not believe the Scriptures or have not actually studied the Bible.

Read Matthew 13:36-42 to see some of what the Lord Himself had to say about hell.

Jesus knew that hell is a real and literal place.

He warned people about hell and desired that no one go there.

Indeed in the New Testament we find:

John 3:16

"For God so loved the world that he gave his one and only Son, that whoever believes in him shall not perish but have eternal life.

1 Timothy 2:3–4

3 This is good, and pleases God our Savior, 4 who wants all men to be saved and to come to a knowledge of the truth.

One might ask how people will hear about being "saved" (being saved presupposes there is something to be saved from) during the Tribulation if believers have been raptured from the earth.

People living at that time will have more information about the truth available than at any time ever before in human history. They will have:

1. All the Bibles still in the world. (The Bible has been the best-selling and most widely distributed book of all time.)

2. All the books, tapes, DVDS, and CDs left behind by believers extolling the virtues of a life committed to Jesus Christ.

3. The witness of the 144,000 Jewish believers during the Tribulation.

4. The two special witnesses spoken of during the Tribulation.

5. The witness of all of the believers they have met or known before or during the Tribulation.

How might parents with starving young children feel during the Tribulation if they know they can feed them by taking the mark of the beast?

How might these same people feel if they realize that their choices will actually be simple and mutually exclusive? That is that they can choose between:

1. Short-term gratification and real and eternal suffering and separation from God. This suffering never ends.

2. Short-term suffering and real and eternal joy, peace and pleasure in the presence of the Living God.

Reread: Revelation 14:12

Also read: Matthew 24:13

In the face of this terrible situation, what must God's holy people do?

1.

2.

3.

4.

How does this relate to believers today? Please explain.

Reread: Revelation 14:13

What does it mean for someone to "die in the Lord?"

What happens to those who "die in the Lord?"

What does it mean that the "deeds of those who die in the Lord will follow them?"

We also read that those who die in the Lord will "rest from their labor." What does this rest mean to you?

It is helpful to know that the word used for this rest in the Greek is *anapauo*. This is the kind of rest experienced by a sailor who has spent his life on the seas and at last comes back home to his family.

Robert Louis Stevenson's epitaph reflects this type of rest.

It reads:

Under the wide and starry sky

Dig the grave and let me lie:

Glad did I live and gladly die,

And I laid me down with a will.

This be the verse you 'grave for me:

Here he lies where he long'd to be;

Home is the sailor, home from the sea,

And the hunter home from the hill.

Many believers have already found this rest, and Revelation 14:13 indicates that many more will find it during the Tribulation.

Application Questions

What does it mean to you, assuming that you have trusted Jesus Christ, that you will someday "rest from your labors?"

If believers are promised a rest from their labors, does this infer that they need to be giving their all for Christ on a minute by minute basis? (After all, there must be something to rest from.)

How can you cultivate faithfulness to Jesus in all of your thoughts and activities on a daily and hourly basis?

Close in Prayer

THE HARVEST IS RIPE
REVELATION 14:14-20

Opening Prayer

Group Warm-Up Question

Why do you think death is often personified as the Grim Reaper?

Read: Revelation 14:14-20

Reread: Revelation 14:14

How did John describe the person he saw in this verse?

What was this person holding?

Who is this person?

For help in figuring this out, in case you haven't already, read the following verses:

Daniel 7:13-14

Revelation 1:13

Revelation 1:7

Acts 1:6-9

Matthew 8:20 (This was Jesus' favorite way of referring to Himself during His earthly ministry.)

It is quite clear that this person is none other than Jesus Christ coming to establish His kingdom in fulfillment of Daniel's prophecy.

(It is interesting that in Revelation 14:14 the crown worn by Jesus Christ is the *stephanos* (in Greek), the victor's crown. We see this alluded to in Matthew 24:30.

Matthew 24:30

And then at last, the sign that the Son of Man is coming will appear in the heavens, and there will be deep mourning among all the peoples of the earth. And they will see the Son of Man coming on the clouds of heaven with power and great glory.

In Scripture this brilliant white cloud symbolizes His glory and majesty (See Revelation 1:7 and Acts 1:9).

Read: Revelation 14:15-16

What did John see next?

What did this angel say to the Lord?

Why did he tell Him to do this?

Hint: This angel is coming out of the temple, from the very throne of God. It appears that he is delivering the message entrusted to him from God the father to the Son of Man.

Note: When this verse speaks of another angel it is referring to the other angels already seen or heard from in this chapter. These angels are not to be confused with Jesus Christ Himself.

The Greek word used for the English word "ripe" actually means ripe to the point of withering, useless, putridness. We can see what this imagery conjured up in the minds of those who understood the language at the time in the following verses where the same word is used:

James 1:11

Matthew 21:19-20

Mark 3:1

Mark 3:3

John 15:6

The grain to be harvested here is well past the point of usefulness and is suited only to be gathered up and burned in the fire. (Matthew 13:40)

What does this imagery and understanding of the Greek tell us about the state of those to be harvested?

For a more complete decoding of what is meant by the harvesting of this grain, read the following excerpts.

Matthew 13:24-30

Matthew 13:36-43

Luke 3:8-17

Please list the things we learn in these passages.

Note: The frightening details of this divine judgment are unfolded in Revelation 16.

Reread: Revelation 14:17-18

How would you describe the next two angels that come on the scene?

What power did each of these angels have?

That Jesus is to be assisted in His final judgment is not new information. We also see it referenced in;

Matthew 13:39

Matthew 13:49

2 Thessalonians 1:7

What does the angel with the power to destroy by fire tell us about the grapes that are to be harvested?

What do you think it means that the grapes are "ripe for judgment?"

Read Joel 3:13 for greater understanding of the symbolism inherent in the grape imagery.

Note: The word "ripe" employed in this verse is not the same as the word employed in Revelation 14:15. The word used in Revelation 14:18 refers to something fully ripe and in its prime. These "grapes" are bursting with wickedness.

Where does this angel come from?

Read Revelation 6:9-11 to remind us of who else was under the altar.

Here we see the fulfillment of the promise made to the martyrs.

Reread: Revelation 14:19-20

What happened to the grapes that were gathered by the angel with the sickle?

This particular angel with the sickle has come to harvest grapes in contrast to Jesus Christ who is harvesting grain.

What are the differences between the harvesting of the grain and the harvesting of the grapes? Please make a list.

How does John describe the volume of blood produced in the winepress?

Note: Most scholars see this imagery as anticipating the "battle of Armageddon."

Read Hebrews 10:31 and Psalm 2:12 to get more of an idea of what is happening here.

The book of Joel, written over 2300 years ago, has an amazing summary of the events occurring at this point in history. In particular, it is profitable to read Joel 3 to see the broad scope of the return of the Jews to their homeland, the battle of Armageddon, and the Millennial Kingdom. We will see more about this history to come as we proceed with our study of the book of Revelation.

Joel 3

1 "In those days and at that time, when I restore the fortunes of Judah and Jerusalem, 2 I will gather all nations and bring them down to the Valley of Jehoshaphat. There I will enter into judgment against them concerning my inheritance, my people Israel, for they scattered my people among the nations

and divided up my land. 3 They cast lots for my people and traded boys for prostitutes; they sold girls for wine that they might drink. 4 "Now what have you against me, O Tyre and Sidon and all you regions of Philistia? Are you repaying me for something I have done? If you are paying me back, I will swiftly and speedily return on your own heads what you have done. 5 For you took my silver and my gold and carried off my finest treasures to your temples. 6 You sold the people of Judah and Jerusalem to the Greeks, that you might send them far from their homeland. 7 "See, I am going to rouse them out of the places to which you sold them, and I will return on your own heads what you have done. 8 I will sell your sons and daughters to the people of Judah, and they will sell them to the Sabeans, a nation far away." The LORD has spoken. 9 Proclaim this among the nations: Prepare for war! Rouse the warriors! Let all the fighting men draw near and attack. 10 Beat your plowshares into swords and your pruning hooks into spears. Let the weakling say, "I am strong!" 11 Come quickly, all you nations from every side, and assemble there. Bring down your warriors, O LORD! 12 "Let the nations be roused; let them advance into the Valley of Jehoshaphat, for there I will sit to judge all the nations on every side. 13 Swing the sickle, for the harvest is ripe. Come, trample the grapes, for the winepress is full and the vats overflow— so great is their wickedness!" 14 Multitudes, multitudes in the valley of decision! For the day of the LORD is near in the valley of decision. 15 The sun and moon will be darkened, and the stars no longer shine. 16 The LORD will roar from Zion and thunder from Jerusalem; the earth and the sky will tremble. But the LORD will be a refuge for his people, a stronghold for the people of Israel. 17 "Then you will know that I, the LORD your God, dwell in Zion, my holy hill. Jerusalem will be holy; never again will foreigners invade her. 18 "In that day the mountains will drip new wine, and the hills will flow with milk; all the ravines of Judah will run with water. A fountain will flow out of the LORD's house and will water the valley of acacias. 19 But Egypt will be desolate, Edom a desert waste, because of violence done to the people of Judah, in whose land they shed innocent blood. 20 Judah will be inhabited forever and Jerusalem through all generations. 21

Their bloodguilt, which I have not pardoned, I will pardon." The LORD dwells in Zion!

Application Question

In what way can you express your gratitude to God this week for sparing you from His wrath?

Close in Prayer

Two Great Songs and The Bowls of Wrath

Revelation 15:1-8

Opening Prayer

Group Warm-Up Question

What is your favorite song of worship? Why?

Read: Revelation 15:1-8

Reread: Revelation 15:1

What great sign did John see in heaven?

What is the significance of the seven last plagues in the plan of God?

Note: The Greek word translated "plague" literally means "a blow" or "a wound." Knowing this, the seven plagues are actually powerful blows from God that will strike the world with deadly effect.

Reread: Revelation 15:2

What objective features did John observe as a part of heaven?

Who did John see standing on this portion of heaven?

What do we know about these people?

(Read the following verses for assistance with your answer.)

Revelation 6:9-11

Revelation 7:9-17

Revelation 12:11

Revelation 12:17

Revelation 13:17

Revelation 13:10

Revelation 14:1-5

Revelation 14:12-13

Why were these people victorious?

Read: Revelation 20:4-6 to see their resurrection and reward.

Read: 1 John 5:4-5

John 16:33

When and how are believers victorious today?

Where were these people in Revelation 15:2 standing?

We have seen this sea of tranquil beauty before.

See: Revelation 4:6

Exodus 24:10

However, this beautiful sea is here mixed with fire. In scripture, such fire is associated with God's Judgment as we see in the references below:

Hebrews 12:29

Numbers 11:1

Numbers 16:35

Deuteronomy 9:3

Psalm 50:3

Psalm 97:3

Isaiah 66:15

2 Thessalonians 1:7-9

2 Peter 3:7

What were these people holding?

If we don't like harp music now, we'd better get used to it. God seems to like it and such music seems to be quite evident in heavenly worship. We can see this in:

2 Samuel 6:5

1 Chronicles 13:8

Psalm 33:2

Psalm 71:22

Psalm 144:9

Psalm 150:3

Revelation 5:8

Revelation 14:2

Reread: Revelation 15:2-4

What were these people doing?

What two specific songs were these people are singing?

What attributes of God are praised in these songs? Please list them.

By what names is God referred in these verses? Please list.

Read 1 Timothy 1:17 and see what you can add to the two lists we have just made.

We can see the original and extended Song of Moses in Exodus 15:1-21.

We also see the thoughts and concepts from the song in Revelation 15:3-4 echoed in the following passages:

Psalm 145:17

Revelation 14:7

Psalm 86:9

Psalm 90:1-2

Psalm 92:5

Psalm 98:2

Psalm 119:9

Note: In Isaiah 11:15-12:6 we see that the singing of the song of Moses as depicted in Revelation was actually prophesized about 2,800 years ago.

We see the extended version of the Song of the Lamb in Revelation 5:9-12.

Read Philippians 2:9-11 to see some of the ideas and concepts incorporated in the song of the Lamb.

By now, you may have realized that portions of these songs and Scripture references are often included as parts of contemporary praise music as well as hymns.

How can singing help us worship God?

Singing as a part of worship seems to be quite important. Why do you think that is so?

What psychological and emotional impact does it have upon a person who sings the type of phrases we see in the song of Moses and the Song of the Lamb? (Look at the specific components of the songs and comment.)

At some point, either alone or in a group, you may wish to sing the Song of Moses and the Song of the Lamb as we see them in Revelation 15:3-4. Below we see them presented in several different versions. Each is profound and beautiful in its expression.

Revelation 15:3–4

3 And they sing the song of Moses the servant of God, and the song of the Lamb, saying, Great and marvellous *are* thy works, Lord God Almighty; just and true *are* thy ways, thou King of saints. 4 Who shall not fear thee, O Lord, and glorify

thy name? for *thou* only *art* holy: for all nations shall come and worship before thee; for thy judgments are made manifest. (KJV)

Revelation 15:3–4

3 They sing the song of Moses, the servant of God, and the song of the Lamb, saying: "Great and marvelous *are* Your works, Lord God Almighty! Just and true *are* Your ways, O King of the saints! 4 Who shall not fear You, O Lord, and glorify Your name? For *You* alone *are* holy. For all nations shall come and worship before You, For Your judgments have been manifested." (NKJV)

Revelation 15:3–4

3 and sang the song of Moses the servant of God and the song of the Lamb: "Great and marvelous are your deeds, Lord God Almighty. Just and true are your ways, King of the ages. 4 Who will not fear you, O Lord, and bring glory to your name? For you alone are holy. All nations will come and worship before you, for your righteous acts have been revealed." (NIV84)

Revelation 15:3–4

3 And they were singing the song of Moses, the servant of God, and the song of the Lamb: "Great and marvelous are your works, O Lord God, the Almighty. Just and true are your ways, O King of the nations. 4 Who will not fear you, Lord, and glorify your name? For you alone are holy. All nations will come and worship before you, for your righteous deeds have been revealed." (NLT)

Revelation 15:3–4

3 and singing the song of Moses, the servant of God, and the song of the Lamb: "Lord God Almighty, how great and wonderful are your deeds! King of the nations, how right and true are your ways! 4 Who will not stand in awe of you, Lord? Who will refuse to declare your greatness? You alone are holy. All the nations will come and worship you, because your just actions are seen by all." (GNB)

Revelation 15:3–4

3 And they sang the song of Moses, the bond-servant of God, and the song of the Lamb, saying, "Great and marvelous are Your works, O Lord God, the Almighty; Righteous and true are Your ways, King of the nations! 4 "Who will not fear, O Lord, and glorify Your name? For You alone are holy; For ALL THE NATIONS WILL COME AND WORSHIP BEFORE YOU, FOR YOUR RIGHTEOUS ACTS HAVE BEEN REVEALED." (NASB95)

Read Revelation 15:4 and Psalm 66:4. These two verses are prophetic and together point toward what we will see as we continue our study in Revelation.

Reread: Revelation 15:5

What did John next see in heaven?

What was happening to this structure?

Note: The temple is mentioned 15 times in the book of Revelation. However, it is not mentioned until after chapter 4, the time many scholars pinpoint as when the Rapture will take place and the church is removed. Chuck Missler points out that from then on God is dealing with and through a people who have had a temple—a replica of things in heaven. (See Exodus 25:40 and Hebrews 9:23)

Reread: Revelation 15:6

Who did John see coming out of the temple?

What did these beings have with them?

How were they dressed? Is this significant? How so?

Reread: Revelation 15:7

Who else came out of the tabernacle?

What did this personage give to the seven angels?

With what were these containers filled?

Reread: Revelation 15:8

What happened in the temple after the angels received their packages?

In Scripture, smoke often symbolizes the glory, majesty, power, and presence of God. This can be seen in the following verses.

Isaiah 6:1-4

Leviticus 16:12-13

Exodus 19:16-18

Exodus 40:34-35

1 Kings 8:10-11

Why could no one enter the temple at this time?

When would it be possible for someone to again enter the temple?

These seven angels with their bowls make it clear that these just judgments proceed from the wrath of God.

Based upon this passage, what new insights do you have about heaven?

Application Questions

What provisions has God provided to us in our battle to be victorious over Satan? (See Ephesians 6:10-18?)

How can you be sure to make singing a part of your worship of God?

Close in Prayer

BEWARE THE WRATH OF THE LAMB
REVELATION 16:1-21

Opening Prayer

Group Warm-up Question

What is the most pain you have ever experienced?

Read: Revelation 16:1-21

Reread: Revelation 16:1

What did John hear from the temple?

What instructions did the seven angels receive?

What was contained in these seven bowls?

Reread: Revelation 16:2

What happened when the first angel poured out his wrath?

How is this first plague appropriate for those who have allowed the mark of the beast to be placed upon their bodies?

Like so much in the book of Revelation, the first bowl of God's wrath points back to a time near the beginning of recorded history, about 3500 years ago. Here we find:

1. A similar use of skin eruptions in Exodus 9:8-11

2. God's command in Exodus 20:3-4

3. An amazing unfulfilled 3500 year old prophecy in the Old Testament coming to fruition in Revelation 16:2. See:

    •   Deuteronomy 28:15

    •   Deuteronomy 28:27

    •   Deuteronomy 28:35

To purposely belabor the point of these skin lesions, is there a cure for them?

Reread: Revelation 16:3-4

What happened when the second angel poured out his vial?

What transpired when the third angel poured out his bowl?

Some people compare this plague to the "Red Tide," a modern day overgrowth of microorganisms sometimes seen in the oceans today. Others liken it to the accidental Exxon Valdez oil spill or the purposeful Persian Gulf Spills unleased by the Iraqi's in 1991. The end result, however, is that sea life dies and the water become blood is foul and detestable.

This hearkens back to what we see in the Old Testament in Exodus 7:20-21

As we read the passage in Exodus as well as Psalm 105:29 there is no indication that the waters in Egypt were turned to anything but literal blood.

How do you think people at this future point in time will react when they turn on the tap for a drink of water and blood comes out?

How do you think they will respond when they try to take a shower and find themselves in a rain of blood?

How do the second and third judgments fit the crimes mankind had committed?

Reread: Revelation 16:5-7

What did the angel who had authority over all water say about the judgments being poured out?

Why were the judgments witnessed by John just?

Reread: Revelation 16:8-9

What happened when the fourth angel poured out his bowl of judgment?

How did the pouring out of this bowl impact the physical well-being of those on the earth?

As a result of their pain, did the earth dwellers call upon God for help, turn from their evil ways, and give God glory?

The fact that the text states these people refused to turn to God indicates that they must have therefore had the opportunity to do so. Why did they not take advantage of this opportunity?

When people today are in great physical or emotional pain, why do some of them refuse to turn to God?

Albert Einstein, one of the most famous scientists of the 20th century and the father of the Atom bomb, said "It is easier to denature plutonium than to denature the evil spirit of man."

What in Albert Einstein's experience might have led him to make such a statement?

Interestingly, we also see the roots of this plague elsewhere in Scripture. Read and discuss the following verses.

Deuteronomy 32:22

Malachi 4:1

Isaiah 24:4-6

Luke 21:25

Reread: Revelation 16:10-11

Specifically where did the fifth angel pour out his bowl?

What happened when the fifth angel poured out his vial of wrath?

Why do you think the text makes a point of telling us that it was "his" kingdom that was plunged into darkness?

Dr. Charles Missler says that in a cultural war, truth is the first casualty. Does this in any way relate to the kingdom of the beast? How so?

Have you ever experienced darkness so intense that you thought you could feel it? How so?

Intense darkness of this sort was reported in Exodus 10:21-23.

The darkness of Revelation 16:10 is predicted in:

Joel 2:31 about 2500 years ago and again by

Jesus Christ Himself in Mark 13:24 about two thousand years ago.

There have also been strange and unexplained periods of darkness in more "modern" human history. Several of these have been noted within the past few hundred years and have *not* been associated with a solar eclipse. This includes:

1. The "Dark Day" recorded on May 19, 1780 in New England.

2. Ten minutes of intense daytime darkness recorded on March 19, 1886 in Central Wisconsin.

3. Intense daytime darkness recorded in Memphis, Tennessee in December of 1904.

4. A similar period of intense daytime darkness recorded in March of 1911 in Louisville, Kentucky.

How did the subjects of the beast react to this intense darkness?

Please specifically list the two things these people did and the two things they refused to do.

What the subjects of the beast did at this point in time.

    1.

    2.

What the subjects of the beast refused to do.

    1.

    2.

Reread: Revelation 16:12

We should, at this point, understand a little bit about the Euphrates River. It is:

1. Mentioned 25 times in the Bible.

2. 1800 miles long.

3. 300-1200 yards wide.

4. 10-30 feet deep.

5. Sometimes deeper or wider depending upon meteorological conditions.

It was:

1. The eastern boundary of the Roman Empire.

2. The eastern boundary of Israel.

3. The great obstacle in the Gulf War of 1991 when the armies of 30 countries bottled up Saddam Hussein's forces against it.

It was and will be:

1. The eastern boundary of Israel. (Genesis 15:18)

What happened to the Euphrates River when the six sixth angel poured out his bowl on it?

What is the stated purpose of what happened to the river?

Why do you think God opened up a path for his enemies so that they could ultimately come and wage war against Him and His people?

Note: Modern readers sometimes have trouble imagining how the great Euphrates River could be dried up. Thinking about this supernaturally we should realize that if God could create the earth and part the Red Sea (Exodus 14), stopping up this river would be "child's play." For those who wonder if Revelation 16:12 is referring to an event in any way brought about by "modern" man it is of interest to note that the great Ataturk dam in Turkey was completed in 1990. This dam can reportedly hold back the Euphrates River to a trickle.

Reading Revelation 16:12 I couldn't help but recall the following e-mail sent to me by a friend associated with the United States Marines.

Sent: Wednesday, September 30, 2009 8:36 PM

Subject: Fwd: Semper Fi

This conversation was overheard on the VHF Guard (emergency) frequency 121.5 MHz while flying from Europe to Dubai. It's too good not to pass along.

The conversation went like this...

Iranian Air Defense Radar: 'Unknown aircraft you are in Iranian airspace. Identify yourself.'

Aircraft: 'This is a United States aircraft. I am in Iraqi airspace.'

Air Defense Radar: 'You are in Iranian airspace. If you do not depart our airspace we will launch interceptor aircraft!'

Aircraft: 'This is a United States Marine Corps FA-18 fighter. Send 'em up, I'll wait!'

Air Defense Radar: (no response ... total silence)

Does this story in any way remind you of what is happening at this point in Revelation? How so?

Reread: Revelation 16:13-14

Specifically where did the three evil spirits mentioned come out of? What do you think this means?

Having arrived at this point in revelation, how would you describe the members of this unholy trinity and their interaction in your own words?

These evil spirits have a three-fold mission. Please enumerate the three specific tasks they are given to accomplish.

    1.

    2.

    3.

Reread: Revelation 16:15

Here we have a statement that goes back to information imparted to us earlier about the event most people refer to as the rapture.

Read: 1 Thessalonians 4:13-18 to see this.

When or how does Jesus say He will come?

Why do you think He reiterates this information at this particular point in time in the book of Revelation?

Who does Jesus say are blessed?

Why are they blessed?

Read: 1 Thessalonians 5:1-4

Who does Jesus say should not be taken unawares and unprepared when this even occurs?

Reread: Revelation 16:16

What did the demonic spirits succeed in doing?

Specifically where were these rulers and armies gathered?

Here we see yet another specific reference to the upcoming battle of Armageddon.

We also see references to this great battle in the Old Testament in places such as:

Zephaniah 3:8

Zechariah 12:11

Zechariah 14:1-2

(A complete reading of Zechariah 12 and Zechariah 14 as well as Joel 3:9-21 gives one a greater picture of this time period.)

Apparently, Armageddon is the "perfect place for a battle." Following are some facts about Armageddon that might be helpful to know.

1. The Bible does not actually use the phrase, "The Battle of Armageddon." This is a title others have given to the event destined to occur in this particular place.

2. The name Armageddon comes from two Hebrew words, *har Megiddo*. *Har* refers to a hill or hill country and *Megiddo* means "place of troops" or "place of slaughter." Since there is no particular hill there this seems to be a reference to the Plain of Megiddo which is surrounded by hills some sixty miles north of Jerusalem.

3. This particular place is also called "The Valley of Jezreel" and "The Plain of Esdraelon."

4. The area itself is approximately 12 miles wide and 38 miles long and forms what Napoleon Bonaparte called "the most natural battlefield of the whole earth."

5. Indeed, this perfect arena for war has been the venue of over 200 major battles in human history to date. A few of the many times when this plain was used in such a fashion follow:

   - It was on this plain that Barak defeated the armies of Canaan. (Judges 5:19)

   - It was here that Gideon met and fought with the Midianites. (Judges 7)

   - It was here that King Saul lost his life. (1 Samuel 31)

   - Titus and the Roman army used this natural corridor in their conquest of the area.

   - The crusaders used this natural corridor as they traveled to the Middle East for battle.

   - The British General Allenby used the area when fighting and subduing the Turkish armies in 1917.

We find the net result of the shocking gathering of the armies of the world to fight against Jesus Christ Himself in Revelation 19:17-21.

Revelation 19:17–21

"17 Then I saw an angel standing in the sun, shouting to the vultures flying high in the sky: "Come! Gather together for the great banquet God has prepared. 18 Come and eat the flesh of kings, generals, and strong warriors; of horses and their riders; and of all humanity, both free and slave, small and great." 19 Then I saw the beast and the kings of the world and their armies gathered together to fight against the one sitting on the horse and his army. 20 And the beast was captured, and with him the false prophet who did mighty miracles on behalf of the beast—miracles that deceived all who had accepted the mark of the beast and who worshiped his statue. Both the beast and his false prophet were thrown alive into the fiery lake of burning sulfur. 21 Their entire army was killed by the sharp sword that came from the mouth of the one riding the white horse. And the vultures all gorged themselves on the dead bodies."

Reread: Revelation 16:17

Where did the seventh angel pour out his bowl?

Read: Ephesians 2:2

What might be the significance of where this last bowl was poured out?

What did the mighty voice from heaven say when this bowl was emptied?

What was meant when the shout from the Temple said "It is done?" What will be done and to whom will it be done when these judgments are finished?

We might also note that this is the last reference to the Temple in the book of Revelation. Why might that be?

Reread: Revelation 16:18-21

A number of terrifying and amazing things happened when the seventh bowl of God's wrath was poured out. Please list them:

1.

2.

3.

4.

5.

6.

7.

8.

9.

10.

11.

12.

13.

14.

15.

This final bowl judgment seems to be associated with the battle of Armageddon. Indeed, the events associated with this are prophesized in the Old Testament. Read the following verses and discuss how they seem to apply:

Isaiah 29:6

Psalm 50:3-4

Haggai 2:6

Jeremiah 4:23-27

Reread: Revelation 16:19

Here we see yet another reference to Babylon. By reading this verse in several versions of the Bible you will likely come to the conclusion that both a city and a system are being referred to. We will learn much more of Babylon in the coming two chapters of Revelation.

Reread: Revelation 16:21

Question: What particular atmospheric calamity do we see mentioned here?

Read Job 38:22-23 to see this mentioned beforehand long ago.

We might note a few things in regard to this hail:

1. A Hebrew talent of silver is said to have weighed about 125 pounds. (Some references put this at 110 pounds.)

2. An ancient Babylonian talent is said to have weighed 125 pounds.

3. A Greek talent is said to have weighed about 86 pounds.

4. One of the reported effects of a nuclear blast is a storm of large hailstones!!!! (There are many who believe that the battle of Armageddon will involve nuclear weapons.)

Hail this size might seem outlandish to some. However, storms of extremely large and destructive hail have been reported in the recent past.

One is reported to have occurred in India on January 31, 2013. The initial short news report said:

31 January 2013

Hailstones the size of boulders have rained down on villages in southern India.

At least nine people were killed when the violent weather hit several villages in the state of Andhra Pradesh.

The hailstorm, which lasted for almost 20 minutes, destroyed crops, houses and livestock, causing devastating financial implications for residents.

The report on the following day gave more details.

February 1, 2013 – INDIA - Hailstones the size of boulders have rained down on villages in southern India. At least nine people were killed when the violent weather hit several villages in the state of Andhra Pradesh. The hailstorm, which lasted for almost 20 minutes, destroyed crops, houses and livestock, causing devastating financial implications for residents. It was once-in-lifetime experience for people living in seven villages in Chevella, Moinabad and Shankarpally. The hailstones started falling from the sky on Tuesday night and covered the entire villages under the snow-like blanket. Some women were seen attempting to sweep up the massive boulders using flimsy brushes more suited to lighter debris. Dr K. Sitarama, director, Meteorological Centre Hyderabad, said: 'The hailstorm was caused by an intense thunderstorm. 'Such occurrences are highly localized and restricted to a small area.' The storm in the south was extremely rare as the deadliest hailstorms, and perhaps the largest hailstones, in the world occur on the Deccan Plateau of northern India and in Bangladesh. Daily Mail.

One can also go to You Tube on the internet and find actual video footage of a recent storm of very large hail in Germany. While these hailstones were only about the size of duck eggs, the impact was devastating.

Read: Leviticus 24:16

The Old Testament penalty for blasphemy was stoning. Do you see this as being in any way related to the hailstorm in Revelation 16:21?

What one simple and yet profound thing did the earth dwellers not do as a result of the pouring out of these seven vials?

Why do you think these people did not (will not) turn from their ways, and ask God for help at this point in history? (Remember Revelation 16:9 infers that they had (and will have) the opportunity and the ability to do so.)

What makes the judgments we see in this passage, as horrible as they are, entirely just?

Application Question

How might the message of this passage spur you on to engage your non-believing friends in conversations about Jesus Christ?

Close in Prayer

Important Homework Assignment

In preparation for the coming two chapters of Revelation wherein Babylon is discussed in detail please read the following chapters of the Bible in one sitting. This will likely take about half an hour and will be well worth the time spent.

Revelation 17

Revelation 18

Isaiah 13

Isaiah 14

Jeremiah 50

Jeremiah 51

THE RELIGION OF MYSTERY BABYLON
REVELATION 17:1-18

Opening Prayer

Introduction

The ancient city of Babylon is identified in Scripture as the origin of all occultic practices. (See Isaiah 47)

As we have seen before, Satan has, on an historic basis, mimicked and attempted to counterfeit and replace the things of God. We see this quite clearly in the religion of ancient Babylon.

The first world dictator was named Nimrod and his queen was named Semiramis. He is shown in the Old Testament as operating in opposition to God. (The KJV translated this as "before," however the actual language translated into modern day English means against. See Genesis 10:8-10) This evil couple had a son name Tammuz who was identified with the Sun god and worshipped at the time of the winter Solstice. (About December 22-23). This entire religious system was transplanted first to Pergamos and later to Rome. Without going into greater detail about the particulars of this religion we can summarize by realizing that this pagan tradition was converted into something positive when believers began to celebrate the birth of Jesus Christ around the same time of year.

We also see something similar regarding Easter. (This is a term we do not see in our Bibles. We do, however, see Passover which was celebrated by Jesus himself. We might also note that the Apostle Paul expected both Jewish and Gentile believers to be celebrating the Passover as we see in 1 Corinthians 5:7–8) The Babylonian fertility goddess Ishtar was associated with eggs, bunny rabbits, and pagan fertility rites of spring. This was supplanted when Christianity became the official state religion of Rome and Easter became a time when the resurrection of Christ was celebrated. The Easter eggs and chocolate bunny rabbits which are so popular today come from but have lost their original occultic significance.

At this point in Revelation we seem to see the false religious systems coming back to where they all began, in Babylon. They all appear to be combined in one world-wide false religion.

As we go through chapter 17 we will see that Satan and the Antichrist use this false religious system to their own ends and then turn upon the system itself. (After they have used it to achieve their goals)

Before delving into this chapter we should say a word about religions and religious systems. Blaise Pascal said that there is a "God shaped hole" in every person. Nikolai Lenin said that "religion is the opiate of the people." Like it or not, they are both in some sense right.

Lenin's claim is correct in relationship to the organized religions he was attacking. These comforting group organizations based upon man's attempt to reach God have nothing to do with a vital personal relationship with Jesus Christ.

Pascal was also right. People have tried to fill the "God shaped hole" he referenced with religions, certain denominational affiliations, possessions, worship of self, worship of science, worship of their own intellect, worship of men, worship of political systems (such as Lenin's communism or enforced paganism), and a myriad of other inferior idols and practices.

As we have found, the only way to fill Pascal's "God shaped hole" is through a vital and transforming personal relationship with Jesus Christ. This is not just some story made up by monks or clerics. A relationship with God through Jesus Christ and the power of His Holy Spirit is authenticated through His Word as well as actual experience. (See Composite Probability theory, for example, in the appendix.) The Judeo-Christian Scriptures, history, archaeology, science, and mathematics all authenticate the reality of Jesus Christ and His Word beyond any doubt.

Nothing else in the world, including any and all false religions and replacements for a true relationship with God, can stand up to honest scrutiny in the same way. They are all wanting and an honest, intelligent investigation into this subject reveals that this is true as we see referenced and confirmed in 1 Timothy 2:5.

1 Timothy 2:5

For there is only one God and one Mediator who can reconcile God and humanity—the man Christ Jesus.

And now on to Babylon.

Group Warm-Up Question

If your life was being threatened and you could choose anyone in the world to be your personal bodyguard, who would you pick?

Read: Revelation 17:1-18

Note: Here the chronology of the book of Revelation pauses while we are taught about Babylon.

Reread: Revelation 17:1

What did the angel tell John he was going to show him?

Note: While Babylon and in fact many cities sit "on many waters," the reference in this verse is not geographic.

Read: Revelation 17:15

What do the many waters symbolize in Revelation 17?

Reread: Revelation 17:2

How did the angel describe the evil committed by the "great prostitute?"

Here we see that the false religion of Babylon will dominate the entire world including unbelievers from the greatest to the least. By the use of the term prostitute or harlot we also see that this system has prostituted itself for personal gain from the triumvirate of Satan, the Antichrist (the Beast), and the false prophet.

Harlotry or prostitution infers false devotion, flatteries, feigned love, pretended affection, intimacy for favors. Real or symbolic harlotry is always spoken of negatively in the Scriptures.

See:

Nahum 3:2-4

Isaiah 23:16-17

Jeremiah 3:6

Jeremiah 3:8

Jeremiah 3:9

Ezekiel 16:32

Hosea 1:2

Isaiah 1:21

Revelation 2:22

Reread: Revelation 17:3

What did John see when the Spirit carried him away?

Reread: Revelation 17:4

How was this woman dressed?

Note: Purple was the predominant color of Roman Imperialism. Every senator and consul wore a purple stripe as a badge of his position. The emperor himself wore robes of purple.

The golden cup in the hands of the woman is not new.

Read Jeremiah 51:7 to learn about it.

The reference to this woman's adulteries or immorality is also not a new concept.

Read Proverbs 2:16-19 and discuss what we learn about any such relationship.

How does this relate to what we are reading in Revelation 17?

Reread: Revelation 17:5

Note: When you see "MYSTERY, BABYLON THE GREAT, THE MOTHER OF HARLOTS AND ABOMINATIONS OF THE EARTH" in capital letters in your bible, this is not a misprint. This is how it is written in the original text.

The use of these capital letters in the Word of God must be for some important reason. What do you think it is?

Harlotry and abominations mentioned in Scripture often have to do with idolatry. Read the following verses to see this:

Judges 2:17

Judges 8:27

Judges 8:33

Ezekiel 16:30-31

Ezekiel 16:36-37

Why do you think these things often occur together?

How do you see this relating to our world and experience today? Please explain.

Reread: Revelation 17:6-7

John said that he could tell that this woman was inebriated. With what was she drunk?

Why did this astonish him?

In response to the astonishment and confusion experienced by John we see that the angel was out to explain the mystery of the woman (Revelation 17:18) and the beast upon which she is riding (Revelation 17:8-17).

Many scholars have felt that John was astonished because this woman, representing a worldwide false religious system, was doing so under the auspices of what he expected to be Christian churches. These same scholars would posit that the worldwide religious organizations and systems in place did not disappear with the Rapture. They were simply then populated by unbelievers.

We would be remiss in not reporting that over the centuries many people have identified the harlot with the Roman church. Two of the best know studies putting forth this view are: *The Two Babylons* written by Alexander Hislop in 1858 and *A Woman Rides the Beast* more recently produced by David Hunt. However, as we see in the text of the Scripture, this woman is identified as the mother of all Harlot(s). This is plural and would seem to show that we are looking at a false worldwide religious system encompassing all sorts of denominations, organizations, and customs.

Revelation 17:18 clearly identifies the woman as the "great city that rules over the kings of the earth." Some commentators have denied that this refers to a literal city, but only to the religious system dominating the earth at that time. Others who have accepted the more literal biblical view that it refers to both a city and a system have thought that the city might variously be Rome, Jerusalem, New York City, or Bejing, among others.

However, throughout Revelation 17 and 18 the angel seems to clearly be referring to the actual city of Babylon on the Euphrates River. This seems to indicate a rebuilt Babylon acting as the center of the kingdom of the anti-Christ. In Revelation 18 we see this literal city being destroyed.

When we tie in the Old Testament prophecies regarding the eventual destruction of the literal city of Babylon on the Euphrates the picture seems to be complete. (See Isaiah 13:1-14:27 and Jeremiah 50-51) While the city was sacked by the Medes and the Persians, the prophecy seems to have only been partially fulfilled at the time. As with many passages of Scripture dealing with prophecy there seems to be a double intent. The prophecies regarding the destruction of Babylon appear to have application both in ancient times as well as the "end times."

Reread: Revelation 17:8

Why will people dwelling upon the earth be astonished at the beast? (Remember from our earlier sessions that this description refers to unbelievers.)

This refers back to the Antichrist's faked death and resurrection which we saw previously in:

Revelation 13:3–4

3 I saw that one of the heads of the beast seemed wounded beyond recovery—but the fatal wound was healed! The whole world marveled at this miracle and gave allegiance to the beast. 4 They worshiped the dragon for giving the beast such power, and they also worshiped the beast. "Who is as great as the beast?" they exclaimed. "Who is able to fight against him?"

The beast is able to deceive those who do not follow Jesus Christ as we see in:

Revelation 13:14

And with all the miracles he was allowed to perform on behalf of the first beast, he deceived all the people who belong to this world. He ordered the people to make a great statue of the first beast, who was fatally wounded and then came back to life.

However, at the same time he will try, but cannot fool the believers as we see in:

Revelation 13:8

And all the people who belong to this world worshiped the beast. They are the ones whose names were not written in the Book of Life before the world was made—the Book that belongs to the Lamb who was slaughtered.

Matthew 24:24

For false messiahs and false prophets will rise up and perform great signs and wonders so as to deceive, if possible, even God's chosen ones.

Reread: Revelation 17:9-11

What attribute do people need to be able to understand these verses?

What is the difference between knowledge and wisdom?

Why is it important for us to be wise today?

Read Proverbs 1:1-7 as you construct your answer.

How can one become wise?

In an attempt to decipher Revelation 17:9-11 we should first understand that mountains in the Old Testament are sometimes used symbolically to represent rule, power, and government. Some of the many verses in which this can be seen are:

Psalm 30:7

Isaiah 2:2

Jeremiah 51:25

Daniel 2:35

Daniel 2:44-45

Applying this to Revelation 17 we can relate it to the great empires the world has known. At the time that John wrote Revelation the five fallen empires would have been:

Egypt

Assyria

Babylon

Persia

Greece

The one empire then in existence would have been Rome.

The empire to come is what some have called Rome II, which appears to encompass the area originally part of the Roman Empire.

The eighth king appears to be the Antichrist ruling over this seventh empire.

Reread: Revelation 17:12-13

What do the ten horns represent?

What do these ten horns do that is of particular interest?

These ten kings seem to represent ten regions or areas of government that were not in existence at the time that John wrote Revelation. Many books have been written in which the author has speculated upon the makeup of this ten kingdom or nation federation. Many have speculated that this will be the European Union, though the number of members in that union is in flux. While this topic is of some interest, too much time spent on it is a useless waste of energy. The makeup of this confederation will be apparent at the right time.

Now we come to a verse that is in some ways at the same time one of the most astonishing and fulfilling in the Word of God.

Reread: Revelation 17:14

What do we see the kings of the earth, in conjunction with the Antichrist, actually doing at this point in time?

What is the result of their action?

Do you find it astonishing that human beings actually decide to take up arms against God?

What do you imagine that these people will be thinking and expecting when they declare war on the Almighty?

Some believers, me included, find great satisfaction in the implication that they will have a part in fighting against and defeating the armies of the Antichrist in this coming battle. Why might they feel this way?

What systems in the world today are hostile to God, Jesus Christ, the Holy Spirit, and the written Word of God?

Reread: Revelation 17:15

As a refresher, what is the significance of the waters the great whore, the universal religious system, is sitting upon?

Reread: Revelation 17:16-18

What does the kingdom of the Antichrist end up doing with the worldwide religious system?

Application Questions

How should it impact your life and actions today to realize that Jesus Christ is the Lord of Lords and King of Kings?

What can you do this week to increase your wisdom?

Close in Prayer

THE FALL OF BABYLON
REVELATION 18:1-24

Opening Prayer

Introduction

In this chapter we witness the destruction of Babylon.

While some people view Babylon as merely a symbol of the Antichrist's whole godless system, the text itself seems to indicate that an actual city is also involved. Babylon is described as a city in Revelation 18:10, 16, 18, 19 and 21 and other features in the text also imply that it is a city. Since the actual text implies that we are dealing with a city as well as the concomitant system it is, of course, safest to assume that the city with its worldwide religious system and commercial ventures will be destroyed.

It is of some note that God has given the people of the world one chance after another to change their ways and turn to Him. He sent His prophets, His Son, His Word, the 144,000 Jewish evangelists in Revelation, the two witnesses of Revelation, a special angel in Revelation proclaiming His gospel message, and still they did not repent. Add to that the billions of books, Bibles, audio and video programs and other media available to the world during the time described in the book of Revelation and this becomes quite astounding. One is forced to ask why God has been so patient and loving as to continue to offer life to those who have rebelled against Him even after all He has done to bring them into His family. We see the culmination of these attempts and many people rejecting them in the following excerpts.

Revelation 9:20–21

20 The rest of mankind that were not killed by these plagues still did not repent of the work of their hands; they did not stop worshiping demons, and idols of gold, silver, bronze, stone and wood—idols that cannot see or hear or walk. 21 Nor did they repent of their murders, their magic arts, their sexual immorality or their thefts.

Revelation 16:9

They were seared by the intense heat and they cursed the name of God, who had control over these plagues, but they refused to repent and glorify him.

Revelation 16:10–11

10 The fifth angel poured out his bowl on the throne of the beast, and his kingdom was plunged into darkness. Men gnawed their tongues in agony 11 and cursed the God of heaven because of their pains and their sores, but they refused to repent of what they had done.

In the end, God's judgment will fall upon Babylon. In this session we will examine seven aspects of God's judgment on the empire of the Antichrist. It is quite fitting that we examine seven aspects of His judgment since we have already seen the seven seal judgments, the seven trumpet judgments, and the seven bowl judgments in the book of Revelation. We would do well to remember that seven is the biblical number of completion.

Group Warm-up Question

What is the most extreme or humiliating fall from power you have ever seen someone undergo?

Aspect 1: Judgment Announced

Read: Revelation 18:1-24

Reread: Revelation 18:1

Who did John see coming down from heaven?

What happened to the earth at this point in time?

Note: This may have been more of a shock than one realizes when coupled with Revelation 16:10 which says:

Revelation 16:10

The fifth angel poured out his bowl on the throne of the beast, and his kingdom was plunged into darkness…

We have seen no statement that this great darkness abated prior to this point (or that it did not). However, if it continued until this arrival of this angel, how might the people dwelling upon the earth have reacted to his arrival?

Reread: Revelation 18:2-3

Also read:

Isaiah 21:9

Revelation 14:8

Why do you think the fall of Babylon is mentioned three times in this portion of scripture?

These verses list a number of major overt reasons for the judgment of Babylon. Please list them.

Aspect Two: Judgment Avoided

Reread: Revelation 18:4-5

What warning is given to believers living in a corrupt and immoral system?

How does this apply to believers today?

Read: Colossians 1:13

How might this apply to what believers are told in Revelation 18:4-5?

Aspect Three: Definition of Judgment

Reread: Revelation 18:6-8

There are a number of component parts of God's judgment upon the corrupt world system listed in these verses. Please list them below.

1.

2.

3.

4.

5.

6.

When finished, see if your list includes the following:

1. It will be done to her as she has done to others.

2. Her penalty for her evil deeds will be doubled.

3. Her terror will be twice the terror she brewed for the world.

4. The way in which she glorified herself and lived in luxury will be matched by her torment and sorrow. (The Greek word for "torment" literally means torture.)

5. These plaques will overtake her in a single day. They will include:

    • Death

    • Mourning referring to the grief produced by her torment.

    • Famine

6. She will be completely consumed by fire.

As we have discussed previously, there is sometimes a double intent in Biblical references that are prophetic. We can see this clearly in several Old Testament passages that seem to apply to this time in history to come. Read:

Psalm 137:8

Jeremiah 50:14-15

Jeremiah 50:29

Furthermore, the cup of terror brewed by Babylon is mentioned in:

Revelation 18:3

Revelation 14:8

Revelation 17:2

Revelation 17:4

Going yet one step further, God's responsive cup of wrath can also be seen in:

Revelation 14:10

Revelation 16:19

As bad as the judgment and deserved suffering of Babylon and the evil world system will be, it pales in comparison to the description we see of hell in:

Revelation 20:10

Luke 16:23-24

Luke 16:8

Matthew 8:12

Matthew 13:42

Do you think it is possible for a human being to comprehend the terrors of hell? Why or why not?

If the terrors of hell are tortuous and continuous perhaps beyond our capacity to understand them, how should believers live their lives today?

With the limited understanding of hell that we have, how should we relate to other people?

How, in particular, should we lovingly admonish, and encourage those we love, knowing that the terrors of hell are real and eternal?

Aspect Four: Judgment Mourned

Reread: Revelation 18:9-19

What groups of people will mourn for Babylon? Please list them.

1.

2.

3.

4.

5.

6.

7.

8.

Reread: Revelation 18:9-10

Why will the kings of the world mourn?

Reread: Revelation 18:11-16

Why will the merchants of the world mourn?

The text mentions a number of specific goods with which the merchants of the world have made money by virtue of their relationship with Babylon. Please list them (You should come up with at least 28):

Reread: Revelation 18:17-19

Why will the ship owners, the captains of merchant ships, and their passengers, sailors, and crews mourn?

All of those mourning over the fall of Babylon have one thing in common. What is it?

What warning should we and all peoples take from this one commonality shared by those who will mourn for Babylon?

Understanding this warning, how should we respond in a positive and pro-active sense in our lives today?

Aspect Five: Rejoicing Over Judgment

Reread: Revelation 18:20

This is the first time in Revelation that the command is given to rejoice. Who specifically is commanded to rejoice?

According to the text, why are these people and groups commanded to rejoice?

Read: Revelation 6:9-11

How do these verses relate to Revelation 18:20?

Aspect Six: The Completion of Babylon's Judgment

Reread: Revelation 18:21-23

While the destruction of Babylon and the system of the Antichrist might come as a surprise to some, it should not be a surprise to students of the Bible.

We see this spoken of prophetically in:

Isaiah 13:19-22

Isaiah 14:22-23

Jeremiah 50:13

Jeremiah 50:39

Jeremiah 51:37

Jeremiah 51:56

Jeremiah 51:59-64

How do you feel when you realize that the defeat of the enemies of God was foretold so long ago? Do you feel imbued with a sense of confidence; of awe; of thankfulness; of fear; of the realization of God's love for you?

Aspect Seven: Judgment Further Explained and Justified

Reread: Revelation 18:23-24

Also Read: Revelation 9:20-21

Galatians 5:19-21

Revelation 19:1-2

In addition to the evil fomented by rulers and merchants, for what other reasons will Babylon be judged?

Application Question

How can you use what we have learned in Revelation 18 to comfort a suffering friend with the knowledge that God sees every injustice and will one day right every wrong?

Close in Prayer

WEEK 32

THE WEDDING FEAST
OF THE LAMB
REVELATION 19:1-10

Opening Prayer

Group Warm-Up Question

What is one of the most memorable weddings or banquets you have ever attended? Why was it so?

Read: Revelation 19:1-10

Reread: Revelation 19:1-4

What was the great roaring sound that John heard coming from heaven?

Note: *Alleluia* is the Greek form of the Hebrew word *Hallelujah,* which means "praise the Lord." This word appears a number of times in the Old Testament; twenty-four times in Psalms alone. However, it will likely surprise many people to know that this word appears only four times in the New Testament, and we just read them today. They mark a momentous event. Read together they appear:

Revelation 19:1

After this I heard what sounded like the roar of a great multitude in heaven shouting: "Hallelujah! Salvation and glory and power belong to our God,

Revelation 19:3

And again they shouted: "Hallelujah! The smoke from her goes up for ever and ever."

Revelation 19:4

The twenty-four elders and the four living creatures fell down and worshiped God, who was seated on the throne. And they cried: "Amen, Hallelujah!"

Revelation 19:6

Then I heard what sounded like a great multitude, like the roar of rushing waters and like loud peals of thunder, shouting: "Hallelujah! For our Lord God Almighty reigns.

In your opinion, why does this special word appear only here in the New Testament, and why does it appear so many times?

Upon an examination of the text it appears that this great "Hallelujah Chorus" is being sung for three reasons:

1. God has judged His enemies. (Revelation 19:1-4)

2. God is reigning. (Revelation 19:5-6)

3. The Bride is ready. (Revelation 19:7-10 and Romans 8:18-23)

What did the twenty-four elders and four living creatures do at this point in time?

What did the four living creatures and the twenty-four elders say?

As we have discussed before, the term "Amen" initially sounds strange to modern ears. In our culture we are probably most familiar with amen as a sort of a benediction at the conclusion of a prayer. However, in the New Testament we see that it means more. It is sometimes used interchangeably with the old English term "Verily." In this context it refers to the truth of a matter. When someone says "amen" after a statement has been made it implies not only agreement, but that the statement is absolutely true. Read the following verses to see five statements of absolute truth in Revelation as indicated by the use of the word "amen." Please list the statements of absolute truth that emanate from these verses as you read them.

Revelation 1:6

Revelation 1:7

Revelation 3:14

Revelation 7:12

Revelation 22:20

Statements of Absolute Truth

(As indicated by the use of amen.)

1.

2.

3.

4.

5.

6.

7.

8.

9.

We should also note that this is the last time we see the twenty-four elders in the New Testament. They are apparently attending the wedding feast as part of the bride.

What is the last thing these elders are recorded as having said prior to the wedding feast of the Lamb? What two words did they speak in combination?

Understanding the original languages as we have discussed today, what exactly did this mean?

How is it significant that this is the last thing we ever hear them saying in the Scriptures?

Reread: Revelation 19:5-6

What did the voice from heaven say that everyone should do?

According to Revelation 19:5, exactly who is to do this?

What definitive statement of fact do we see in Revelation 19:6?

The evil system of the world has been destroyed and the Lamb, the great Lion of Judah, is coming to take control. We will see this happening in the second half of this chapter of Revelation.

In 1719 the English hymn writer, Isaac Watts, wrote a song that became very popular about the second coming of Jesus Christ. He published this in *The Psalms of David: Imitated in the language of the New Testament, and applied to the Christian state and worship.* The lyrics were based on Psalm 98 which reads:

Psalm 98

1 Sing to the LORD a new song, for he has done marvelous things; his right hand and his holy arm have worked salvation for him. 2 The LORD has made his salvation known and revealed his righteousness to the nations. 3 He has remembered his love and his faithfulness to the house of Israel; all the ends of the earth have seen the salvation of our God. 4 Shout for joy to the LORD, all the earth, burst into jubilant song with music; 5 make music to the LORD with the harp, with the harp and the sound of singing, 6 with trumpets and the blast of the ram's horn— shout for joy before the LORD, the King. 7 Let the sea resound,

and everything in it, the world, and all who live in it. 8 Let the rivers clap their hands, let the mountains sing together for joy; 9 let them sing before the LORD, for he comes to judge the earth. He will judge the world in righteousness and the peoples with equity.

Watts wrote the words of his song as a hymn glorifying Christ's triumphant return at the end of the age.

Surprisingly, this great song, entitled *Joy to the World,* is now normally sung as a popular Christmas Carol to celebrate the first coming of Jesus Christ.

It is somewhat of a paradox to see this wonderful hymn used as both a celebration of the first and second coming of the Lamb.

The lyrics follow.

(If you feel up to it, you may enjoy singing this song right now. It has become so popular over the years that most everyone in the western world knows the tune.)

Verse 1

Joy to the world! the Lord is come;

Let earth receive her King;

Let every heart prepare him room,

And heaven and nature sing,

And heaven and nature sing,

And heaven, and heaven, and nature sing.

Verse 2

Joy to the world! the Saviour reigns;

Let men their songs employ;

While fields and floods, rocks, hills, and plains

Repeat the sounding joy,

Repeat the sounding joy,

Repeat, repeat the sounding joy.

Verse 3 *(optional)*

No more let sins and sorrows grow,

Nor thorns infest the ground;

He comes to make His blessings flow

Far as the curse is found,

Far as the curse is found,

Far as, far as, the curse is found.

Verse 4

He rules the world with truth and grace,

And makes the nations prove

The glories of His righteousness,

And wonders of His love,

And wonders of His love,

And wonders, wonders, of His love.

Reread: Revelation 19:7-10

Reread: Revelation 19:7

Why did the great multitude say that the entire assemblage should rejoice?

Unlike most weddings in the western hemisphere, the focus in this wedding is not on the bride, but on the groom.

Just so we are all on the same page regarding who the players are in this wedding please read:

2 Corinthians 11:2

Ephesians 5:22-23

John 3:29

Jesus is the Lamb and the Bridegroom.

The believers from every kindred and tribe are the bride.

Reread: Revelation 19:8-9

Why was the bride given white linen to wear?

Specifically who is blessed and why are they blessed?

Read: Revelation 3:20

While this was written to the church at Laodicea, many people believe it has a double meaning and also applies to the offer Jesus Christ makes to every living person. What do you think?

Before proceeding, a little background on Jewish weddings might help us all gain a greater appreciation for just what is happening at this point in Revelation.

A traditional Jewish wedding took place in several parts.

1. First, there was the betrothal or the *shiddukhin*. This was usually arranged by the parents. It involved the bridegroom traveling from his father's house to that of his prospective bride. He would at that time pay the purchase price for the bride thus establishing a marriage covenant called a *ketubah*. This marriage covenant was binding and any unfaithfulness during this period was regarded as adultery.

See:

1 Corinthians 6:19-20

Ephesians 5:25-27

1 Corinthians 1:2

1 Corinthians 6:11

Hebrews 10:10

Hebrews 13:12

There is great symbolism in this betrothal as it relates to Jesus Christ and believers. Please list the many different ways you see this to be symbolic.

1.

2.

3.

4.

5.

6.

7.

2. The next step in a traditional Jewish wedding involved he bridegroom departing for his father's house. During this time he prepared the living accommodations for his bride in the house of his father. He would then come for his bride at a time not known exactly to her. However, the bride lived in the daily expectation of the return of the bridegroom.

See: John 14:1-6

What symbolism to you see in this part of the wedding ceremony? Please list what you see below.

1.

2.

3.

4.

5.

3. When the bridegroom returned by surprise to claim his bride the wedding ceremony (huppah) took place. The bridegroom returned to consummate the

marriage, celebrate the wedding feast for the next seven days, and to take the bride back to his father's house where he had prepared a place for her.

See: Isaiah 26:6-10

Isaiah 26:19

Luke 22:15-16

John 17:24-26

Again, this is filled with symbolism. Please list the ways in which you understand this to apply to Jesus Christ as the bridegroom and to His bride.

1.

2.

3.

4.

5.

Read what John the Baptist had to say in John 3:29

John 3:29

The bride belongs to the bridegroom. The friend who attends the bridegroom waits and listens for him, and is full of joy when he hears the bridegroom's voice. That joy is mine, and it is now complete.

What direct analogies can you draw from this verse as it relates to the wedding feast of the Lamb?

Read the parable Jesus told alluding to his own wedding feast to come in Matthew 22:1-13.

Matthew 22:1–13

1 Jesus spoke to them again in parables, saying: 2 "The kingdom of heaven is like a king who prepared a wedding banquet for his son. 3 He sent his servants to those who had been invited to the banquet to tell them to come, but they refused to come. 4 "Then he sent some more servants and said, 'Tell those who have been invited that I have prepared my dinner: My oxen and fattened cattle have been butchered, and everything is ready. Come to the wedding banquet.' 5 "But they paid no attention and went off—one to his field, another to his business. 6 The rest seized his servants, mistreated them and killed them. 7 The king was enraged. He sent his army and destroyed those murderers and burned their city. 8 "Then he said to his servants, 'The wedding banquet is ready, but those I invited did not deserve to come. 9 Go to the street corners and invite to the banquet anyone you find.' 10 So the servants went out into the streets and gathered all the people they could find, both good and bad, and the wedding hall was filled with guests. 11 "But when the king came in to see the guests, he noticed a man there who was not wearing wedding clothes. 12 'Friend,' he asked, 'how did you get in here without wedding clothes?' The man was speechless. 13 "Then the king told the attendants, 'Tie him hand and foot, and throw him outside, into the darkness, where there will be weeping and gnashing of teeth.'

How would you explain this in your own words?

Reread: Revelation 19:10

What mistake did John make at this point?

What did the angel say he shared with John?

What important concept does the angel explain to John at the end of verse 10?

Is it helpful for you to know that all prophecy in the Bible ultimately points to Jesus Christ?

What thoughts and feelings do you have when you realize that the whole of Scripture in the end points to Jesus Christ?

Application Question

In what way can you honor Jesus Christ in your conversations this week?

Close in Prayer

WEEK 33

THE RETURN OF THE KING
REVELATION 19:11-21

Opening Prayer

Group Warm-Up Question:

Who, in our opinion, has been the greatest military leader of all time? Why do you feel that way?

Read: Revelation 19:11-21

Reread: Revelation 19:11

What did John see at this point in his vision?

What was the name of the person that John saw?

How does His name tie in to:

Revelation 1:5

Revelation 3:7

Who exactly is this rider?

If the identity of this rider is not immediately obvious read:

Revelation 1:5

Revelation 3:7

Revelation 19:16

This event is spoken of throughout Scripture. It is interesting to see Jesus partially quoting one of the Old Testament references to himself in Luke.

Luke 4:10–21

10 For the Scriptures say, 'He will order his angels to protect and guard you. 11 And they will hold you up with their hands so you won't even hurt your foot on a stone.'" 12 Jesus responded, "The Scriptures also say, 'You must not test the LORD your God.'" 13 When the devil had finished tempting Jesus, he left him until the next opportunity came. 14 Then Jesus returned to Galilee, filled with the Holy Spirit's power. Reports about him spread quickly through the whole region. 15 He taught regularly in their synagogues and was praised by everyone. 16 When he came to the village of Nazareth, his boyhood home, he went as usual to the synagogue on the Sabbath and stood up to read the Scriptures. 17 The scroll of Isaiah the prophet was handed to him. He unrolled the scroll and found the place

where this was written: 18 "The Spirit of the LORD is upon me, for he has anointed me to bring Good News to the poor. He has sent me to proclaim that captives will be released, that the blind will see, that the oppressed will be set free, 19 and that the time of the LORD's favor has come." 20 He rolled up the scroll, handed it back to the attendant, and sat down. All eyes in the synagogue looked at him intently. 21 Then he began to speak to them. "The Scripture you've just heard has been fulfilled this very day!" (NLT)

Luke 4:10–21

10 For it is written, He shall give his angels charge over thee, to keep thee: 11 And in *their* hands they shall bear thee up, lest at any time thou dash thy foot against a stone. 12 And Jesus answering said unto him, It is said, Thou shalt not tempt the Lord thy God. 13 And when the devil had ended all the temptation, he departed from him for a season. 14 And Jesus returned in the power of the Spirit into Galilee: and there went out a fame of him through all the region round about. 15 And he taught in their synagogues, being glorified of all. 16 And he came to Nazareth, where he had been brought up: and, as his custom was, he went into the synagogue on the sabbath day, and stood up for to read. 17 And there was delivered unto him the book of the prophet Esaias. And when he had opened the book, he found the place where it was written, 18 The Spirit of the Lord *is* upon me, because he hath anointed me to preach the gospel to the poor; he hath sent me to heal the brokenhearted, to preach deliverance to the captives, and recovering of sight to the blind, to set at liberty them that are bruised, 19 To preach the acceptable year of the Lord. 20 And he closed the book, and he gave *it* again to the minister, and sat down. And the eyes of all them that were in the synagogue were fastened on him. 21 And he began to say unto them, This day is this scripture fulfilled in your ears. (KJV)

You will notice, however, that Jesus did not complete the quote from Isaiah. He purposely stopped before completing the portion that refers to his second coming. We can see this in Isaiah 61:1-2

Isaiah 61:1–2

1 The Spirit of the Lord God *is* upon me; Because the Lord hath anointed me to preach good tidings unto the meek; He hath sent me to bind up the brokenhearted, To proclaim liberty to the captives, And the opening of the prison to *them that are* bound; 2 To proclaim the acceptable year of the Lord, And the day of vengeance of our God; To comfort all that mourn; (KJV)

Why do you think Jesus only quoted the portion of Isaiah that referred to his first coming in the reference from Luke?

Now, at this point in Revelation, we see the prophecies of both the first and second coming of Jesus Christ fulfilled.

Reread: Revelation 19:11

What two very specific things does this verse tell us that the rider will do?

As we have discussed before, the first coming of Jesus Christ is attested to in over 300 Old Testament prophecies. On an empirical and mathematical basis this makes His identity and His Word impossible to refute.

However, what many people don't know is that for every prophecy of the first coming of Jesus Christ there are eight prophecies of His second coming. Even as we move through the New Testament we see these references continue to proliferate. This means that even the enemies of Jesus Christ knew that He said this day would come. Read the following verses to get an inkling of this:

Matthew 24:29-30

Acts 1:11

2 Thessalonians 1:7-10

Revelation 12:12

How do you explain the enemies of Yeshua Ha-Maschiach, Jesus Christ, the Jewish Messiah and our Lord continuing to oppose Him knowing:

    A. He said that he would return in this fashion?

    B. His word is always true?

Reread: Revelation 19:12-13

What is the appearance of this Rider?

Read: Matthew 28:18

Note: The crowns on His head are diadems, those of a ruler.

What does this mean to you in your every-day life?

What is the Rider called in these verses?

What do you see as the significance of the other descriptors of the Rider that we see in Revelation 19:12-13? Please comment on the ones listed below:

A: His eyes were bright like flames of fire. (See Revelation 1:14 and Revelation 2:18)

B: A name was written on him, and only he knew what it meant.

C: He was clothed with a robe dipped in blood.

Reread: Revelation 19:14

Read the following verses to see this predicted before it happens:

Zechariah 14:5

Matthew 13:41

Matthew 25:31

2 Thessalonians 1:7

Jude 1:14-15 (It is of particular note that this is the oldest prophecy in the Bible. It was uttered *before* the flood of Noah.)

What do you make of the fact that the oldest prophecy in Scripture deals with the return of Jesus Christ? What does this mean to you?

Who do we see coming with Jesus Christ in these verses?

Read the following verses to see who else will be coming with Him:

1 Thessalonians 3:12-13

2 Thessalonians 1:10

Colossians 3:4

Zechariah 14:5

Read: Revelation 17:14

How does it feel to know that you may have the opportunity to be a part of this great and momentous battle?

Reread: Revelation 19:15

What is coming out of the rider's mouth?

What will He do with this weapon in tow? Please make a list.

Of what significance might this be?

Read the following verses and comment:

Isaiah 11:4

2 Thessalonians 2:8

Revelation 1:16

Revelation 2:16

Isaiah 49:1-2

Hebrews 4:12

Ephesians 6:17

Do believers have this same weapon available to them today?

If this weapon is available to believers today, how might they best use it?

Revelation 19:15 also speaks of an iron rod.

Read the following verses to see this concept elsewhere in Scripture.

Psalm 2:9

Revelation 12:5

Revelation 2:26-27

Revelation 20:6

How will those who are victorious believers be involved in the process of ruling?

Reread: Revelation 19:16

What does this verse mean to the world?

What does this verse mean to you?

Reread: Revelation 19:17-19

What message did the angel mentioned in these verses deliver?

What will the birds of carrion consume?

Who is fighting against Jesus Christ and His army?

Are you part of the army of Jesus Christ? How do you know?

Reread: Revelation 19:20-21

Who wins this battle?

What happens to the beast and the false prophet?

In our study on Revelation 6 we said, in relationship to a person ending up in hades or ultimately hell:

This is a grievous, serious, eternal, mournful and irreversible event. It could be accurately stated that losing one's soul in hades is absolutely the worst thing that can happen to a person. Nothing else is more terrifying, painful, or permanent.

A book entitled *Heaven is For Real* by Todd Burpo was recently published. Whether or not you like the book, the premise, that heaven is for real, is undisputedly true. One cannot wish it away through some cleverly conceived pseudo-intellectual games. By the same token, the converse is true. Hell is for real. One also cannot wish it away for whatever reason they might find the idea distasteful or abhorrent.

Unbelievers, when they die, go to Hades, the unseen world, the (temporary) realm of the dead. Believers go immediately into the presence of the Lord. (Philippians 1:19-23; 2 Corinthians 5:6-8). Hades will be emptied of its dead in Revelation 20:13.

How will it impact the actions of so many people on earth at the time of this battle when they know that hell is real? Surely they must, by this point in time, understand the reality of the Supernatural struggle in which they are engaged.

Why do you think these people will actually fight against Jesus Christ and his followers?

Is there any greater height of arrogance than a person or group of persons deciding to make war on their creator?

As strange and bizarre as it is for human beings to make war on God, it is recorded prophetically beforehand.

Read Psalm 2:1-9 for a quick summary of this.

In addition, this is referenced many other places in the Old Testament including, but not limited to:

Joel 2

Daniel 11

Isaiah 24

Ezekiel 38-39

These passages and others are dealt with in many books on prophecy and many people have found it profitable to embark upon such a study. However, this must be done with a word of caution. Such study must lead not just to knowledge, but to a victorious contemporarily experienced life in Jesus Christ and to the sharing of the life available in Him with others.

Reread: Revelation 19:21

What specifically was involved with the death of the armies of the anti-Christ?

What do you understand this to mean? What role might the Word of God, the actual Scriptures themselves, have in the death of these people?

This is it. **The big event.** Jesus Christ has returned and will begin His reign, starting with His 1000 year rule on earth. As we know, all Scripture ties together and this was spoken of beforehand in:

Isaiah 9:6–7

6 For to us a child is born, to us a son is given, and the government will be on his shoulders. And he will be called Wonderful Counselor, Mighty God, Everlasting Father, Prince of Peace. 7 Of the increase of his government and peace there will be no end. He will reign on David's throne and over his kingdom, establishing

and upholding it with justice and righteousness from that time on and forever. The zeal of the LORD Almighty will accomplish this.

Luke 1:32–33

32 He will be great and will be called the Son of the Most High. The Lord God will give him the throne of his father David, 33 and he will reign over the house of Jacob forever; his kingdom will never end."

Application Questions

For what confrontations or battles in the cause of Jesus Christ to you need to prepare this week?

How can you effectively do so?

Close in Prayer

THE MILLENNIUM
REVELATION 20:1-6

Opening Prayer

Group Warm-Up Question

Why do you think people in general seem to be more and more interested in Satan and the occult in the world today? (You may wish to think of the firestorm of drug abuse, abuse of individuals even to modern-day slavery and torture, and hedonism as evidences of this.)

This study deals with what is called the Millennium. While there are many views of this period, three of the main ones are listed below.

Postmillennialism by which it is believed that through Christian influence the world will get better and better until Christ returns to rule after his followers have set up a utopian society. This view is now held by very few people since it is patently obvious that this is not the direction in which humanity is headed.

Amillennialism by which it is assumed that references to this period of time are allegorical and that Christ will rule in the hearts of his people but not literally on the earth.

Premillennialism by which it is assumed that there is a real rapture, a real tribulation and a real millennium on the earth. This millennial kingdom will be centered in Jerusalem and will last for 1000 years. After this time the world as we know it will be destroyed and a new heaven and earth will be created.

One's view of Scripture and their view of the veracity of God's Word influences the view one has of the Millennium. The more a person trusts the Word of God the more they will find that the literal view of a real millennium on earth is the one with the ring of truth. This is, in fact, the one and only view Jesus Christ had of this period of time, the view put forth in the Scriptures, and the view most often and generally adhered to today by those who seriously and diligently hold the Word of God in high regard and who study this material.

Going one step further, one's view of Scripture and the Millennium is normally also directly related to their view of the timing of the rapture. Most, but not all students who hold to a Premillennial view also adhere to the view of a Pre-Tribulation rapture or secondarily to a Mid-Tribulation rapture. I have attempted to illustrate this on the chart below.

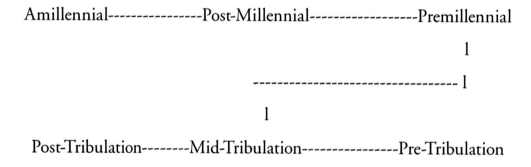

```
    Amillennial---------------Post-Millennial-----------------Premillennial

                                                                  l

                        --------------------------------- l

                              l

    Post-Tribulation--------Mid-Tribulation----------------Pre-Tribulation
```

The more literal one is in their view of the text the closer they will find themselves to the right side of this diagram.

At this point you may be asking yourself how these differing ways of viewing the Millennium came to be. For insight into this we might consider:

1. Christianity became the official religion of the Roman Empire under Constantine.

2. Augustine, an early church father, interpreted much of Scripture allegorically. He had a great personal interest in doing so. He was, in effect, an employee of the state. It would not have gone well for him if he had followed the example of Jesus, the writers of the New Testament, and Scripture as a whole if he had literally interpreted the passages about:

   • Jesus coming to rule from Jerusalem for one thousand years,

   • the importance of Israel as the capital of the world in times to come,

   • and the role of the Jews as God's chosen people.

3. During the reformation, many of the problems with allegorical interpretation were corrected. Indeed, grace was realized to be through faith as we see clearly in Ephesians 2:8-9.

4. However, their scholarship at the time of the reformation did not extend to their Eschatology or their view of Israel and the Jews. If it had done so many of the problems with the Millennium as well as those with the Israel even leading up to the holocaust in World War II might have been avoided.

5. While this may seem easy for us today in hindsight, God actually used the difficulties as part of His plan. We can see this clearly in the reestablishment of the modern state of Israel as literally foretold in the Scriptures. And, we can see this as the book of Revelation and prophecy both become more clear as we near "the end of the age" as Bible believing scholars interpret God's Word as Jesus did. (See How to Avoid Error in the Appendix.)

Many people actually avoid the study of the Millennium specifically and the book of Revelation as a whole since it can be an arduous task necessitating the utilization of the Word of God from beginning to end. This can also be a daunting task, though as we said at the outset of our study of this book of the Bible, it need not be so.

Read: Revelation 20:1-6

Reread: Revelation 20:1

What did John see a mighty angel carrying?

Here we are faced with another question that bears answering; that is "What is the Abyss?" The Greek word for this place is *Abousso* and means "bottomless pit." We see this term used 9 times in the New Testament and 30 times in the Old Testament. Seven of the times we see the term in the New Testament are in Revelation.

Abyss in Revelation

Read:

Revelation 9:1

Revelation 9:2

Revelation 9:11

Revelation 11:7

Revelation 17:8

Revelation 20:1

Revelation 20:3

For further information on the functioning of the *Abousso* see:

Genesis 6:2 to learn about angels who stepped over their authority.

Genesis 6:4 to again see these disobedient angels.

Isaiah 24:21-22 to see the fate of these beings prophesized.

Luke 8:31 to see that the demons themselves feared the *abousso*; the bottomless pit.

Revelation 20:1 to see a mighty angel with the keys to the bottomless pit.

Revelation 20:3 to see Satan confined to bottomless pit for a thousand years.

This bottomless pit, *the abousso*, always appears as reference to a temporary place of incarceration for certain demons or for Satan himself.

The lake of fire is the final awful destiny of these demons and the enemies of God. Take a look at:

Matthew 13:40-42 to see the fiery furnace as the terrible destiny of those who do evil.

Matthew 13:49-50 to see the involvement of this place of torment in the future.

Revelation 19:20 to see that the Antichrist and the false prophet are at this point in Revelation already in the lake of fire.

Revelation 20:10 to see the future destiny of the "star" we read about in Revelation 9:1-2

Reread: Revelation 20:2-3

Whom did the mighty angel seize?

What four names does the Word of God use for our enemy in this verse?

Read Revelation 12:9 to see this individual referred to in exactly the same fashion.

Since we know that nothing in Scripture is there by chance we now have another short riddle to unravel. That is, why is our enemy referred to by these particular four names in these important places? What exactly do they mean?

1. Here and elsewhere in Revelation he is called the dragon a total of 12 times. This would seem to be a reference to his ferocity and cruelty.

2. Calling him "the ancient serpent" or "serpent of old" reminds us of his temptation of Eve in the garden of Eden seen in Genesis 3:1-6.

3. The term "devil" means "slanderer" or "malicious gossip."

4. "Satan" means "adversary" and is quite appropriate since he is the enemy of God, Jesus Christ, the Holy Spirit, all believers and seemingly all believing Jews in particular.

What did the mighty angel do with him?

For how long was Satan locked up?

Note: The mighty angel had to have bound Satan securely since our adversary is an extremely powerful being (Ezekiel 28:14).

What impact did it have upon the people living on earth to have Satan locked up for a thousand years?

What must happen after the thousand years?

Reread: Revelation 20:4

What else did John see in his vision at this point?

For what reasons had some of the believers referenced in this verse died?

How had these Tribulation believers defied the beast?

What great honor was accorded these Tribulation believers?

These Tribulation saints remained faithful unto death and we see them in:

Revelation 6:9

Revelation 7:9-17

Revelation 12:11

Read 1 Peter 2:9 to see another famous reference to those who will rule and reign with Christ during this thousand year period.

Are you part of this group? How do you know?

Reread: Revelation 20:5-6

What happens to the rest of the dead, that is the unbelieving dead?

To whom is the first resurrection limited? (John calls the resurrection of the saints from all ages "the first resurrection." This is a category, not a single event.)

This resurrection is, of course, mentioned throughout Scripture. Read the following verses for some particular references to it. Please comment on any insight you gain from each reference.

Luke 14:13-14

Acts 24:14-15

John 5:28-29

1 Corinthians 15:21-23

Hebrews 11:35

Here we must understand:

- The thrones are literal.

- The martyrs are literal.

- Jesus is literal.

- The resurrection is literal.

- The thousand years are literal.

There are Four Classes of Believers involved in the category termed "first resurrection" and who will be ruling and reigning with Jesus Christ on the earth. They are:

1. Believers from the Old Testament. These are often called Old Testament Saints. (See Daniel 12:1-4 and Isaiah 25:7-9.)

2. Believers since the coming of Christ. (Sometimes called the "church") (See Revelation 5:10, Revelation 2:26-28, Revelation 3:12, Revelation 3:21, 1Thessalonians 4:13-18, 2 Timothy 2:12.)

3. Tribulation martyrs. (See Revelation 6:9)

4. Living Tribulation saints who have not worshipped the beast.

Note: We will later see the second resurrection in Revelation 20:11-15. This is the resurrection of the unbelieving dead who are headed for judgment and damnation; the lake of fire. Again, as we said in our study of Revelation 6:

Hades or Hell claims the soul. This is a grievous, serious, eternal, mournful and irreversible event. It could be accurately stated that losing one's soul in hades is absolutely the worst thing that can happen to a person. Nothing else is more terrifying, painful, or permanent.

What honor is accorded *all* resurrected believers during this period of one thousand years?

What power does the second death have over those who have trusted Jesus Christ?

It has been said that those who have not trusted Jesus Christ are born once and die twice. Those who have trusted him die once and are born twice. How would you explain this in your own words?

From the Old Testament we learn a number of things about this period of time when Jesus Christ and his followers rule the earth.

1. This will be a period of righteousness and peace.

   - Isaiah 32:17

2. This will be a time of joy.

   - Isaiah 12:3-4

   - Isaiah 61:3

   - Isaiah 61:7

3. The curse will be lifted.

   - Isaiah 11:7-9

   - Isaiah 30:23-24

   - Isaiah 35:1-2

- Isaiah 35:7

4. Food will be plentiful.

- See Joel 2:21-27

5. Physical health will be the norm.

- Isaiah 33:24

- Isaiah 35:5-6

6. Long life will be enjoyed. (Isaiah 65:20)

The millennium will be astounding. Satan will be bound. However, this does not mean that people living in the millennium will be incapable of sinning. In fact, as we will see in our succeeding studies, a large part of the population, born of those entering the kingdom, will reject the King. They will be dealt with severely as we see in Revelation 2:27, Revelation 12:5 and Psalm 2:9.

For Further Study: A great deal has been written about the millennium and we have time to only touch upon it here. One of the popular topics addressed is that of the Millennial Temple. However, one need not wonder what this will be like to any great degree. You can simply read Ezekiel 40-48 where it is described in great detail. There is no doubt that this will be a real temple and is no mere allegorical illustration. There are also a number of verses that speak of His throne as they relate to the temple at this time. You may want to read:

Isaiah 16:5

Matthew 25:31

Zechariah 6:12-13

Jeremiah 3:16-17

Application Questions

What can you do to try and be sure that those you love participate in the first resurrection and have the privilege ruling with Yeshua Ha-Maschiach for a thousand years?

Do you think of this differently when you ask yourself how you can help them avoid the terrible fate of those who end up in the fiery furnace? How so?

Close in Prayer

SATAN'S FINAL REBELLION AND DOOM

REVELATION 20:7-10

Opening prayer

Group Warm-Up Question

In things you have read or seen, who, in your opinion, is the worst villain of all time? (Exclusive of Satan or the Antichrist)

Read: Revelation 20:7-10

Reread: Revelation 20:7

What surprising thing will happen when the millennium is over?

How is the Abyss where Satan was confined described?

Why do you think God will permit Satan to be released?

Reread: Revelation 20:7-8

What will Satan do as soon as he gets out of prison?

Where does Satan go to gather his army?

The phrase used here is the same one we see in:

Revelation 7:1

Isaiah 11:12

It indicates that this force will be gathered from all over the globe; north, south, east and west.

How large an army is Satan able to gather?

Note: There have been 1000 years of peace, plenty, and prosperity on the earth as we saw in our previous study. Although the world's population had greatly declined prior to the millennium, it increased greatly during the thousand years. Not only will it be populated by God's people, but by many others who must reproduce at exponential rates given the wonderful living conditions.

Is it possible that the army that Satan gathers will be the largest ever seen on the planet earth?

How is it possible that so many people are both unbelievers and deceived at this point in history that Satan is able to do this? Read Romans 8:6-7 as you construct your answer.

It appears that during the Millennium unbelievers and children of believers will still have to make a personal decision to follow or not follow Jesus Christ.

How can it be that anyone might decide to fight against Jesus Christ after having lived in His millennial kingdom and having heard or read about all of history up until this point? What else does this tell us about human nature? Read Jeremiah 17:9 as you think about your answer.

What is Satan's purpose in gathering this force?

With what two names do we see this large force identified?

Note: The names Gog and Magog are the same two associated with Ezekiel 38 and 39 which describes the invasion force that comes against Israel at the end of the Great Tribulation. (Revelation 19:11-20) By this time, after the Millennium, the names appear to be utilized idiomatically for enemies of God's people.

Interestingly, we see a swarm of locusts in Amos 7:1. At least one translation names "Gog" as their king. When we tie this in with Revelation 9:2-11 some people believe that one of the leaders of Satan's army in Revelation 20 will be actually be a demon identified as Gog.

The scriptures seem to make it clear that Ezekiel references what is often called the battle of Armageddon and that the battle so named is different from what occurs after the Millennium. In the battle depicted in Ezekiel 38-39 and Revelation 19 God's enemies are destroyed on the mountains of Israel. (See Ezekiel 39:4 and Ezekiel 39:17)

In Revelation 20 they will be defeated on a broad plain as we will momentarily see. They are, in fact, attacking Jesus Christ and his followers in Israel and in particular in His Holy City, Jerusalem. In the Old Testament we read about Israel and the way God feels about this country, this people, and indeed Jerusalem. Read the following verses to see this:

Genesis 12:3

Zechariah 2:8

Psalm 121:3-4

This again causes many to ask why anyone would be so arrogant and stupid as to attack the very Creator of the universe in the place He loves so dearly.

How does Satan try and deceive even believers today?

How does Satan try and use distractions to try and deceive believers today?

How does Satan try and use misdirection to try and deceive both believers and nonbelievers today?

What can you do to keep from being deceived, distracted, or misdirected in your life?

How are you encouraged by the way God acts on behalf of His people? (This includes you if you have trusted Jesus Christ.)

How does knowing the end of history affect the way you feel and live in the present?

Can you think of any modern day examples when someone has been released from incarceration and immediately gone back to their old ways?

Why do you think someone released from prison today, which is supposed to somehow rehabilitate them, might go back to their old way of life?

Reread: Revelation 20:9

What battle plan will Satan follow at this point in time?

How is he defeated?

How long and difficult a battle does this appear to be for Jesus Christ?

Reread: Revelation 20:10

What happens to the devil after he is defeated in this battle?

How can we draw encouragement from the certainty of Satan's doom?

Who else is already in the fiery lake?

For how long will Satan, the false prophet and the Antichrist be tormented in hell?

Why is it just and fair that Satan will be "tormented" day and night forever and ever?

In contemplating this topic we should realize anew some of the characteristics of this terrible place. Please list as many as you can think of.

After constructing your list see if it includes:

1. Those there are tormented.

2. Those there are in great pain.

3. There is no relief from their pain.

4. There is not sleep.

5. Those there are tormented every day.

6. Those imprisoned there are tormented every night.

7. The torment never stops.

8. The suffering is forever and ever.

We might note that the same phrase that tells us that this torment does not end is used to describe the existence of Jesus Christ and the life that believers have. Read the following verses to see this.

Revelation 1:18

2 Thessalonians 1:9

Matthew 25:46

How do you think and feel when you contemplate this terrible place called hell and the fate which will befall all who choose to go there?

Why might it be said that people actually *choose* to go to this terrible place?

As a counterpoint, those who have decided to follow Jesus are already citizens of God's kingdom. Their relationship with God through Jesus Christ is as eternal as the punishment of those who oppose the one true Lord of all. See the following verses:

Philippians 3:20

But our citizenship is in heaven. And we eagerly await a Savior from there, the Lord Jesus Christ,

1 Thessalonians 2:11–12

11 For you know that we dealt with each of you as a father deals with his own children, 12 encouraging, comforting and urging you to live lives worthy of God, who calls you into his kingdom and glory.

Colossians 1:13–14

13 For he has rescued us from the dominion of darkness and brought us into the kingdom of the Son he loves, 14 in whom we have redemption, the forgiveness of sins.

1 Peter 1:3–4

3 Praise be to the God and Father of our Lord Jesus Christ! In his great mercy he has given us new birth into a living hope through the resurrection of Jesus Christ from the dead, 4 and into an inheritance that can never perish, spoil or fade—kept in heaven for you,

Application Questions

What can you do to try and make sure that those you love and care about end up with God and not in torment?

A number of years ago Hal Lindsey wrote a book entitled *Satan is Alive and Well on Planet Earth.* Obviously he was right. What can you do today to make a dent in the following and power that Satan possesses and enjoys?

If you are in a desperate situation today and feel surrounded by the enemy, what step of faith and what actions do you need to take?

Close in Prayer

THE GREAT WHITE THRONE JUDGMENT

REVELATION 20:11-15

Opening Prayer

Group Warm-up Question

What is one time you remember getting into trouble as a child?

Read: Revelation 20:11-15

At the outset of this passage we need to differentiate between the Great White Throne Judgment and the Bema Seat Judgment in Scripture.

As we proceed we will see:

1. The Great White Throne Judgment described at this point in Revelation impacts those who have not trusted Jesus Christ.

2. The Bema Seat Judgment impacts those who have trusted Him.

The Bema Seat Judgment

First, we need to further differentiate between the Bema seat and the Bimah. These terms are sometimes confused because they sound very much alike and because they are both important to Jews.

The Bimah is a raised platform in a synagogue where the reading of the Torah takes place. In the United States today this is normally in the front center of the Synagogue. However, on an historic basis different groups within Judaism have argued that it should be on the eastern or western side of the Synagogue. For our purposes here today, it doesn't matter. All we need to do is to realize that it has nothing to do with the Bema Seat.

The concept of the Bema Seat comes primarily from ancient Greek athletic games. Contestants would compete under the careful scrutiny of judges to be sure every rule of the contest in question was obeyed (2 Timothy 2:5) and to determine and reward the winners. The victor of an event who participated according to the rules was led by the judge to a platform called the *Bema*. Here the winner would be rewarded with a laurel wreath that placed upon his head as a symbol of victory. (1 Corinthians 9:24-25)

In a race, for example, a judge would sit on the Bema Seat at the finish line. This would enable him to determine who came in first, second, third and so on and to then give out the appropriate rewards. This is, perhaps, the best example of the imagery behind the Bema Seat.

The same word for the Bema Seat is used in Acts and the gospels when a ruler sat to make judgment. (Matthew 27:19 and John 19:13)

There is some debate as to the exact timing of the Bema Seat Judgment. Some understand it to take place at the moment of death for every believer. Some understand it to take place at pretty much the same time as the Great White Throne Judgment in Revelation 20. And, some even understand it to take place at the time of the Rapture, though this construct does not work logically in concert with the rest of the book of Revelation or indeed the whole of Scripture.

Suffice it to say that all who have truly trusted Jesus Christ will appear before His Bema Seat.

Scripture teaches us many things about this Bema judgment:

1. It is described in 1 Corinthians 3:11-15.

2. It is only for believers.

    • John 3:16

    • Romans 10:9-10

3. Jesus Christ already paid the penalty for believers who have trusted Him and accepted His gift of life.

    • Colossians 2:3

    • Ephesians 2:8-9

4. Each believer will have to give an account of their life.

    • Romans 14:10-12

5. Every believer will receive what is due them.

    • 2 Corinthians 5:9-10

6. We have choices about what rewards we will or will not receive at the Bema seat.

    •   I John 2:28

7. We must be sure to hold on to our rewards. One can apparently lose them by wrong action.

    •   Revelation 3:11-12

8. We can and should continue to "lay up treasure for the coming age."

    •   1 Timothy 6:18-19

    •   Matthew 6:19-22

The Coin of the Realm: My wife and I are, at this writing, planning a trip to Israel with a number of friends. When we go there we will have to convert our dollars into shekels so that we can live and travel in the country. When we or others have gone to different countries we have always had to convert our money to the currency of that country. In a similar fashion, all believers have the opportunity to convert what we are doing in this life to the treasure that will benefit us in the future, the coin of the realm, mentioned in 1 Timothy 6:18-19 and Matthew 6:19-22.

Great White Throne Judgment

The Great White Throne Judgment is described in Revelation 20:11-15. We also see it referenced throughout Scripture where we learn:

1. It is expected and accepted in the Old Testament.

    •   Daniel 7:9-11

    •   1 Kings 22:19

2. Yeshua Ha-Maschiach, Jesus Christ, the Jewish Messiah is the Judge.

- John 5:22
- John 5:27
- John 5:29
- Acts 10:42

3. It will not involve believers; those who have trusted in Jesus Christ.

- John 5:24

4. It will involve some people who masqueraded as believers.

- Matthew 7:22-23

Read Revelation 20:11-15 again.

Reread: Revelation 20:11

How does creation react to the Great White Throne Judgment?

Why do you think this might be so?

Reread: Revelation 20:12-13

Where does this judgment take place?

What book will be opened up?

The Book of Life is seen throughout Scripture. It is apparently a compendium of the names of those who have truly trusted Jesus Christ. Read the following passages and make a list of the things we learn about this book.

Exodus 32:32-33

Psalm 69:20-28

Revelation 21:22-27

Philippians 4:3

Revelation 13:8

Revelation 17:8

Luke 10:20

Malachi 3:16

1 Corinthians 3:14-15 (Please also relate this to Rewards at the Bema Seat Judgment)

In reading Revelation 13:8 and 17:8 we need to combine the concept of God's foreknowledge with our responsibilities and free will to choose. How would you put this in your own words?

The other books to be opened up at this point also contain lists. What do they seem to record?

Reread: Revelation 20:14-15

How is each person judged?

What will happen to those whose name is not found in the Book of Life?

What does it mean that death and hades were thrown into the lake of fire?

What does it mean when it says that being thrown into the lake of fire is "the second death?"

Why are those found in the Book of Life spared judgment based upon their works?

How does the concept of believers receiving rewards for their works at the Bema seat tie into whether or not one's name is recorded in the Book of Life?

How exactly does one make certain that they will be in the Book of Life? See the following verses as you construct your answer:

Romans 5:9

1 Thessalonians 1:10

1 Thessalonians 5:9

John 3:16

John 14:6

How should it impact us to know that we will be judged for the way in which we live?

Hell

Hell is a real place.

At times in the New Testament Hell is described as Gehenna. This was a terrible place. Gehenna is another name for the valley of Ben-Hinnom or Topheth, located somewhat to the southwest of Jerusalem. (See 2 Kings 23:10; Isaiah 30:33; Jeremiah 7:31-32; Jeremiah 19:6)

In Old Testament times this valley was a place of unspeakable evil and revulsion. It was there that some idolatrous Israelites burned their children alive in sacrifice to pagan gods. (Jeremiah 19:2-6)

In the time of Jesus this was the site of Jerusalem's garbage dump. It was filled with trash, rotting food, the bodies of criminals who had been dumped there, and maggots. This dump had also caught fire and was constantly smoldering and giving off a horrendous stench and smoke.

The Scriptures tell us a great deal about Hell. And, being the most reliable documents in existence, we need to pay close attention to what they say on any subject. Here is a smattering of the verses that teach us something about the Lake of Fire:

Matthew 5:22

But I tell you that anyone who is angry with his brother will be subject to judgment. Again, anyone who says to his brother, 'Raca,' is answerable to the Sanhedrin. But anyone who says, 'You fool!' will be in danger of the fire of hell.

Matthew 5:29–30

29 If your right eye causes you to sin, gouge it out and throw it away. It is better for you to lose one part of your body than for your whole body to be thrown into hell. 30 And if your right hand causes you to sin, cut it off and throw it away. It is better for you to lose one part of your body than for your whole body to go into hell.

Matthew 10:28

Do not be afraid of those who kill the body but cannot kill the soul. Rather, be afraid of the One who can destroy both soul and body in hell.

Matthew 18:9

And if your eye causes you to sin, gouge it out and throw it away. It is better for you to enter life with one eye than to have two eyes and be thrown into the fire of hell.

Matthew 23:15

"Woe to you, teachers of the law and Pharisees, you hypocrites! You travel over land and sea to win a single convert, and when he becomes one, you make him twice as much a son of hell as you are.

Matthew 23:33

"You snakes! You brood of vipers! How will you escape being condemned to hell?

Mark 9:43

If your hand causes you to sin, cut it off. It is better for you to enter life maimed than with two hands to go into hell, where the fire never goes out.

Mark 9:45

And if your foot causes you to sin, cut it off. It is better for you to enter life crippled than to have two feet and be thrown into hell.

Mark 9:47

And if your eye causes you to sin, pluck it out. It is better for you to enter the kingdom of God with one eye than to have two eyes and be thrown into hell,

Luke 12:5

But I will show you whom you should fear: Fear him who, after the killing of the body, has power to throw you into hell. Yes, I tell you, fear him.

Matthew 25:41

"Then he will say to those on his left, 'Depart from me, you who are cursed, into the eternal fire prepared for the devil and his angels.

Matthew 22:13

"Then the king told the attendants, 'Tie him hand and foot, and throw him outside, into the darkness, where there will be weeping and gnashing of teeth.'

2 Peter 2:17

These men are springs without water and mists driven by a storm. Blackest darkness is reserved for them.

Isaiah 66:24

"And they will go out and look upon the dead bodies of those who rebelled against me; their worm will not die, nor will their fire be quenched, and they will be loathsome to all mankind."

Matthew 8:12

But the subjects of the kingdom will be thrown outside, into the darkness, where there will be weeping and gnashing of teeth."

Matthew 13:42

They will throw them into the fiery furnace, where there will be weeping and gnashing of teeth.

Matthew 24:51

He will cut him to pieces and assign him a place with the hypocrites, where there will be weeping and gnashing of teeth.

Matthew 25:30

And throw that worthless servant outside, into the darkness, where there will be weeping and gnashing of teeth.

Luke 13:28

"There will be weeping there, and gnashing of teeth, when you see Abraham, Isaac and Jacob and all the prophets in the kingdom of God, but you yourselves thrown out.

As we said in earlier sessions:

Hell claims the soul. This is a grievous, serious, eternal, mournful and irreversible event. It could be accurately stated that losing one's soul in hades or hell is absolutely the worst thing that can happen to a person. Nothing else is more terrifying, painful, or permanent.

Application Questions

Are there any steps you need to take today to be sure that your name is written in the Book of Life?

How can you help a friend or loved one avoid a future in the lake of fire?

A word on reincarnation: Some people even in our postmodern world find the concept of reincarnation to be attractive. However the Judeo-Christian documents which we call the Bible teach otherwise. Their commentary on the subject is summed up in Hebrews 9:27.

Hebrews 9:27

And as it is appointed for men to die once, but after this the judgment,

While we do not wish to take away from the seriousness of our eternal destiny, one almost cannot help but enjoy the humorous poem entitled Reincarnation by Wallace McRae available in his book *Cowboy Curmudgeon and Other Poems.*

Close in Prayer

THE NEW JERUSALEM
REVELATION 21

Opening Prayer

Group Warm-Up Questions

What is the most beautiful place you have ever been?

What is the most beautiful or exotic jewelry you have ever seen?

Read: Revelation 21:1-27

In many ways we are now seeing the whole of Scripture and the whole of human history tied together from Genesis to Revelation. Look up the following references and confirm this for yourself.

Genesis	Revelation
Genesis 1:1	Revelation 21:1
Heavens and earth are created.	New Heavens and earth are created.
Genesis 1:16	Revelation 21:23
The sun is created.	There will be no need for the sun.
Genesis 1:5	Revelation 22:5
Night is established.	Night is eliminated.
Genesis 1:10	Revelation 21:1
The seas are created.	There is no longer any sea.
Genesis 3:14-17	Revelation 22:3
The curse enters human experience.	The curse is gone.
Genesis 3:19	Revelation 21:4
Death enters history.	Death itself is defeated.
Genesis 3:24	Revelation 22:14
Man driven from the Garden.	Believers permitted to enter the Holy City.
Genesis 3:17	Revelation 21:4
Human suffering begins.	There are no more tears or pain.

What are the implications for our everyday lives if this present earth and everything in it will pass away?

Reread: Revelation 21:1

What did John first see at this point in time?

What happened to the first heaven and earth?

What happened to the sea?

The end of the old things was spoken of thousands of years ago. Read the following verses and discuss what they mean. (This is only a smattering of the many references to these events in the Scriptures.)

2 Peter 3:7-12

Hebrews 12:26-27

Hebrews 1:10-12

Matthew 24:35

Conversely, we also see the new heavens and earth referred to in God's Word over the millennia. Please read and discuss:

Isaiah 65:17

Isaiah 66:22

Hebrews 11:13-16

Reread: Revelation 21:2

What else did John see coming down out of heaven?

What comparison does John make?

What does this comparison imply taking into account what you now know about Jewish weddings?

Note: We see here that the New Jerusalem is an actual city. John MacArthur describes it as "the capital city of the eternal state. The new Jerusalem is not heaven, but heaven's capital."

In Hebrews we see that while this city comes down out of heaven it does not necessarily touch the earth.

Hebrews 11:10

Abraham was confidently looking forward to a city with eternal foundations, a city designed and built by God.

Hebrews 11:16

But they were looking for a better place, a heavenly homeland. That is why God is not ashamed to be called their God, for he has prepared a city for them.

Furthermore, Scripture seems to imply that this place already exists and is populated by believers who have died.

Hebrews 12:22–23

22 No, you have come to Mount Zion, to the city of the living God, the heavenly Jerusalem, and to countless thousands of angels in a joyful gathering. 23 You have come to the assembly of God's firstborn children, whose names are written in heaven. You have come to God himself, who is the judge over all things. You have come to the spirits of the righteous ones in heaven who have now been made perfect.

Revelation 21:10

So he took me in the Spirit to a great, high mountain, and he showed me the holy city, Jerusalem, descending out of heaven from God.

John 14:1–3

1 "Don't let your hearts be troubled. Trust in God, and trust also in me. 2 There is more than enough room in my Father's home. If this were not so, would I have told you that I am going to prepare a place for you? 3 When everything is ready, I will come and get you, so that you will always be with me where I am.

These concepts also seem to fit with the concept that the Bema seat judgment of believers as referenced in our previous study takes place at the moment of physical death for one who has trusted Jesus Christ. (As adhered to by some Bible scholars.)

However, to be fair, we must again state that many Bible scholars also believe that the Bema seat judgment takes place when Jesus Christ returns. (Revelation 20:12) Either way, we had better be ready.

Reread: Revelation 21:3-4

What did the voice from the throne announce?

How was this new situation described? Please make a list of the primary characteristics you find in these verses.

    1.

    2.

    3.

    4.

    5.

    6.

    7.

Reread: Revelation 21:6

What great sense of power do you feel as you read this verse?

What great promise do you see in this verse? Please put this in your own words.

Reread: Revelation 21:7

What benefit specifically inures to those who overcome?

Early in the book of Revelation Jesus Christ himself repeatedly speaks about the reward of one who overcomes. Who, from your study, would be defined as an overcomer? Be sure to read 1 John 5:4 as you construct your answer.

Reread: Revelation 21:8

This is, for many, the most frightening verse in the Bible. Why might this be?

Does this clearly state that these practices not only keep people out of heaven, but condemn them to the fiery lake of burning sulfur *forever*?

Who, specifically, do we find on this list? Please enumerate.

Read: Mark 4:40

What clue do you find in this verse that tells you how the people mentioned in Revelation 21:8 got on the worst possible list?

What do we learn about believers from the following verses in contrast to those on the terrible list?

John 14:27

2 Timothy 1:7

2 Timothy 1:8

Reread: Revelation 21:8

How is the fate of those whose conscious and overt choices cause them to end up in the lake of fire summed up in only a few words at the end of the verse?

How does it impact you when you realize that this "death" is not eternal unconsciousness or sleep, but eternal wakefulness and experience?

What a tragedy it is that anyone chooses this fate for themselves, especially when we know that life is available for the asking.

Read Ephesians 2:8-9 to remind ourselves of this gift.

Read 1 Timothy 2:5-6 to see that this is available to all people.

Read 2 Peter 3:9 to see that the Lord wants everyone to choose life.

Read 2 Corinthians 6:2 to see that one should never delay this decision.

Reread: Revelation 21:9-10

Who offers to give John a closer look at the Holy City?

How are the occupants of the city described?

Note: The bride of the Lamb was a title initially given to the church, but is now expanded to encompass the redeemed of all ages. (See Revelation 19:7)

Reread: Revelation 21:11-14

How is the New Jerusalem first described?

We should be sure to note the symbolism that hits us in the face as we read these verses. God is again tying His plan together in this description and the construction of the city. One enters the city through gates associated with one of the twelve tribes of Israel. We are reminded that from the beginning God promised to bless the world through the Jews. This included both the Messiah, Yeshua Ha-Maschiach and His Word. Both were brought to the world through Israel as an instrument of God. (See Genesis 12:3 and John 4:22)

Reread: Revelation 21:15-17

How did God quantify the size of this city to John?

In measurements common in North America the surface size of this city is 1400 miles by 1400 miles or 1,960,000 square miles. By comparison:

1. If you examine the contiguous states in the United States of America and remove the 7 largest including California, Texas, Montana, New Mexico,

Arizona, Nevada, and Colorado you have a surface area roughly equivalent to the surface area of the New Jerusalem.

2. India, the second most populous country on earth, is only 64% as large as the New Jerusalem.

3. You could fit 14 countries the size of Germany, a large industrially and technologically advanced nation, into the surface area occupied by the New Jerusalem.

4. If we examine the country of Mexico we would need a nation almost three (2.6) times as large to be equivalent in surface area to the Holy City.

So we have established that the New Jerusalem is really, really big.

Right?

However, we have only touched the surface.

Reread: Revelation 21:16

The city is not squared. It is cubed.

If we do the math we find that New Jerusalem contains 2,744,000,000 cubic miles. (That is billion with a "B.")

The planet earth has 196,939,900 square miles in surface area. If we wish to extrapolate this further we might make an imaginary comparison to the "living space" on earth as compared to the New Jerusalem. If we do this we are in most cases being unfair to Jerusalem. On the earth we have essentially unlimited air space above the planet in a practical sense as it relates to activities of normal daily life. However, if we think about activities of normal daily living we can likely agree that nobody on the earth needs more than a mile over their head to give them room to live. If we assume this to be true in the New Jerusalem and in a sense assume that there are figurative floors or stories we find that actual living space there is 14 times greater than the surface area of the earth. (2,744,000,000 divided by 196,939,900)

However, upon further examination we find that there are only 57 Million square miles of land on earth. The rest is water. In this case we find that there is 48 times the living space in the New Jerusalem as on the land of the earth. (2,744,000,000 divided by 57,000,000)

Taking this to one more level, let's assume that a person on the earth really doesn't need a mile of air above their head to be comfortable. Let's assume we only need 52.8 feet. (We get this by dividing the number of feet in a mile by 100) If a person needs only 52.8 feet above their head to comfortable and we try to extrapolate this to the New Jerusalem we find that this wonderful city will have the living space that is equivalent to 4,800 earths. (2,700,000,000 divided by 57,000,000 times 100)

When I made these calculations I had to keep checking and rechecking my numbers. They are just so large that they seem almost impossible to understand in normal human experience.

Why do you think God revealed so many details about the size and appearance of the New Jerusalem?

Having gone through this little exercise, what do you think and feel about the size of the New Jerusalem?

Is it possible for a human being to correctly conceptualize and comprehend the immensity of this city?

Do you think there will be enough room for all those who have trusted Jesus Christ?

Read: John 14:2

Does this verse along with the calculations we have made give you greater insight into what Jesus was talking about at this point in his ministry?

Do you think His listeners had any idea what he meant as quoted in the book of John?

Reread: Revelation 21:18-21

How else did John describe the New Jerusalem?

Did anything jump out at you as being different than you might expect?

Reread verses 18 and 21. Most readers, upon reading that the gold was "as clear as glass," simply skip over the phrase and ignore it. However, "modern" science tells us that gold in the most refined form is indeed as clear as glass. This form of gold is used in high level telecommunications equipment where maximum conductivity is required. One would not use it in jewelry, where the traditional colors springing from impurities in the metal are desired. Indeed, in a small group Bible study session a few years ago, Scott Swart, a former Marine with a White House security clearance, told us how he personally saw gold on very advanced electronic equipment in a highly refined state when in the military. It was clear, albeit a little smoky. Further refinement reportedly makes it just as referenced in Revelation.

Perhaps just as interesting is that John, the writer of Revelation, was simply writing down what he heard and saw. He had no idea what "modern science" would tell us about gold. He just reported the facts. As with the rest of God's Word, this particular fact was simply corroborated later when our ability to understand things caught up to the reality revealed in the Scriptures.

This instance, like all others of the same nature, should simply serve to put us more in awe of the Word of God and help us to realize its supernatural nature.

Reread: Revelation 21:22-27

Reading these verses and recalling the others in this chapter, in what way does the New Jerusalem reflect God's glory and holiness? Please make a list.

What will be the source of light in the New Jerusalem?

What do you think it means that the kings of the earth will "bring their splendor into the city and that the nations will walk by its light?"

Why do you think God revealed so many details about the New Jerusalem?

Who or what will never enter the New Jerusalem?

What class of people, and only what class, will enter the New Jerusalem?

Read: Ephesians 2:4-7

Do you think at this point in Revelation 21 God has accomplished what He said he would do?

Application Question

How can you use the information from Revelation 21 to bring comfort to someone facing death, great pain or sadness? Please think of one specific instance where you can do this now.

Close in Prayer

INSIDE THE NEW JERUSALEM
REVELATION 22:1-6

Opening Prayer

Group Warm-Up Question

How do you imagine the existence of a believer in heaven? What, in your opinion, will you be doing? What do you want to be doing?

Read: Revelation 22:1-6

Reread: Revelation 22:1

From whence does the River of Life flow?

How is the River of Life described?

What symbolism do you find here?

Read: John 4:7-15

What does one need to do to be sure they receive this living water both now and in the future?

Reread: Revelation 22:2

Where does the River of Life flow?

What else do we know about the course of this river? (See Revelation 21:21)

What do we see growing by the river?

Where have we seen this tree before? (Take a look at Genesis 3:22-24.)

How do you feel knowing that mankind once gave up an existence like this?

How do you feel knowing that God restores his servants to such a place?

How are the leaves of this tree used?

What do you think this means?

Could this have anything to do with the new earth?

Read: Genesis 3:14-19

Reread: Revelation 22:3

What happened to the curse?

What will God's people be doing in heaven?

Reread: Revelation 22:4

What will God's servants see?

Note: This is somewhat different than what people were to expect if they saw the face of God in His Glory as referenced in the Old Testament. (See Exodus 33:18-23)

How will all of God's servants be marked?

Read Revelation 7:3-8 to see this first happening to the special appointed Jews during the great tribulation.

Why do you think God so marks His servants in heaven?

Might they have tasks to perform as part of their service that require them to have the mark for some reason?

Read: Revelation 22:5

How will those in heaven receive their light?

What will God's servants be doing as part of their service to Him?

Read Ephesians 1:1-10 to see this spoken of in advance.

Reread: Revelation 22:6

How did the angel reassure John?

Why, according to this verse, did God provide all of the information in the book of Revelation to John?

While the book of Revelation and the Judeo-Christian Scriptures as a whole tell us a ton about heaven and our long-term existence, they also leave some things out. Why do you think God does not reveal all the details in advance?

We know that God always keeps His promises. We know that His Word is true and consistent. We know that we can trust Him. What then can you extrapolate about the general characteristics of the rest of the things you will learn about heaven when you arrive? (This assumes, of course, that you have trusted Jesus Christ.)

Read:

Hebrews 11:10

Hebrews 11:13-16

Hebrews 12:2

The Old Testament patriarchs looked forward to this city. New Testament believers and we are also admonished to also look forward to heaven.

How did taking the long-term view of reality impact the daily lives and actions of the people we see in the Bible? (See Hebrews 11:32-40)

How should taking the long-term view of reality impact our day-to-day lives?

Read Ephesians 4:22-30 in the Good News translation.

Ephesians 4:22–30

22 So get rid of your old self, which made you live as you used to—the old self that was being destroyed by its deceitful desires. 23 Your hearts and minds must be made completely new, 24 and you must put on the new self, which is created in God's likeness and reveals itself in the true life that is upright and holy. 25 No more lying, then! Each of you must tell the truth to one another, because we are all members together in the body of Christ. 26 If you become angry, do not let your anger lead you into sin, and do not stay angry all day. 27 Don't give the Devil a chance. 28 Those who used to rob must stop robbing and start working, in order to earn an honest living for themselves and to be able to help the poor. 29 Do not use harmful words, but only helpful words, the kind that build up and provide what is needed, so that what you say will do good to those who hear you. 30 And do not make God's Holy Spirit sad; for the Spirit is God's mark of ownership on you, a guarantee that the Day will come when God will set you free.

Application Question

What can you do today to show that you have God's "mark of ownership" upon you?

Close in Prayer

HE IS COMING BACK
REVELATION 22:7-21

Opening Prayer

Group Warm-Up Question

What is your most memorable experience upon "returning home?"

Read: Revelation 22:7-21

Reread: Revelation 22:7

Also read: Revelation 1:3

What promise does Jesus make?

Who in particular did Jesus say will be blessed?

What do you think this means?

What does it mean to you that Jesus ties the whole of the book of Revelation together by saying something similar at both the beginning and ending of the book?

Read:

Deuteronomy 4:2

Proverbs 30:5-6

What further insights do you gain from these verses?

Read: Revelation 22:8-9

What mistake does John make?

This is the same error we saw John making in Revelation 19:10. Why do you think he did this?

Read Revelation 1:17 and discuss any insight you find in regard to this question.

Do people today sometimes revere leaders both within and outside of the church too highly? How so?

Reread: Revelation 22:10

What was John commanded to do and why?

Why do you think the Holy Spirit communicated this by telling John what not to do instead of directly what to do?

What psychological impact does it have upon a person if a command is given in this fashion?

Read: Revelation 22:11

What does this verse mean to you? Please explain.

Why do you think this verse is positioned here where we find it in the last book of the Bible?

Reread: Revelation 22:12

What does Jesus say he will bring with him when he comes?

How does this make you feel?

How do you relate this to the Bema seat judgment we discussed in previous sessions?

Reread: Revelation 22:13

What titles does Jesus use of Himself in this verse?

Why are these titles significant?

Why is it significant that Jesus uses these titles at this place in Scripture?

Reread: Revelation 22:14

Also Read: Revelation 7:12-14

How must one "wash their robe?"

What exactly does this mean?

What characteristics would you expect to see in the lives and practice today of those who have done this?

What right inures to those who have "washed their robes" in this manner?

Reread: Revelation 22:15

First, let's understand the use of the imagery of dogs in Scripture. Look up the following verses where we find that dogs were the scavengers of the ancient world and were considered unclean.

Isaiah 66:3

Matthew 7:6 (Be sure to see the KJV)

Psalm 22:16

Psalm 22:20

Jeremiah 15:3

Deuteronomy 23:18 (See the KJV)

2 Peter 2:22

Read: Matthew 15:21-28

What do we learn about dogs in this passage?

We should note that many Jews who considered themselves and their God the source of all that was good looked upon Gentiles as dogs. With that knowledge, what insight do you gain from these verses in Matthew?

Finally, we see Paul referring to the Judaizers as dogs in Philippians 3:2.

What did he mean by this?

Read Revelation 22:15 again.

Also read:

Revelation 21:8

Revelation 21:27

Here we find a very interesting list of people who will not be found in heaven. Please enumerate the characteristics of such people. (This involves, but also goes far beyond the things they are doing.)

What is the consequence of living a life of disobedience to God, no matter what it involves?

Knowing this, how should we be living now? Or, as Francis Shaffer put it so simply, "How shall we then live?"

Reread: Revelation 22:16

How did Jesus get the message of the book of Revelation to the churches then as well as to us today?

How is it possible that Jesus is both the root and the offspring of David at the same time? Please explain.

Reread: Revelation 22:17

What invitation is given by the Spirit and the Bride?

To whom is this invitation addressed?

Is there any restriction placed upon whom may receive this invitation?

How, specifically, does one take advantage of this invitation? What must one do?

How does it impact you to know that even in this last book of the Bible, having detailed God's character, righteousness, judgment, power and glory that His Spirit and His bride still invite all people to come to Him?

What bearing on your life and interactions with others ought this to have?

Read: Revelation 22:18-19

Also Read:

Revelation 1:3

Revelation 22:7

2 Peter 3:15-16

Deuteronomy 4:2

Proverbs 30:5-6

Psalm 138:2

How seriously does God regard the keeping and preservation of His Word?

What does this tell us about the attempts that people sometimes make to twist, turn, shape and allegorize the Word of God to fit their own agendas?

In what other ways might a person "take away" from the Word of God?

What do we learn from the fact that God deals with this subject several times in the last book of the Bible?

Read:

2 Timothy 3:16-17

Hebrews 4:12

Acts 17:11

What must faithful followers of Jesus Christ always do in relationship to the Word of God?

Reread: Revelation 22:20-21

What final words do we see from the Lord Jesus Christ in these verses?

What does John, the writer of the book of Revelation, have to say about this?

How does the Holy Spirit then close the last book of God's Word?

What does it mean to you that He closes the Scriptures in this fashion?

Application Questions

How can you be certain to hear and apply God's Word to your life each and every day?

Are you looking forward to the coming of Jesus Christ with joyful anticipation?

On August 16th, 2014 my wife Sally and I attended a reception for Franklin Graham. During his remarks he said that he believes we are "in the final minutes on God's clock." What do you think? Are you ready?

Our Coming King

Partially excerpted from a summary by Chuck Missler
who was inspired by Pastor S. D. Lockridge

He is King of the Jews; King of Israel; King of all the Ages; King of Heaven; King of Glory; King of Kings.....and Lord of Lords.

He is a prophet before Moses; a priest after Melchizedek; a champion like Joshua; an offering in place of Isaac; a king from the line of David; a wise counselor above Solomon; a beloved/rejected/exalted son like Joseph. And yet far more.........

He is the "I AM that I AM;" The voice in the burning bush.

He is the Captain of the Lord's Host; the conqueror of Jericho. He is enduringly strong, entirely sincere, and eternally steadfast; He is immortally graceful, imperially powerful, and impartially merciful.

In Him dwells the fullness of the Godhead bodily, the very God of very God. He is our Kinsman-Redeemer and He is our Avenger of Blood; He is our City of Refuge, Our Perfect High Priest, Our Personal Prophet, and Our Reigning King.

He's the loftiest idea in Literature.

He's the highest personality in Philosophy.

He's the fundamental doctrine of Theology.

He's the Supreme Problem in "higher criticism!"

He's the Miracle of the Ages; the superlative of everything good.

We are the beneficiaries of a love letter that was written in blood, on a wooden cross erected in Judea 2,000 years ago.

He was crucified on a cross of wood, yet He made the hill on which it stood.

By Him were all things made that were made; without Him was not anything made that was made; by Him are all things held together!

What held him to the cross? It wasn't the nails! It was His love for you and me.

He was born of a woman so that we could be born of God.

He humbled Himself so that we could be lifted up.

He became a servant so that we could be made co-heirs.

He suffered rejection so that we could become His friends.

He denied Himself so that we could freely receive all things.

He gave Himself so that He could bless us in every way.

His Offices are manifold. His Reign is righteous. His Promises are sure. His Goodness is limitless. His Light is matchless. His Grace is sufficient. His Love never changes. His Mercy is everlasting. His Word is enough. His Yoke is easy and His burden is light.

He is indescribable, incomprehensible, irresistible and invincible.

The Heaven of heavens cannot contain Him; man cannot explain Him; the Pharisees couldn't stand Him (and learned that they couldn't stop Him); Pilate couldn't find fault with Him; the witnesses couldn't agree against Him; Herod couldn't kill Him; death couldn't handle Him; the grave couldn't hold Him!

He has always been and always will be.

He had no predecessor and will have no successor.

You can't impeach Him and He isn't going to resign!

His name is above every other name in heaven and on earth.

At the name of Yeshua every knee shall bow and every tongue confess that Jesus Christ is Lord!

His is the kingdom, the power, and the glory forever, and ever...Amen!

Close in Prayer

APPENDIX 1

HOW TO AVOID ERROR
(Partially excerpted from *The Road to Holocaust* by Hal Lindsey)

1. The most important single principle in determining the true meaning of any doctrine of our faith is that we start with the clear statements of the Scriptures that specifically apply to it, and use those to interpret the parables, allegories and obscure passages. This allows Scripture to interpret Scripture. The Dominionists (and others seeking to bend Scripture to suit their purposes) frequently reverse this order, seeking to interpret the clear passages using obscure passages, parables and allegories.

2. The second most important principle is to consistently interpret by the literal, grammatical, historical method. This means the following:

    1. Each word should be interpreted in light of its normal, ordinary usage that was accepted in the times in which it was written.

    2. Each sentence should be interpreted according to the rules of grammar and syntax normally accepted when the document was written.

    3. Each passage should also be interpreted in light of its historical and cultural environment.

Most false doctrines and heresy of Church history can be traced to a failure to adhere to these principles. Church history is filled with examples of disasters and wrecked lives wrought by men failing to base their doctrine, faith, and practice upon these two principles.

The Reformation, more than anything else, was caused by an embracing of the literal, grammatical, and historical method of interpretation, and a discarding of the allegorical method. The allegorical system had veiled the Church's understanding of many vital truths for nearly a thousand years.

Note 1: It is important to note that this is how Jesus interpreted Scripture. He interpreted literally, grammatically, and recognized double reference in prophecy.

Note 2: It is likewise important that we view Scripture as a whole. Everything we read in God's Word is part of a cohesive, consistent, integrated message system. Every part of Scripture fits in perfectly with the whole of Scripture if we read, understand, and study it properly.

Note 3: Remember to Appropriate the power of The Holy Spirit.

Read: Luke 11:11-12   Read: I Timothy 4:15-16
Read: Luke 24:49   Read: II Peter 2:1
Read: John 7:39   Read: Mark 13:22
Read: John 14:14-17, 26

Appendix 2

Understanding Composite Probability and Applying It to the Judeo-Christian Scriptures

TO BETTER UNDERSTAND one of the ways the Creator of the Universe has validated His Word and the work and person of Jesus Christ, it is helpful to get a grasp on composite probability theory and its application to the Judeo-Christian Scriptures.

We are indebted to Peter W. Stoner, past chairman of the Department of Mathematics and Astronomy at Pasadena City College as well as to Dr. Robert C. Newman with his Ph.D. in astrophysics from Cornell University for the initial statistical work on this topic. Their joint efforts on composite probability theory were first published in the book *Science Speaks*.

Composite Probability Theory

If something has a 1 in 10 chance of occurring, that is easy for us to understand. It means that 10 percent of the time, the event will happen. However, when we calculate the probability of several different events occurring at the same time, the odds of that happening increase exponentially. This is the basic premise behind composite probability theory.

If two events have a 1 in 10 chance of happening, the chance that both of these events will occur is 1 in 10 x 10, or 1 in 100. To show this numerically this probability would be 1 in 10^2, with the superscript indicating how many tens are being multiplied. If we have 10^3, it means that we have a number of 1000. Thus 104 is equivalent to 10,000 and so on. This is referred to 10 to the first power, 10 to the second power, 10 to the third power, and so on.

For example, let's assume that there are ten people in a room. If one of the ten is left handed and one of the ten has red hair; the probability that any one person in the room will be left handed and have red hair is one in one hundred.

We can apply this model to the prophecy revealed in the Bible to figure out the mathematical chances of Jesus' birth, life and death, in addition to many other events occurring in the New Testament by chance. To demonstrate this, we will consider eight prophecies about Jesus and assign a probability of them occurring individually by chance. To eliminate any disagreement, we will be much more limiting than is necessary. Furthermore, we will use the prophecies that are arguably the most unlikely to be fulfilled by chance. I think you will agree that in doing so, we are severely handicapping ourselves.

The first prophecy from Micah 5:2 says, "But you, O Bethlehem Ephrathah, are only a small village in Judah. Yet a ruler of Israel will come from you, one whose origins are from the distant past." (NLT) This prophecy tells us that the Messiah will be born in Bethlehem. What is the chance of that actually occurring? As we consider this, we also have to ask: What is the probability that anyone in the history of the world might be born in this obscure town? When we take into account all of the people who ever lived, this might conservatively be 1 in 200,000.

Let's move on to the second prophecy in Zechariah 9:9: "Rejoice greatly, O people of Zion! Shout in triumph, O people of Jerusalem! Look, your king is coming to you. He is righteous and victorious, yet he is humble, riding on a donkey---even on a donkey's colt" (NLT). For our purposes, we can assume the chance that the Messiah (the king) riding into Jerusalem on a donkey might be

1 in 100. But, really, how many kings in the history of the world have actually done this?

The third prophecy is from Zechariah 11:12: "I said to them, 'If you like, give me my wages, whatever I am worth; but only if you want to.' So they counted out for my wages thirty pieces of silver" (NLT). What is the chance that someone would be betrayed and the price of that betrayal would be thirty pieces of silver? For our purposes, let's assume the chance that anyone in the history of the world would be betrayed for thirty pieces of silver might be 1 in 1,000.

The fourth prophecy comes from Zechariah 11:13: "And the Lord said to me, 'Throw it to the potter'---this magnificent sum at which they valued me! So I took the thirty coins and threw them to the potter in the Temple of the Lord" (NLT). Now we need to consider what the chances would be that a temple and a potter would be involved in someone's betrayal. For our statistical model, let's assume this is 1 in 100,000.

The fifth prophecy in Zechariah 13:6 reads: "And one shall say unto him, What are these wounds in thine hands? Then he shall answer, Those with which I was wounded in the house of my friends: (KJV). The question here is, "How many people in the history of the world have died with wounds in their hands?" I believe we can safely assume the chance of any person dying with wounds in his or her hands is somewhat greater than 1 in 1,000.

The sixth prophecy in Isaiah 53:7 states, "He was oppressed and treated harshly, yet he never said a word. He was led like a lamb to the slaughter. And as a sheep is silent before the shearers, he did not open his mouth" (NLT). This raises a particularly tough question. How many people in the history of the world can we imagine being put on trial, knowing they were innocent, without making one statement in their defense? For our statistical model, let's say this is 1 in 1,000, although it is pretty hard to imagine.

Moving on to the seventh prophecy, Isaiah 53:9 says "He had done no wrong and had never deceived anyone. But he was buried like a criminal; he was put in a rich man's grave" (NLT). Here we need to consider how many people, out of all the good individuals in the world who have died, have died a criminal's death and been buried in a rich person's grave? These people died out of place. (Some might also infer that they were buried out of place, though that is not necessarily true.) Let's assume the chance of a good person dying as a criminal and being buried with the rich is about 1 in 1,000.

The eighth and final prophecy is from Psalm 22:16: "My enemies surround me like a pack of dogs; an evil gang closes in on me. They have pierced my hands and feet" (NLT). Remember this passage and all the other prophetic references to the crucifixion were written before this form of execution was invented. However, for our purposes, we just need to consider the probability of someone in the history of the world being executed by crucifixion. Certainly, Jesus wasn't the only person killed by being crucified. We will say that the chances of a person dying from this specific form of execution to be at 1 in 10,000.

Calculating the Results

To determine the chance that all these things would happen to the same person by chance, we simply need to multiply the fraction of each of the eight probabilities. When we do, we get a chance of 1 in 10^{28}. In other words, the probability is 1 in 10,000,000,000,000,000,000,000,000,000. Would you bet against these odds?

Unfortunately, there is another blow coming for those who do not believe the Bible is true or Jesus is who He said He was. There are not just eight prophecies of this nature in the Bible that were fulfilled in Jesus Christ------there are *more than three hundred* such prophecies in the Old Testament. The prophecies we looked at were just the ones that we could *most easily* show fulfilled.

If we deal with only forty-eight prophecies about Jesus, based on the above numbers, the chance that Jesus is not who He said He was or the Bible is not true is 1 in 10^{168}. This is a larger number than most of us can grasp (though you may want to try to write it sometime). To give you some perspective on just how big this number is, consider these statistics from the book *Science Speaks* by Peter Stoner:

- If the state of Texas were buried in silver dollars two feet deep, it would be covered by 10^{17} silver dollars.

- In the history of the world, only 10^{11} people have supposedly ever lived. (I don't know who counted this.)

- There are 10^{17} seconds in 1 billion years.

- Scientists tell us that there are 10^{66} atoms in the universe and 10_{80} particles in the universe.

- Looking at just forty-eight prophecies out of more than three hundred, there is only a 1 in 10^{168} chance of Jesus not being who He said He was or of the Bible being wrong.

In probability theory, the threshold for an occurrence being absurd---translate that as "impossible"---is only 10^{50}. No thinking person who understands these probabilities can deny the reality of our faith or the Bible based on intellect. Every person who has set out to disprove the Judeo-Christian Scriptures on an empirical basis has ended up proving the Bible's authenticity and has, in most cases, become a believer.

These facts are more certain than any others in the world. However, not everyone who has come to realize the reliability and reality of these documents has become a believer. These intelligent people who understand the statistical impossibility that Jesus was not who He claimed to be and who yet do not make a decision for Christ are not insane; they generally just have embedded emotional issues. They allow these issues to stop them from enjoying the many experiential benefits that God offers them through His Word and the dynamic relationship they could have with Him, not to mention longer-term benefits. These people, of course, deserve love and prayer, because this is not just a matter of the intellect.

If it were, every intelligent inquirer would be a believer. Rather, it is very much a matter of the heart, the emotions, and the spirit.

The truth of this statement was brought home to me in one very poignant situation. In this case, someone very near and dear to me said, "But dad, this could have been anybody." No, this could not have been just anybody. The chance these prophecies could have been fulfilled in one person is so remote as to be absurd. That is impossible. Only one person in human history fulfilled these prophecies and that person is Jesus Christ. To claim otherwise is not intelligent, it is not smart, it is not well-considered, and it is not honest. It may be emotionally satisfying, but in all other respects it is self-delusional.

APPENDIX 3

EZEKIEL PREDICTED WHEN ISRAEL WOULD BE RE-ESTABLISHED

Bible passage: Ezekiel 4:3-6

Written: between 593-571 B.C.

Fulfilled: 1948

In Ezekiel 4:3-6, the prophet said the Jews, who had lost control of their homeland, would be punished for 430 years. This prophecy, according to Bible scholar Grant Jeffrey, pinpointed the 1948 rebirth of Israel. Here's a summary of Jeffrey's theory:

1. Ezekiel said the Jews were to be punished for 430 years because they had turned away from God. As part of the punishment, the Jews lost control of their homeland to Babylon. Many Jews were taken as captives to Babylon.

2. Babylon was later conquered by Cyrus in 539 B.C. Cyrus allowed the Jews to leave Babylon and to return to their homeland. However, only a small number returned. The return had taken place sometime around 536 B.C., about 70 years after Judah lost independence to Babylon.

3. Because most of the exiles chose to stay in pagan Babylon rather than return to the Holy Land, the remaining 360 years of their punishment was multiplied by 7. The reason is explained in Bible's book of Leviticus.

(Leviticus 26:18, Leviticus 26:21, Leviticus 26:24 and Leviticus 26:28). In Leviticus, it says that if the people did not repent while being punished, the punishment would be multiplied by 7. And, by staying in pagan Babylon, most exiles were refusing to repent.

4. So, if you take the remaining 360 years of punishment and multiply by 7, you get 2,520 years. But, Jeffrey says those years are based on an ancient 360-day lunar calendar. If those years are adjusted to the modern solar calendar, the result is 2,484 years.

5. And, there were exactly 2,484 years from 536 BC to 1948, which is the year that Israel regained independence.

(In this Bible passage, Ezekiel is asked by God to symbolically act out the 430 years of punishment)

Ezekiel 4:3-6

... Then take an iron pan, place it as an iron wall between you and the city and turn your face toward it. It will be under siege, and you shall besiege it. This will be a sign to the house of Israel. "Then lie on your left side and put the sin of the house of Israel upon yourself. You are to bear their sin for the number of days you lie on your side. I have assigned you the same number of days as the years of their sin. So for 390 days you will bear the sin of the house of Israel. "After you have finished this, lie down again, this time on your right side, and bear the sin of the house of Judah. I have assigned you 40 days, a day for each year.

Source: Watchmanbiblestudy.com

CPSIA information can be obtained at www.ICGtesting.com
Printed in the USA
BVOW06s0946130415

395648BV00002B/5/P